Allah or God

RELIGIOUS FALLACIES

MICKEY RAY MULLEN

Allah or God
Copyright © 2022 by Mickey Ray Mullen

All rights reserved. No part of this book may be reproduced or transmitted in any form or by any means, electronic or mechanical, including photocopying, recording, or by any information storage and retrieval system without express written permission from the author, except in the case of brief quotations embodied in critical reviews and certain other noncommercial uses permitted by copyright law.

Printed in the United States of America.

Brilliant Books Literary
137 Forest Park Lane Thomasville
North Carolina 27360 USA

Chapter 1

Muhammad

This book shows the discrepancies of the two major religions, Islam and Christianity. It goes on into mostly, what is known as the infallible word of God that is fallible, believe it or not. It is a mess to put it mildly, with verses added that shouldn't be there, and Paul's gospel with his disciples, were not sanctioned by God, can it get any worse than that for mankind? Extraordinary claims require extraordinary evidence but the K J Bible of 1611 is all I have.

For religious expansion, War is the goal of the Muslim faith, the crusades has never ended until the entire world is in submission. The agreement between Muslims and Christians are that Allah and God are not the same entity. That Allah's existence is based on sound doctrine, but the author hasn't found that to be true.

Muhammad's mother, Halima, thought that he was possessed by the devil, but Muhammad's wives thought otherwise, and a perfect example to be followed.

If you love Allah, that is the way that he forgives your sins. On T V the preacher said that the difference between Islam and the Christian is 'love.' When it reads that God grieved in His heart that He made man on the earth, perhaps the preacher should look at the world with new glasses. Scheming people out of their hard earned money is considered almost normal, not only from individuals but corporations. Men are creating famines, global warming, wars, that are involving thousands of people, and countries, just to name a few things of biblical proportion.

Islam teaches that Judas, Iscariot took the place of Jesus. The author has every reason to believe that Judas started out as Judy. There theology is women are intellectually inferior, because of the deficiency of a women's mind. According to them they don't have a soul that must be the reason women like to be a Muslim, how convenient.

At the last day, or Judgment day, is when a person will find out, if they're admitted to Paradise, except by the three other ways, when you can go directly there. If you become a Martyr you get 72 virgins, die for a cause, or recite the ninety nine names of Allah.

I can see now it is best to die by jihad instead of getting old, a person tends to lose body functions if they live long enough. If a person soils themselves with urine, it can be reason enough, to keep a person out of paradise.

A fever, according to Muhammad is from the furnace of Hell.

For twenty five years Muhammad had only one wife Khadija but she died, and after that he took several wives. One was six when she moved in, and they consummated the marriage when she was nine, I'm not sure how anybody knew that?

In the Christian Bible people felt the need to improve it, and it is the same with the Qur'an. It seems to be a trait that humanity has. It leads to a lot of false doctrine that leads to the detriment of mankind. They say Muhammad changed Allah's wisdom to his own, on several occasions.

Muhammad lost the ability to make a living so the Muslims raided caravans for financial gain. The attributes of Satan in the Christian Bible coincide with the Islam faith.

Either a person is a Moslem or they deserve death, and whoever kills an infidel no harm should come to them.

According to the Christian Bible, if Muhammad wanted to sin a little, he would get revelations from Allah. Therefore, 'Muhammad received a lot of revelations from Allah.'

Focusing on a stone in Mecca, Islam was born. Jesus unifies sinners through his own death and resurrection. No one questions the influence of both men, but their influence is as different as the difference between peace and war.

Jihad (holy war) is completed only when the entire world is placed under the submission of Allah, and there laws are in place.

The Qur'an is the final revelation from Allah' and I'm not sure where the Book of Mormon stands in the equation. If anything, both books are a personal revelation of just how brilliant Lucifer is. The Word of God, our King James Bible of 1611 that Jesus spoke about was with God from the beginning of time, according to St John, the Word existed in heaven before Jesus was born. "In the beginning was the Word, and the Word was with God, and the Word was God." St John 1:1 "To him that overcometh (from false doctrine) will I grant to set with me in my throne, even as I also overcame, and am set down with my Father in his throne." Revelation 3:21 "And the Word was made flesh, and dwelt among us, (and we beheld his glory, the glory as of the only begotten of the Father,) full of grace and truth." St John 1:14

The collection of the Qur'an texts or 'revelations' fell to Muhammad's companions, he couldn't read nor write. The difference is, the Gospels that Jesus spoke, were from His Father God, and each of His disciples were named.

The Law of Moses and the Gospel of Jesus, is just a guide for mankind. It is Islam's belief that Allah sent the Old and New Testament, as a precursor to the Qur'an. That Christians worship three gods: the Father, the Mother (Mary) and the Son (Jesus). Left out of the equation is the Spirit or Holy Ghost, and it is the only thing needed for a person to enter into the kingdom of God. Jesus received it when He was baptized by John in St Matthew 3:16 it never, "lighted on Him" but went in His mouth, and down His throat. My Bible tells me that Mary was not blessed but equal to any one that shall do the will of God "For whosoever shall do the will of my Father which is in heaven, the same is my brother, and sister, and mother." St Matthew 12:50

The Qur'an says that one angel came to Mary, that clears that up, it was only the announcement of conception, It usually takes something to get a baby started, the one angel, is it hinting something? It was the Spirit in Genesis 1:2 that impregnated Mary, and it wasn't the Holy Ghost as it reads in St Matthew 1:18 but the other Spirit. There are two Spirits.

If you're a prophet you are without sin in Islam, I'm not sure what a messenger or priest is? It reads Muhammad was a messenger.

In the Christian Bible man was made from the ground, but the Qur'an has a little different version, a blood clot, burned clay, nothing, earth, or a drop of thick fluid.

Every Muslim will go to hell (for some period) while other numerous texts state that those who die in Jihad go immediately to paradise. That means the Moslem's and Catholic's will be in the same place, purgatory. If a person received a new heart and new Spirit as I did, does it make any common sense that they will to go to purgatory, to get straighten out? This is explained further in the book.

Some of the sound doctrine of medical virtues is camel urine and there milk, if you drink it, your body will become healthy, and a housefly in one's cup is a sign of guaranteed health.

The rejection of Jesus' claim to lordship is a principle doctrine in Islam.

I never thought of it before but evidently the Islam faith doesn't believe there is a Satan or Lucifer, and Spirit or The Holy Ghost, which is the other Spirit. It reads that Allah is the cause of evil.

There are three ways to enter Paradise directly, Jihad, martyrdom, or memorize the ninety nine names of Allah.

A healthy baby boy receives these words, there is no god but Allah and Muhammad is the messenger of Allah. I'm not sure what an unhealthy boy receives or a girl?

The ablution or wudu (cleansing in the Qur'an) Wash their hands up to the wrist three times. Rinse out the mouth three times. Clean the nostrils by sniffing water three times. Wash the face from forehead to chin and from ear to ear. Wash the forearms up to the elbows three times. Pass a wet hand over the whole head. Wash the feet up to the ankles three times, the right then the left. It could be today they just take a bath, but make sure to sniff. Allah does not accept the prayer of a person who has released gas until he makes a new ablution. (Above)

People like structure, so prayer is repeated five times a day. My God tells me, He knows what I need before I ask Him.

Muslims only hope that Allah will show favor of them at the end time with no guaranty, even Muhammad said he didn't know for sure where he was going.

A black stone thought to be a meteorite in Mecca is a building called the Ka'aba that is the direction that a man faces when a prayer is given.

Ishmael threw stones at the Devil resisting temptation, so once in a lifetime a good Moslem must travel to Mina to do the same. With a heartfelt, (literal and physical) Christian Redemption, as in this book I see no reason to go anyplace on the earth.

The Muslim faith and other religions have the intense desire of one main purpose, the ultimate forgiveness of sin. It is as if the desire is inside of man, no matter what the religion is.

Saying the Shahada is accepting the creed of Islam. It sounds like what the sinner's prayer does for the Christian, and in this book it will shed some light on the redemption method.

I'm not sure where I read it, but people like structure. That is the arrangement of all the parts of a whole or to put together systematically; an organization. That must be why the Catholic Church and Islam thrive. They like to be told to put on the right shoe first, clean your nostrils, or throw rocks at the Devil, light a candle, and go to a confessional to get rid of sin. Not long ago a Priest was explaining how this is so important on a TV program.

You wonder why there are so many women in the faith of Islam according to the Qur'an they don't have souls, and that would be an asset when it comes to Paradise or the Christian heaven, but I see no reason to think it is true. I'm not sure why it reads men are reincarnated into what? And they believe in Paradise. The Christian religion, because man were made in the image of God they will stay about the same or somehow be changed to a Spirit. There is a verse that says God is a Spirit.

There are different sects of Islam just as we have in the Christian Religions. In Islam the Shiites, I have read, are worse than the Jew. That division started when Muhammad never chose a successor.

The Christian ideal is the Word of God the King James Bible of 1611, it is the basis upon which ethical decisions are made, and it is believed, all people have the opportunity to be redeemed, but sorry to say that is not the case. The sacrifice of His Son on the cross was only the beginning, there is the matter of being chosen, and drawn, but do we want to throw that part of the Bible away? A person must become righteous, and it has nothing to do with love or St John 3:16. (Explained in the book) In Pakistan a nation of millions of Moslems a preacher from that country, was so delighted that the government allowed a Christian television program on the air.

He showed the verse that he believed in, and was spreading it all over Pakistan. "For God so loved the world, that he gave his only begotten Son, that whosoever believeth in him should not perish, but have everlasting life." St John 3:16 It is a play on the fifteenth verse (a parable) by someone that was helping God out. First of all it grieved God in His heart that He made man on the earth Genesis 6:6 Second of all, why "should is used?" If God wrote the verse, He would have used the words 'shall not perish.' That means everybody that is saved. The preachers seem to believe, everybody or whosoever believeth. In other words, God would be obligated for all that believe to enter into the kingdom of God, but there is the biblical problem with chosen and drawn when you are on this earth.

Muslims and Christians believe in the afterlife, but with the different doctrines of the different religions just common sense should reveal to a person there is something drastically wrong. Our King James Bible of 1611 has books, chapters, and individual verses, that I hope will shed some light on what I have learned in the Qur'an, and what I know about the Bible to be true in later chapters.

Honoring and worshiping Allah, warfare is necessary, that is why the crusades has never ended

It is a death sentence for a person to change into another religion from the Islamic faith, and some women have been killed dating a person, of a different religion.

Jihad is the quickest way to Paradise, fighting to the death, but after the author has become older some of the rules laid down by Muhammad would be hard to achieve, in some of the rules in the Qur'an.

In the Qur'an, to reach Paradise is with the sword.

Truth is devastating that is why Jesus spoke allegorically or in parable form, He had to get to the cross, and God made it easy when those around Him never knew what He meant when He spoke. Jesus recognized that; "Even so, Father: for so it seemed good in thy sight." St Matthew 11:26 This was after Jesus recognized, only those that become saved would understand the parables or the allegorical spoken Word, In the 25 verse it is those that believe they have the truth, a person can feel sorry for them as the martyrs in the Islam faith, and the different denominations without the true doctrine.

If Allah is to be honored it is through warfare, as being necessary to be favored for eternities sake, as presented from the time of Muhammad.

In the Qur'an, Muhammad had no qualms in demonstrating himself as a warrior' it was part of being a true Moslem. In Islam they wondered why Jesus went stoically to the cross. He died so that mankind could become redeemed so they would have a way to gain righteousness, so they could live with God in His kingdom.

How can the Word of God be corrupted by man? From the beginning man has had free will and that has been his down fall. God has never been able to control what is in the KJB of 1611 it is a mess to put it mildly. St John 3:16 should not be in the Bible, and it is the most famous verse in the universe.

It is Lucifer or the Devil that is in charge of the earth and all that is in it at this time. That should answer most of the questions. God looked in the heart of Lucifer, and what did He see? "For thou hast said in thine heart, I will ascend into heaven, I will exalt my throne above the stars of God: (churches and religious organizations) I will sit also upon the mount (all) of the congregation, (churches) in the sides of the north:" Isaiah 14:13 (America) Can it be written any plainer than that? "I will ascend above the heights of the clouds; I will be like the most High." (God) 14 If he is going to be like God wouldn't Lucifer need an advocate as Jesus was to God. Wouldn't that be Paul and Lucifer? Jesus said "Hereafter I will not talk much with you: for the prince (Lucifer) of this world cometh, and hath nothing in me." St John 14:30 It doesn't take a rocket scientist to figure out who he is referring too. This should answer two of the questions but Jesus said the parables or allegorical speech is a mystery to the unsaved. "And the disciples came, and said unto him, Why speakest thou unto them in parables?" St Matthew 13:10 "He answered and said unto them, Because IT IS GIVEN UNTO YOU TO KNOW THE MYSTERIES OF THE KINGDOM OF HEAVEN, BUT TO THEM IT IS NOT GIVEN." 11 That should answer the third question.

Intelligent people who care about faith in God should awaken, from their biblical and theological slumber. Perhaps they will be inspired to open their own Bibles after reading this book and read what the Scripture actually says, 'Truth is immortal.' The problem is the above verse and St Matthew "At that time Jesus answered and said, I thank thee, O Father,

Lord of heaven and earth, because thou hast (hid) these things from the wise and prudent, (exercising sound judgment in practical matters; sensible;) and hast REVEALED THEM TO BABES". St Matthew 11:25 The people not to bright; but who Jesus has transformed them, by being born again and have received the Holy Ghost; they are the ones that know the mystery.

'Truth is immortal,' That is the most truthful three letter words. I have spent thousands of dollars on those three words but, when a person butts heads with the (intelligent people) what can a couple of carpenter's do like Jesus and Mickey? The intelligent people have St John 3:16, what more do you need? It keeps the lights on. "And because I (Jesus and Mickey) tell you (intelligent people) the truth, ye believe us not." St John 8:45 Yes; truth is immortal, and those that find the truth will be immortal, but it reads few will find the way.

Theological Arguments

A religion is only as stable as the foundation. Before Muhammad there was no foundation to base the Qur'an or Islam religion on. The authenticity of Islam rises and falls with the substantial claim of Muhammad, that the Bible is corrupt and the Qur'an is the perfect word of Allah."

Many churches fail to heed the Bible, and many so called Christians feel no sense of shame or fear for their sin patterns. I know of no preacher in any church, radio, television, or any religious organizations doctrine that is about the Gospel at this time, that Jesus died for. "Gird yourselves, and lament, ye priests: howl, ye ministers of the Alter: come, lie all night in sackcloth, ye ministers of my God: for the meat offering and the drink offering is with holden from the house of your god." Joel 1:13 If, you are not of the God of Jesus Father, your father is of the devil. "Ye are of your father the devil, and the lusts of your father ye will do. He was a murderer from the beginning, and abode not in the truth, because there is no truth in him. When he speaketh a lie, he speaketh of his own: for he is a liar, and the father of it." St John 8:44 "And because I tell you the truth, ye believe me not." 45

Chapter 2

Paul and Romans

From The Acts through Jude I don't study it, and most of what I know comes from the Radio or Television programs, it's about all the preachers preach on. Jesus spoke in parables and Paul wrote plainly, that should tell the preachers something. Nothing seems to be of God in all of the books, even James, Peter, and the others John 1. 2. 3. Etc. I have decided to include some of these books of the New Testament in this book.

The name Saul is mentioned at the stoning of Stephen as being there, "and the witnesses laid down their clothes at a young man's feet, whose name was Saul." A little kinky but what is life without a little kinky. This happened before it reads Saul or Paul was saved. Saul hated the so-called Christians at that time, did he ever change? I say that he never changed even after his so-called made up conversion. Why was Paul's conversion different from when I was saved? The light that gave me a 'New Heart,' was the power of God or Spirit as when He created the heavens and earth. It reads, about Paul, "there shined round about him a light from heaven:" No power just a light. Some preachers say that the light was Jesus, and would He be allowed back to earth before the end time? I don't think so.

When I received my new heart outside of a gas station talking on a pay telephone, I stopped sinning, and the Lord put a fast on my body three days and nights. The explanation is further in the book. What that does is begin the cleaning process of your body to get it ready to receive the

Spirit or Holy Ghost. It doesn't mention that Paul endured any cleaning process. It was because of the original disobedience of Adam and Eve, plus a person's accumulative sin that is in the heart.

It reads that Ananias who was killed in chapter five of The Acts, because he held back part of his tithes from God, entered into the house where Saul was at, and putting both hands on (Brother Saul?) so that he could be filled with the Holy Ghost. Then Paul was baptized in water, we don't want to forget that, even when it is not necessary. The preachers say there are no contradictions, and Peter said a person will receive the Holy Ghost when they are baptized in water but hear Paul received the Holy Ghost first, by the laying on of hands. Jesus was baptized by John because God would know at the correct time when Jesus was going to receive the Holy Ghost or Spirit, when he took His first breath. It was (like a dove) that went in His mouth and down His throat. That was the way I received it but the Lord put a vision on me, and when I said the word BOY out loud going to work in a 1959 Ford Thunderbird it came through the windshield, and went in my mouth down my throat. It never "lighting on Him" as it reads in St Matthew 3:16.

Some of the things I have heard over the years, and Paul never let those around him forget he came of God's will, but that wasn't true he came on his own without the approval of God. "I am come in my Father's name, and ye receive me not: (Jesus) if another shall come in his own name, him ye will receive." (Believe, Paul) St John 5:43, "How can ye believe, which receive honor one of another, (why worry, be happy) and seek not the honor that cometh from God only?" 44 John the Baptist said, "A man can receive nothing, except it be given him from heaven." St John 3:27 It is a true statement, but hard to believe unless it happens to you.

Paul's salvation plan seems to be faith, grace, and believe, and walk not after the flesh, but after the Spirit. The only way to get the Spirit is the way Jesus received it after your body is clean in the mouth. There doesn't seem to be anybody that knows how to receive the Spirit. It certainly isn't the way Peter described it in the second chapter of The Acts. I'll get into more detail in, the chapter on Peter.

It is written, "(all) the Bible" is by the inspiration of God. Which is not true, the Bible is a mess but it is the only thing that we have. Luke tried to cover for Paul, I understand he was with Paul a lot, and wrote Luke, and The Acts. In Luke 4:4 and St Matthew 4:4 are verses about this. Luke said go by all the Bible where Matthew said only go by what came out of the mouth of Jesus. It reads God but that isn't true. God never died on the cross it was His Son Jesus.

Several times those around Paul wondered about what he was saying?

The diverse of gifts, slay me. But it reads they are from the same Spirit, which is not true.

Paul gives us the way of love, but it has nothing to do with anything. The reason Jesus had to die on the cross was because of the righteousness of God, and that has nothing to do with love. It reads in Genesis that it grieved God in his heart that He made man on the earth. 6:6 God said go and love everybody, but He couldn't very well say go and hate everybody.

Paul said he speaks with tongues more than ye all. Yes, Paul because you were of Satan.

It reads this corruptible must put on incorruption, that is true but a person can't do this with a corrupt heart where sin is located. The corrupt ministers prove this to be true. The Spirit from above can remove a person's heart giving them a new heart that is incorruptible. "---And the Spirit of God moved upon the face of the waters." Genesis 1:2 It is also the Spirit that saves a person.

It reads gather together and smell each other's socks. Which church? At this time I don't know of any that has the right doctrine. It reads of Noah's and Jesus generation so what is meant when it reads in St Matthew "Verily I say unto you, all these things shall come upon this generation." St Matthew 23:36 I believe it means all the other generations were chopped liver, except maybe those designated to be saved in the Old Testament. The generation that is designated for all things from salvation to the end time could be my generation from 1937. (The New Testament has verses about, "this generation.") "Ye serpents, ye generation of vipers, how can ye escape the damnation of hell?" ST Matthew 23:33 "O generation of vipers, how can ye being evil, speak good things? For out of the abundance of the heart the mouth speaketh." St Matthew 12:34 "---An evil and adulterous generation seeketh after a sign; and there shall no sign be given to it, but the sign of the prophet Jonah:" 39 (Or the death, burial, and resurrection of Jesus) "The men of Nineveh shall rise in judgment with this generation, and shall condemn it: because they repented at the preaching of Jonah; and, behold, a greater than Jonah is here." St Matthew 12:41 (Nineveh was only a few thousand people, but now we are talking about the whole earth at this present day in 2018) "---O faithless (unbelieving) generation, how long shall I be with you? How long shall I suffer you" ---. (put up with you) St Mark 9:19 It sounds like Jesus was ready to go to His Father in heaven. "Verily I say unto you, this generation shall not pass, till all things be fulfilled." St Matthew 24:34 "Heaven and earth shall pass away, but my words shall not pass away." 35 Recently I was told, 'see' all the Bible is God's Word. Come and see me after studying this nonfiction book.

That is the reason that Jesus spoke in parables or allegorically, if He would have said it is not meant for you it is for the generation in 1937, I believe they would have packed their bags and went home. All this was sanctioned by the Father God. "At that time Jesus answered and said, I think thee, O Father, Lord of heaven and earth, because thou hast hid these things from the wise and prudent, and hast revealed them unto babes." St Matthew 11:25 "Even so, Father: for it seemed good in thy sight." 26 "All things are delivered unto me of my Father: and no man knoweth the Son, but the Father: and no man knoweth the Son, but the Father; neither knoweth any man the Father, save (except) the Son, AND HE TO WHOMSOEVER THE Son WILL REVEAL HIM." 27 To be born again and receiving the Holy Ghost is physical. That is what it means a person will have no doubt that God is on the throne, when a person receives salvation. "But if I with the finger of God (power) cast out devils, (get rid of Adams sin and your accumulative sin) no doubt the kingdom of God is come upon you." St Luke 11:20

In one of the books it reads how they loved Paul and Paul loved them. Is that biblical? If a person preaches the truth of the parables, and what they mean, according to the Bible a person will be hated of all men. "And ye shall be hated of all men for my name's sake: but he that endureth to the end shall be saved." St Matthew 10:22

It reads and there was great joy in that city. Is this verse biblical? "Verily, verily, I say unto you, that ye shall weep and lament, but the world shall rejoice: (or those that follow Paul) and ye shall be sorrowful but your sorrow shall be turned into joy." St John 16:20 Preachers will tell you, you must not be saved if you're not joyful, loving, generous with your time, and money especially the money. This one preacher wasn't bashful he wanted 1,000 people to send him $1,000 to promote (his) gospel. A preacher said, 'if you don't have joy you don't have grace.'

Paul, he never let those around him forget who he said he was. In my KJB of 1611 is all the people and organization that wrote different bibles or worked on the written word, and not one time have I seen where anyone questioned if Paul was legitimate. It goes something like this. "This Jesus that I preach unto you is Christ." "I have lived in all good conscience before God until this day." "Paul a servant of Jesus Christ, called to be an apostle, separated unto the gospel of God." "I say the truth in Christ, I lye not, my (conscience) also bearing witness in the Holy Ghost. Am I not an apostle? Am I not free? Have I not seen Jesus Christ our Lord? Are not ye my work in the Lord?" "Be ye followers of me, even as I also am of Christ." "Moreover brethren, I declare unto you the gospel which I preached unto you, which also ye received, and wherein ye stand; etc. etc. etc."

It reads Paul saw a light shine around about him. Preachers say that it was Jesus. Why didn't it say Jesus, because it was a made up story in the first place.

I'm not sure how Ananias got so religious it reads "he put his hands on Paul so that he might receive his sight, and be filled with the Holy Ghost." The Acts 9:17 When I was saved or received the Holy Ghost I was blind but I could see, "if that makes any sense to you?" I can't remember which one it was; receiving the new Heart, or Holy Ghost in my mouth, when I was blinded. I kept driving to work, and when I found out I was blind, is when I walked into the main superintendent of the factory. Shortly thereafter scales fell off my eyes.

Paul it reads received the works before he was baptized? Peter said that when you are baptized you will receive the works?

The book is about Allah or God, in Islam they believe Paul existed but he gave a watered down version of the Gospel of Christ. There can't be a watered down version, either your saved or not, pregnant or not, alive or not, received the Holy Ghost or not.

Muslim scholars charge that Paul and his companions altered the message that Jesus spoke almost immediately following Jesus' ascension, In an attempt to win over non Jews. They said Paul denounced the Hebrew Torah, revised the Gospels, and cheapened salvation. Modern Christians are following Paul, not Christ." Jesus said this would happen, "I am come in my Father's name, and ye receive me not: (Jesus) if another shall come in his own name, him ye will receive." (Believe, Paul) St John 5:43

Romans Travesty

He never let people forget, "Paul, a servant of Jesus Christ, called to be an apostle, separated unto the gospel of God, Romans 1:1 ("Which he had promised afore by his prophets in the Holy Scriptures.") 2 I find this not to be the case in St John it reads that the person that comes after me, (Jesus) he will come on his own, without God. (Paul) "Hereafter I will not talk much with you: for the prince of this world cometh and hath nothing in me." (Satan) St John 14:30 He needed an advocate which was Paul. "I will ascend above the heights of the clouds; I will be like the most High." Isaiah 14:14

It seems to me when Christ is used with Jesus, it is referring to God, or Jesus is God. I'm not sure where the preachers get that from in the KJB of 1611. The sad part is they can show you verses that proclaim it. To my knowledge in prophesy of the Old Testament, Paul was never mentioned as coming after Jesus, except in St John in the New Testament

"---Jesus Christ our Lord, which was made of the seed of David according to the flesh;" Romans 1:3 (It sounds like he is referring to Mary as being impregnated by an earthy person and not the Spirit from God.) It reads "And Jacob begat Joseph the husband of Mary, of whom was born Jesus, who is called Christ." ST Matthew 1:16 Joseph never touched Mary according to the Bible so how could He be of the seed of David? It even reads according to the flesh. That is true but Jesus only resembled man without his sinful nature.

"By whom we have received grace and apostleship for obedience to the faith among all nations, for his name:" Romans 1:5 (received grace for obedience to the faith?) Jesus said if a person is not born again and receive the Spirit they cannot enter into the kingdom of God. St John 3:3-5 He brought up all nations, and it reads all nations will be deceived in revelation.

"Among whom are ye also the called of Jesus Christ:" 6 Jesus also said many are called but few chosen. We have to consider, are you one of the chosen and drawn to Him to be saved. "No man can come to me, except the Father which hath sent me draw him:" St John 6:44

"To all that be in Rome, beloved of God, called to be saints: grace to you and peace from God our Father, and the Lord Jesus Christ." Romans

1:7 Most churches say that Jesus was God but here is mentioned God our Father, separate from the Lord Jesus Christ. I hate to think that Paul got something right. Peace won't come to the child of God until the end time in St John It takes more than,' just to be called' to be saints.

"---your faith is spoken of throughout the whole world" 1 Romans 1:8 It's too bad that Paul was never born again he would have found out faith has nothing to do with anything.

"---without ceasing I make mention of you always in my prayers;" 9 That was nice of you Paul; it reads God knows what you need before you ask Him.

"---Paul needed a prosperous journey by the will of God to come unto you." 10 It is too bad he was on his own without God.

"---that I may impart unto you some spiritual gift," Does it make any sense, that a person can impart a spiritual gift, to the end that ye may be established;" 11 (made strong)

"---be comforted together with you by the mutual faith both of you and me." 12

"---(The Gospel) it is the power of God unto salvation---;" 16 that is true the power of God is the only one, that can cause a person to be born again through the Spirit. But Paul said "to everyone that believeth:" (that is true but a person must believe in your heart or very soul, one of the works that Jesus did) "Believe me that I am in the Father, and the Father in me: or else believe me for the very works sake." St John 14:11 also 10:37-38

"---The just shall live by faith." 17 (I was saved in one or two minutes I don't have to live some kind of holy life.)

"Wherefore God also gave them up to uncleanness through the lusts of their own hearts," Romans 1:24 (heart) (it isn't so much the lusts of your own heart, is a big problem, it is getting rid of the original sin of Adam by removing the heart that your born with, and giving a person a new heart from God, 'in doing so' it will get rid also your accumulative sin sense birth. All these sins mentioned, 'have fun,' Jesus came to save the sinner, (not) those that believe they are righteous by living a clean life or sinful life. Ezekiel 36:26

"---Whosoever thou art that judgest: for wherein thou judgest another, thou condemnest thyself; for thou that judgest doest the same things." Romans 2:1. Is he saying that a person must believe everything spoken to them by every Tom, Dick, and Harry or Mary? It reads you can judge righteously or biblically. "Thou hypocrite, first cast out the beam out of thine own eye: and then shalt thou see clearly to cast out the mote out of thy brother's eye."St Matthew 7:5 A person then can judge righteously.

Who judgest not "---that thou shalt escape the judgment of God?" 3 In the last days the elect will be removed, they are already saints and perfect as God is perfect they don't have to be worried about facing the judgment of God. "Be ye therefore perfect, even as your Father which is in heaven is perfect." St Matthew 5:48 Can a person work his way into perfection? No.

The judgment that we have in the court system is based according to what rule of law is broken and severity of the crime. The Bible mentions that those that haven't been removed from the earth will be judged. The question I have is, will there be different tiers of punishment from minor to sever. I know that they say all Catholics will go to purgatory first, even the priests, 'the cream of the crop,' does this make any common sense on paper? The way they are flawed in their personal life they need to go to purgatory, but what is it going to take to get them out?

"---not knowing that the goodness of God leadeth thee to repentance?" Romans 2:4 Goodness is the state or quality of being good. What about where it reads God is righteous? He is virtuous, or chaste it seems to me than being righteous is more than just being good. "But seek ye first the kingdom of God, (Born again and Holy Ghost) and his righteousness." St Matthew 6:33 A child is either being good or naughty. I don't think it is at the same level as God.

"Who will render to every man according to his deeds:" 6 Those that become saved, I don't think they will be judged like or with everybody else.

(Those that do good will have eternal life) 7 Good luck.

"But unto them that are contentious, and do not obey the truth, but obey unrighteousness, indignation and wrath." 8 Seeking the truth, that is what I'm doing seeking truth, and so far I haven't found any in Romans.

"Tribulation, and anguish, upon every soul of man that doeth evil, of the Jew first, and also of the Gentile;" 9 Jesus said He came to save the sinner, so what is this?

"But glory, honor, and peace, to every man that worketh good,---" 10 (contrary to what the Bible says) a person can't work their way into salvation, and what is more important than that? I believe it is about one of the things, "feeding the poor." On most Indian reservations the percentage of high school graduates is extremely low, the very thing that they need. Not always, but it is some of the decisions that people make, create the problems, your work is never going to end. "For ye have the poor always with you; but me ye have not always." St Matthew 26:11

"For not the hearers of the law are just before God, but the doers of the law shall be justified." Romans 2:13 I believe he is saying live a nice way, and be charitable. In about thirty days I received God's righteousness and I don't believe a person needs anything else. "But seek ye first the kingdom of God, and his righteousness;" St Matthew 6:33

"---The Gentiles---having not the law, are a law unto themselves." Romans 2:14 I wish he would have used the words, "not the commandments" that seems more biblical. God said in Genesis that a person would be as gods, knowing good and evil. "if ye love me, keep my Commandments." St John 14:15 "For all the prophets and the law prophesied until John." St Matthew 11:13 Wouldn't this be those in "that" dispensation were under the law, but under 'this' dispensation they would be called the commandments. "If ye love me, keep my commandments." St John 14:15 This love is, you have been born again and have received the Holy Ghost physically, is the commandments that Jesus is referring to here.

"Which show the work of the law written in their hearts (s)" Romans 2:15 What about total heart replacement, it is biblical in Jeremiah. "I will put my law in their inward parts, and write it in their hearts; and will be their God, and they shall be my people."Jeremiah 31:33

"In the day when God shall judge, the secrets of man by Jesus Christ according TO MY GOSPEL." 16 (Paul's Gospel?) Judge the secrets of man? "---the word that I (Jesus) have spoken, the same shall judge him in the last day." St John 12:48 I can't understand why theologians can't see the difference in the Gospels and what Paul says.

"Even the righteousness of God which is by faith of Jesus Christ unto all and upon all them that believe: ---" Romans 3:22 That is true IF you are one of the chosen, drawn to him, and have believed in your heart of one of the works that Jesus did. It triggers the Spirit of Genesis 1:2 to act as a catalyst to remove the heart, "with sin in it" AND REPLACE IT with a new heart from God.: "I speak not of you all: I know whom I have chosen: but that the scripture may be fulfilled," St John 13:18 "No man can come to me, except the Father which hath sent me draw him:" St John 6:44 "But if I do, though ye believe not me, believe the works: that ye may know and believe, that the Father is in me, AND I IN HIM." St John 10:38 "A new heart also will I give you; ---and I will take away the stony heart out of your flesh, and I will give you a heart of flesh." Ezekiel 36:26 (From God, who created the first Spirit but under His command in Genesis 1:2)

"For all have sinned, and come short of the glory of God:" 23 That is true but what about the sin of Adam, the only way to get rid of it is in Ezekiel It gets rid of both yours and his.

"Being justified freely by his 'grace', through the redemption, that is in Christ Jesus:" 24 Grace is between God, and the fact that He sent Jesus, so that man could receive His (God's) righteousness. It has nothing to do with mankind. The only place grace is mentioned in the Gospels is in St John 1:14, 16 and 17 and Luke 2:40, and some of the minister's, use the word grace, a lot, "with grace as the mainstay of their ministry."

"---to declare his righteousness for the remission of sins, that are past, through the forbearance of God." 25 To be born again is physical you can't just declare (your righteousness or God's righteousness.)

"Therefore we conclude that a man is justified (correct?) by faith without the deeds of the law.," 28 There is the old faith word again. What about, if you are not born again, and not receive the Spirit, you will not enter, into the kingdom of heaven. St John 3:3-5 and Ezekiel 36:26-27

"But to him that worketh not, but believeth on him that justifieth the ungodly, his faith is counted for righteousness." Romans 4:5 Faith has nothing to do with being righteous. When God made the heavens and the earth, we can walk on it, or see it, consisting of matter that God put together physically. Why would He change for salvation? Here is the, 'only the believeth on Him, again.'

Paul wonders around more than once in the Old Testament prophets and circumcision, he seems to like the word, but if you asked him, he wouldn't know what he was talking about, just blowing smoke. It reads the Law ended with John the Baptist. This dispensation has nothing to do with the Old Testament laws for salvation, Jesus would tell you that. Until Jesus, they were under the law of Leviticus, and the animal sacrifices. I'm not sure how Noah was found perfect in his generation he lived before Leviticus.

"---if we believe on him (I'm not sure how God got in the picture) that raised up Jesus our Lord from the dead;" Romans 4:24 It reads that a person must believe on His Son Jesus, which worked for me, but I had to believe in my heart on one of the works that Jesus did. "Believe me that I am in the Father, and the Father in me: or else believe me for the very works; sake." St John 14:11

"But God commendeth his love toward us, in that, while we were yet sinners, Christ died for us." 5:8 Love has nothing to do with achieving righteousness. It grieved God in His heart that he made man on the earth Genesis 6:6 Yes, that was the plan of God that Jesus was the perfect sacrifice, so as it reads Christ (according to Paul he used the word Christ, and if you could ask him he would tell you, it means God died for us.)

Jesus died for our sin but that doesn't make a person automatically saved. Paul wrote it as being released from blame, guilt or sin. 5:1-11

Sin through Adam Salvation through Christ

That is true but when Adam sinned his body was changed along with Eve, so salvation is physical. A person must be changed back as before Adam was at the beginning. He was made perfect but lost that status, when he disobeyed God. Salvation only comes from being born again and receiving the new Spirit as in St John with the explanation in Ezekiel. Ezekiel never wrote it as it happens to a person, the old timers would say he got the cart before the horse. "A new heart also will I give you, (drawn and chosen) And I will take away the stony (sinful) heart out of your flesh, and I will give you a heart of flesh. (Not spirit but flesh) Then will I sprinkle clean water upon you, (born again) and ye shall be clean: from all your filthiness, and from all your idols, will I cleanse you. And a new Spirit will I put within you: And I will put my Spirit within you, and cause you to walk in my statutes, and ye shall keep my judgments and do them." Ezekiel 35:26-25-27

Chapter 6 in Romans
Freedom from sin's power

Baptism in water has nothing to do with getting rid of a person's sin. Paul speaks of Jesus death as a means of getting rid of a person's sin when it's an up close and personal, or a physical thing between God and yourself. 6:1:13

"But God be thanked that ye were the servants of sin, but ye have obeyed from the heart that form of doctrine which was delivered you." 6:17 (Obeyed from the heart) In Ezekiel it reads God will give a person a new heart, and I found out He removes the heart you are born with first. It reads in St Matthew "Ye do err, not knowing the scriptures nor the power of God." St Matthew 22:29

How could Paul get the scriptures to match what Jesus said, he never met Him nor at that time there were nothing written down to study? Reading about his conversion he wasn't saved or transformed either. It never came close to what happened to me. (The Acts 9th chapter)

"Being then made free from sin, ye became the servants of righteousness." Romans 6:18 "Know ye not brethren, (for I speak to them that know the law,) how that the law hath dominion over a man as long as he liveth?" Romans 7:1 No, it doesn't, the law ended with John the Baptist as a viable truth for salvation. For this dispensation, salvation is the way of the Gospels, after Jesus left. "For all the prophets and the law prophesied until John." St Matthew 11:13

"For the law of the Spirit of life in Christ Jesus, hath made me free from the law of sin and death." 8:2 I have no way of knowing what Paul is referring to, "the law of the Spirit of life in Christ Jesus?" The Spirit, Holy Ghost, Comforter, is a separate Spirit that a person must receive before they can enter into the kingdom of heaven as it reads. It is known as a Him, or He, the teacher of man, and the Spirit of truth. "But ye know him for he dwelleth with you, AND SHALL BE IN YOU". St John 14:17 I RECEIVED THE Holy Ghost in my mouth as Jesus did in water in St Matthew 3:16. Paul said the Spirit of life in Jesus hath made me free from the law of sin and death. The Spirit of life in Jesus' has nothing to do with a person's New Spirit in their own body.

"For what the law could not do, in that it was weak through the flesh, God sending his own Son in the likeness of sinful flesh and for sin, condemned sin in the flesh:" ? 8:3 We have Paul separating God and His Son that is the main crucible here. What about all three in one as the preacher's will tell you? Even Islam can't understand that, and neither can I, by the preacher's standards.

"That the righteousness of the law, might be fulfilled in us, who walk not after the flesh, but after the Spirit." 4 A person must be physically made righteous from above as John stated, so I don't know what this is referring to. I quit sin on 12/1/1968 at 9 pm, of drinking, smoking, swearing, etc. and have had no desire, for such things sense, I received my new heart. It took thirty days to clean my body to get it ready to receive the Holy Ghost or New Spirit as in Ezekiel 36:26-27. If, people think they can be nice, or good, and be a child of God that is not biblical in the Gospels.

"For they that are after the flesh do mind the things of the flesh; but they that that are after the Spirit, the things of the spirit" 8:5 (If, having received the Spirit, or Holy Ghost, and Paul never received it) or the things of the Spirit.

"For to be carnally minded is death; but to be spiritually minded is life and peace." 6 What about the heart, it reads sin is in the heart. I received a new heart from above that made me spiritually minded, because I got rid of my sin. (It reads those in the world will have joy and peace.) "Verily, verily, I say unto you, that ye shall weep and lament, but the world shall rejoice: and ye shall be sorrowful, but your sorrow shall be turned into joy." St John 16:20 (At the end time, death, or end of days)

"But ye are not in the flesh, but in the Spirit," (if, the Spirit of God, Holy Ghost dwells in you.) I'm sure that Paul means the Spirit IS God, but the Spirit (Holy Ghost) is a separate individualist being known as him or he. "Now if any man, have not the Spirit of (Christ) he is none of his." 9 That is true and the Spirit is controlled by God. "And I will pray the Father, and he shall give you another (after the new heart or born again) Comforter, (Holy Ghost) that he may abide with you forever:" St John 14:16 also 15-26

"Peace I leave with you, my peace I give unto you: not as the world giveth, give I unto you. Let not your heart be troubled, neither let it be afraid." St John 14:27 (Peace, is knowing you're saved from hell) no earthly person can give you spiritual peace.

"And if Christ be in you, the body is dead because of sin; but the Spirit is life because of righteousness." Romans 8:10 It is not Christ in you but the Holy Spirit or Holy Ghost. The body became dead in the time it took to replace my heart, and afterward you become alive in knowing that God is alive if nothing else. Because God is righteous a person must be born again and receive the Holy Ghost to become righteous as He is. "Be ye therefore perfect, even as your Father which is in heaven is perfect." St Matthew 5:48

"But if the Spirit of him that raised up Jesus from the dead dwell in you, he that raised up Jesus from the dead shall also quicken your mortal bodies by his Spirit that dwelth in you." Romans 8:11 It was the Spirit in Genesis 1:2 that did the work of raising Jesus. The Spirit you need is the Holy Ghost which is a different Spirit. "He that raised up Christ (Jesus the Son of God) from the dead shall also quicken your mortal bodies by his Spirit that dwelleth in you." The same Spirit that brought Jesus back to life is the same Spirit that gave me a new heart or born again. That Spirit, does not dwelleth in you, but comes from heaven above to give a person a new heart. It evidently helped God in the creation of the heaven and earth in Genesis 1:2 and 26. It is the Holy Ghost or the other Spirit that dwells in you, and received separately.

"For as many as are led by the Spirit of God, they are the sons of God." 8:14 To receive the Holy Ghost a person must be born again first, that is something that is never mentioned that I know of, from The Acts - Jude. There are two spirits', the first one is found in Genesis 1:2 it helped in the creation of the earth, the other one is called a Spirit or Holy Ghost it is only for those that become saved, or born again first. "Nevertheless I tell you the truth; It is expedient for you that I go away: for if I go not away, the Comforter will not come unto you; but if I depart, I will send him unto you." St John 16:7 Paul and his disciples never understood this.

"The Spirit itself beareth witness with our spirit, that we are the children of God." 8:16 After I was born again thirty days later I received a new Spirit, my spirit that I was born with was replaced by the New Spirit. "And I will put my Spirit (Holy Ghost) within you, and cause you to walk in my statutes, and ye shall keep my judgments, and do them." Ezekiel 36:26-27 A person truly becomes a part of God. "And I will pray the Father, and he shall give you another Comforter, that he may abide with you forever;" St John 14:16 "Even the Spirit of truth; whom the world cannot receive, because it seeth him not, neither knoweth him: but ye know him; for he dwelleth with you, and shall be in you." 17

"And not only they, but ourselves also, which have the first fruits of the Spirit, even we ourselves groan within ourselves, waiting for the adoption, to wit, the redemption of our body." Romans 8:23 12/1/1968 at 9pm I received the New Heart and thirty days later received the New Spirit, the Holy Ghost, I believe I have been redeemed. (I have no idea what the first fruits of the Spirit are, that he is referring to.)

"For we are saved by hope: but hope that is seen is not hope: for what a man seeth, why doth he yet hope for?" 24 Because he hasn't seen anything spiritually, hope has no place in you, after a person is saved physically.

"What shall we say then? That the Gentiles which follow not after righteousness, have attained (arrived at) to righteousness, even the righteousness which is of faith." Romans 9:30 Faith has nothing to do with a person being righteous. It reads seek ye first the kingdom of God and his righteousness in St Matthew 6:33. "Except a man be born of water (born again 3rd verse, H2O has nothing to do with being saved) and of the Spirit, (Holy Ghost) he cannot enter into the kingdom of God." St John 3:5 When you (enter) into the kingdom of God you are righteous. It is physical, as in Ezekiel 36:26-27

"For they (Israel and others) being ignorant of God's righteousness, and going about to establish their own righteousness, have not submitted themselves unto the righteousness of God." Romans 10:3 It is physical and matter, the same as God creating the heavens and the earth. Paul is saying that Israel has a zeal for God but no knowledge. Paul, in the fourth verse said that every one that believeth has the righteousness of God, and that couldn't be further from the truth. It reads in Genesis that man will be his own god creating his own righteousness. Genesis 3:5 Paul was a good example of that.

"For Christ is the end of the law for righteousness (to everyone that believeth)" 4 This is true but you have to believe in one of the works that Jesus did. I believed that I could heal my mother, and it triggered the Spirit to act, it removed the heart I was born with and gave me a new heart as it reads St John 10:37-38 and 14:11 The King James Bible of 1611 says that John the Baptist was the end of the Law. St Matthew 11:13 There is more to being righteous then just believing, with the mind as in St John. "For

God so loved the world, (it grieved God in His heart that He made man on the earth) That he gave his only begotten Son, (that is true) that whosoever believeth (what about drawn and one of the chosen) in him should not perish (redemption is physical) but have everlasting life. St John 3:16

"For Moses describeth the righteousness which is of the law, that the man which doeth those things shall live by them." Romans 10:5 This is true under that dispensation, but not this dispensation, after Jesus came to earth the first time, when the time was right.

"But what saith it? The word is nigh thee, even in thy mouth, and in thy heart: that is the word of faith, which we preach." Romans 10:8 Go back to the third verse above. "That if thou shalt confess with thy mouth the Lord Jesus, and shalt believe in thine heart, that God hath raised him from the dead, thou shalt be saved." 10:9 "For with the heart man believeth unto righteousness: and with the mouth confession is made unto salvation." 10 (These three verses are false doctrine)

I sensed that when I was seeking salvation there was something wrong with the statements made in 8-9-10, and I was physically saved at a gas station after I left the protestant church's Alter, as I have explained before. (It even gets easier) "For whosoever shall call upon the name of the Lord shall be saved." 13 (False doctrine)

Thirteen is easy enough "For whosoever shall call upon the name of the Lord shall be saved." At the end of one's life is that all a person must do, to spend eternity with God in His kingdom is call out either Spirit, Holy Ghost, Lord, or even Jesus, or Jesus Christ, according to their trinity of being all the same thing. Islam added Mary as part of the trinity, and left out the Holy Ghost which is the only game in town. (False doctrine)

(The preachers like this verse) "How then shall they call on him in whom they have not believed? And how shall they believe in him of whom they have not heard? And how shall they hear without a preacher?" Romans 10:14 After I was 'physically saved' I don't need a preacher, Bible, church group or anything else. "And the gospel must first be published among all nations." St Mark 13:10 The preachers never mention this verse.

"---How beautiful are the feet of them that preach the Gospel (of peace), ---".10:15 To preach the Gospel, a person should know what it contains, and it doesn't contain anything that has to do with peace except for a person's own soul and well being. The things that are going on in the world, does not bother me at all, because I know God is on the throne. In this day and age which religious doctrine are we referring to, Islam, Buda, Hindu, or the United Pentecostal Church or Baptist?

"So then faith cometh by hearing, and hearing by the word of God'." 10:17 Who is preaching the, word of God? Who has received what Ezekiel says, 'except me?' It reads few will find the way. "Because strait is the gate, and narrow is the way, which leadeth unto life, and few there be that find it." St Matthew 7:14

"For if the first fruit be holy, (Jesus) the lump is also holy: and if the root be holy so are the branches." Romans 11:16 BUT the branches must be made holy by being born again and receiving the Holy Ghost.

"---If thou continue in his goodness: otherwise thou also shalt be cut off." 11:22 "And they also, if they abide not still in unbelief, shall be grafted in: for God is able to graft them in again." 23 It is a procedure to become a child of God He doesn't just graft a person to him out of the blue, as it seems to say. The Holy Ghost when received, is inside a person, so you can't just be cut off, it is in you forever. "And I will pray the Father, and he shall give you another Comforter, that he may abide with you forever." St John 14:16

"For, who hath known the mind of the Lord---?" Romans 11:34 If a person is saved they will be closer in knowing the mind of the Lord as anyone on the planet with the understanding of the parables. "Not that any man hath seen the Father, save (except) he which is of God, he hath seen the Father." St John 6:46 As good as it gets is, when you receive the new Heart, and Holy Ghost (new Spirit) in the mouth physically. "At that day ye shall know that I am in my Father." (same goals) and ye in me, and I in you." St John 14:20

"I beseech you therefore, (brethren?) by the mercies of God, that ye present your bodies a living sacrifice, holy, acceptable unto God, which is your reasonable service." Romans 12:1 (I was drunk, as much of the time from fourteen to thirty until the night I was saved) Who did Jesus say He came to save the righteous (believe they are righteous) or the sinner? "For the Son of Man (Jesus) is come to save that which was lost." St Matthew 18:11 "---I am not come to call the righteous, but sinners to repentance." (Salvation or redemption) St Matthew 9:13

"And be not conformed to this world: but be ye transformed by the renewing of your mind, that ye may prove what is that good, and acceptable, and perfect, will of God." Romans 12:2 In other words Paul is saying quit drinking, smoking, swearing, and pornography, to show God, your sincere, that will really impress Him. Sin is in the heart and has nothing to do with the mind, according to the Bible. It is beyond comprehension but is God lying?

The service of the love to all
Romans 12:3-21

"But seek ye first the kingdom of God, and his righteousness and all these things shall be added unto you." St Matthew 6:33 "Not everyone that saith unto me, Lord, Lord, shall enter into the kingdom of heaven; but he that doeth the WILL of my Father which is in heaven." 7:21

Honor authority

"Let every soul be subject unto the higher powers. For there is no power but of God: the powers that be are ordained of God." Romans 13:1 What about Satan, Devil, or Lucifer? Is he going to stay down at the bar and have a few? It reads in Isaiah that it is Lucifer that is in charge of the mount (all) the congregation, churches and religious organizations. Isaiah 14:13-14 Could the Devil deceive all the nations without his part in the Bible? Satan is a spirit could he do anything without an advocate such as Paul and Peter? "And the great dragon was cast out, that old serpent, called the Devil, and Satan, which deceiveth the whole world: he was cast out into the earth, and his angels were cast out with him." Revelation 12:9

"Whosoever therefore resisteth the power, (the power?) resisteth the ordinance of God: and they that resist shall receive to themselves damnation." Romans 13:2 If a person does not become saved, I believe this is what is being referred to here, and I will go along with that. "---Ye do err not knowing the scriptures, nor the power of God." St Matthew 22:29

"---do that which is good, and thou shalt have praise of the same:" Romans 13:3 (the devil) There is a matter of being born again and receiving the new Spirit,.which is physical from God.

Walk in love

God couldn't very well have said hate everybody, but the problem is that is about all you hear on Christian radio is, love, family, money, children, like Focus on the family etc..

"Owe no man anything, but to love one another: for he that loveth another hath fulfilled the law." Romans 13:8 I'm not sure why Paul is trying to fulfill the law when it ended with John the Baptist. This dispensation, I believe commandments are a better word. "If ye love me, keep my commandments." St John 14:15 Salvation is an individual accomplishment, and has nothing to do with loving another to fulfill the law.

"And that, knowing the time, that now it is high time to awake out of sleep: for now is our salvation nearer than when we believed." 13:11 When I believed in my heart and received the new heart in 1968 as far as salvation goes that was all I needed, for being in the kingdom of God outside of receiving the Holy Ghost thirty days later. I'm ready to live with God in His kingdom, so does purgatory make any sense now. I don't know what Paul is writing about?

"The night is far spent, the day is at hand: let us therefore cast off the works of darkness, and (let us) put on the armor of light." 12 When the power of God removed the heart I was born with and replaced it, it was done by a light, with power behind it. When this happened at that time I, "cast off the works of darkness." I'm glad Paul said (let us) because he needed that, long before he started his ministry.

You don't need to put on the Lord Jesus Christ, because there is no such thing, it is the Holy Ghost that will enter your mouth, and it will be with you for eternity. "But put on the Lord Jesus Christ, (I question this) and make not provision for the flesh, to fulfill the lusts thereof." 13:14 At the time I was saved the lusts for anything in this world left me on 12/1/1968 at 9pm.

"For whether we live, ---or die, we are the Lord's." 14:8 Jesus said His body is a temple. If you deface the temple of your body would you still be one of the chosen? It reads many are called but few chosen, and a person must be drawn to the Father to be saved it says in St John 6:44 "So the last shall be first, and the first last: for many be called, but few chosen." St Matthew 20:16

"For it is written, as I live saith the Lord, every knee shall bow to me, and every tongue shall confess to God." Romans 14:11 "So then every one of us shall give account of himself to God." 12 With my new heart and Holy Ghost already, there is no way that I'm going to be judged at the last day, with everybody else, I'm already in the kingdom of God by being born again and receiving His Spirit. It reads in St John; "---Except a man be born of water (born again 3rd verse) and of the Spirit, he cannot enter into the kingdom of God." St John 3:5 to be (born again) cleans the body to receive the Spirit that might be why water is used here. Water was used also in Ezekiel 36:25 but it reads there, how your filthy body will be clean from the inside out not outside in.

"Let us not therefore judge one another anymore---." Romans 14:13 Do we except all religions on the earth? Jesus said that we could judge righteously, and if a person has the beam removed from their own eyes they can see clearly to judge others. St Matthew 7:5

"But if thy brother be grieved with thy meat, (the truth of the verses) ---Destroy not him with thy meat, for whom Christ died." 15 (Keep the truth away from him, and leave him alone, 'until the day of judgment' when it is going to be too late) Does this make any common sense to you, it doesn't me?

"For the kingdom of God is not meat and drink; but righteousness, and peace and joy in the Holy Ghost." 17 Jesus used meat and drink allegorically of born again and receiving the Spirit as it reads in St John 6: 31-58. Without the meat and drink there is no righteousness. Peace and joy will only come for those that have been redeemed at the end of their life. The Holy Ghost mentioned, Paul nor Peter, never received it, at least the true Spirit or Holy Ghost.

"For he that in these things serveth Christ (as Paul would put it God) is acceptable to God, and approved of men." 18 Yes, the old a-man corner, if a person preaches the truth it reads they will be hated by all men. That is what we have now the preachers have found a way to appease all men, that's where the money is.

"Let us therefore follow after the things which make for peace, and things wherewith one may edify another." (For God's sake don't offend anybody.) Romans 14:19 "For meat destroy not the work of God. All things indeed are pure: but it is evil for that man who eateth with offense." 20

"It is good neither to eat flesh, nor to drink wine, nor anything whereby thy brother stumbleth, or is offended, or is made weak. 21 "Many will say to me in that day, Lord; Lord, have we not prophesied in thy name? (preached) And in thy name have cast out devils ? and in thy name done many wonderful works?" St Matthew 7:22 "And then will I profess unto them, I never knew you: depart from me, ye that work iniquity." 23

"We then that are (full of it) strong ought to bear the infirmities of the weak, and not to please ourselves." Romans 15:1 Are there two kinds of Gospel one for the weak and the truth? It reads that Paul weakened the gospel, in the Islam religion, but he never knew the Gospel of Jesus in the first place.

"Let every one of us please his neighbor for his good to edification." 15:2 (Build up) Every person is on their own, I'm not going to nullify what is the truth for anybody. Islam or the Qur'an said Paul and his disciples did that. It could be why they call the U. S. the great Satan, which I believe is true..

"For whatsoever things were written afortime were written for our learning, that we through (patience and comfort) of the scriptures might have hope." 15:4 (Before I was saved I never had a Bible in the house, nor needed one, nor did I need a Bible afterward, because I was physically transformed) Finding verses that coincided with my experiences gave me peace of mind afterward, "only." In teaching my fellow man the verses helped, but who wants the truth, as long as a person has St John 3:16? There is a catholic billboard not far from my house it reads "We trust you Jesus." Salvation is built on the physical, and not trust, grace or hope. The truth of the scriptures, are harsh, that is why Jesus spoke allegorically or in parables. If He spoke the truth, He would have never made it to the cross. For instance which generation was He referring to? The disciples thought they were in the generation of deliverance.

"That ye may with one mind, (what about the weak) and one mouth glorify God, even the Father of our Lord Jesus Christ." 15:6 They have Jesus separated from His Father here but who noticed that? Yes, isn't that true today, all the churches are speaking one message with one King James Bible of 1611 especially The Acts through Jude.

"---Jesus Christ was a minister of the circumcision for the truth of God, to confirm the promises made unto the fathers:" 8 (If he is writing about the Old Testament fathers here, they had very little to say after Jesus was born) Circumcision was a physical thing, is it referring to receiving the new heart?

(What would all the Gentiles be doing praising the Lord when 99.99% are not saved?)

"Praise the Lord, all ye Gentiles, and laud (praise) him, all ye people."11

"---There shall be a root of Jesse, and he that shall rise to reign (Paul) over the Gentiles, (heathen) in him shall the Gentiles trust." 12 Do the heathen trust Paul, yes they do. Only those that have been redeemed know beyond any doubt that Jesus lived and God is in heaven. This is one of the few verses that seems to mean a person by the name of Paul, will the Gentiles trust and believe in.

"Now the God of hope fill you with all joy and peace in believing," (unless you receive the new heart the God of hope is not going to work for you, I'm sorry) "that ye may abound in hope, through the power of the Holy Ghost." 15:13 The problem is a person doesn't receive the Holy Ghost at the sinner's prayer' you have to be born again first, that cleans your body to get it ready to receive the Spirit. Ezekiel 36:26--27 Tongues has nothing to do with the Holy Ghost.

"---because of the grace that is given to me (Paul) of God," 15 That isn't what St John says it reads that Paul came on his own without God. St John 5:43 It reads also the prince of this world will come after I (Jesus) leaves. That would be the Devil but he is a spirit so he needed Paul as his advocate."Hereafter I will not talk much with you: for the prince of this world cometh and hath nothing in me." St John 14:30 OR as it reads in Isaiah 14:13 and 14 It reads of Lucifer being in mount (all) of the congregation, (churches) and religious organizations. Lucifer said in his heart that he would be like the most High. He needed Paul and Peter as his advocates.

Paul said he was sanctified by the Holy Ghost. Romans 15:16 (He never received it) It was," as a blob" that went in Jesus mouth, that was the Holy Ghost. St Matthew 3:16

"For I will not dare to speak of any of those things which Christ hath not wrought by me, to make the Gentiles obedient by word and deed." 18 It is the Holy Ghost that is the teacher of the Word, and not Christ except what is written in the Gospels, they were not written down at the time when Paul was expressing what he believed to be the truth.

"And I am sure that when I come unto you, I shall come in the fullness of the blessing of the gospel of Christ." 29 (Paul seemed to like to use the word Christ, I believe he meant God, and he is partially right, God gave Jesus what to say and do, but without it written down how could Paul get it right? "For I have not spoken of myself; but the Father which sent me, he gave me a commandment, what I should say, and what I (should) speak." St John 9:49

"---my service which I have for Jerusalem may be accepted of the saints:" 31(I believe I would be more concerned of my service being acceptable to God.)

"That I may come unto you with joy by the will of God, and may (with) you be refreashed." 32 Back to joy, when it is not to be until death or the end time for the saints. St John 16:20

Personal greetings

(Paul never neglected the girls he knew were his bread and butter came from.) There was Phoebe, Priscilla, Aquila Epene-tus, Mary, Andronicus, Junia, etc. etc..Chapter 16

"Salute one another with a holy kiss, the churches of Christ salute you." Romans 16:16 (I was told one time the name, "Church of Christ" was in the Bible. I wonder what a holy kiss is? The Church of Christ, and others, do a lot of wasteful things, but I have never seen the holy kiss.

"Now I beseech you, brethren, mark them (did Paul mean kill them) which cause divisions and offenses contrary to the doctrine which (ye) have learned;(from us) and avoid them." 17 It is no wonder that the true Gospel is so difficult to get to the world, that statement really helps Elijah the prophet. In the last day he was to explain the meaning of the parables or allegorical speech that Jesus spoke "Behold, I will send you Elijah the prophet before the coming of the great and dreadful day of the Lord:" Malachi 4:5 "And he shall turn the heart of the father's to the children, and the heart of the children to their fathers, lest I come and smite the earth with a curse."6

"For they that are such serve not our Lord Jesus Christ but their own belly; and by good words and fair speeches (the same as Paul) deceive the hearts of the simple." Romans 16:18 (The reference is sincere, the false doctrine is in the Bible that is the biggest problem) That sounds like what the preachers are doing, Paul never knew what the Gospel of Jesus was about.

Concluding Doxology

"Now to him that is of power to stablish you according to (my) gospel, and the preaching of Jesus Christ, according to the revelation of the mystery, which was kept secret since the World began." 25 Jesus said in his Gospel that there was a mystery about salvation, and those that weren't saved would never know what the mystery was. That was Paul's problem he never knew what the mystery was. "And the disciples came, and said unto him, Why speakest thou unto them in parables?" St Matthew 13:10 "He answered and said unto them, because it is given unto you to know the mysteries of the kingdom of heaven, but to them it is not given." 11

Who is wise

"But I say unto you, That it shall be more tolerable for the land of Sodom in the day of judgment than for thee. St Matthew 11:24 "At that time Jesus answered and said, I think thee, O Father, Lord of heaven and earth, because thou hast hid these things from the wise and prudent, and hast revealed them unto babes." 25

In Paul's conversion there was no power as I experienced, that was why I knew that Paul was never saved. Ezekiel 36:26-25-27 Your body must be clean before the Holy Ghost will enter it. The 25th verse should have been put after verse 26 and not before. "Then will I sprinkle clean water upon you, (born again) and ye shall be clean from all your filthiness, and from all your idols, will I cleanse you." 25

Show me where Paul ever received a clean body, and speaking in other tongues has nothing to do with the Holy Ghost.

CHAPTER 3

1 PETER'S TRAVESTY

Did Peter ever understand what Jesus spoke about? Outside of being chosen as a disciple according to my concordance it was in St Matthew, Jesus had walked on the water' and Peter asked Him if he could walk to him on the water. He walked on the water to go to Jesus, but was afraid, and beginning to sink, he cried out, Lord save me. How many steps did he take?

Jesus told Peter that he was Ce'phas, which is by interpretation, a stone. St John 1:42 What does St Matthew say about Peter the first Pope of the Catholic Church? Jesus asked Peter who am I, "Thou art the Christ, the (Son) of the living God." It really gets murky after that, does it make any common sense that God would, "build my church" on any individual when salvation is on a one on one bases. It even reads the gates of hell shall not prevail against it. It reads I will give you Peter, the keys of the kingdom of heaven: and whatsoever you will bind on earth shall be bound in heaven: and whatsoever thou shall loose on earth shall be loosed in heaven. That is why that denomination actually believe, they are in the favor of God with all their rhetoric=artificial eloquence, or a comrade in arms, never mind what the Bible says, that if a person speaks the truth they will be hated of all men.

It never took Peter long to fall out of favor, Jesus was telling His disciples He was to be killed, but Peter said no Lord that can't happen.

"But he turned, and said unto Peter, Get thee behind me, Satan: thou art an offense unto me: for thou savorest not the things that be of God, but those that is of men." St Matthew 16:23 It is what I believe in Peter's entire life, he never showed, that he understood what the Gospel of Jesus was about at any time.

In St Matthew we find Peter sucking up to the high priest's palace, to see the end, after they had already arrested Jesus. St Matthew 26:58 "---A damsel came unto him, (Peter) saying, Thou also was with Jesus of Galilee." 69 "But he denied before them all, saying, I know not what you are sayest." 70

"Jesus said unto him. Verily I say unto thee, That this night, before the cock crow, thou shalt deny me thrice." St Matthew 26:34 "Peter answered and said unto him, through all men shall be offended because of thee, yet will I never be offended." 33 "And Peter remembered the word of Jesus, which said unto him, before the cock crow, thou shalt deny me thrice. and he went out, and wept bitterly."75

In the book of Acts the first chapter there is a lot of it mentioned with Peter in the thick of it, and beyond. It was written by Luke who is not one of my favorite disciples it reads that he traveled with Paul. The trouble starts in St Matthew "Go ye therefore, and teach all nations, baptizing them in the name of the Father, and of the Son, and of the Holy Ghost:" St Matthew 28:19

Water baptism has never been a priority of the salvation Gospel. The baptism spoken of in the Gospels by Jesus, is baptism in the Holy Ghost, the way Jesus and I both received it, in the mouth as a blob or, 'Like a dove' in St Matthew 3:16.

At the end of every Gospel are verses that are suspect, in validity in comparison to the rest of the Word that Jesus spoke.

"He that believeth and is baptized (water) shall be saved; but he that believeth not shall be damned." St Mark 16:16 A form of believe is a condition for the Spirit of Genesis to act or a catalyst. I say the Spirit of Genesis because there are two Spirits the other is the Holy Ghost which is a Spirit for those that have been born again, and their body clean. Ezekiel and St John "---Who then can be saved?" St Matthew 19:25 "---With men this is impossible; but with God all things are possible." 26 "---A man can receive nothing, except it be given him from heaven." St John 3:27 I found out that's true.

"And these signs shall follow them that believe; in my name shall they cast out devils; they shall speak with new tongues; St Mark 16:17 "They shall take up serpents; and if they drink any deadly thing, it shall not hurt them; they shall lay hands on the sick, and they shall recover." 18 There has never been a documented case of a person that was healed by a preacher laying hands on someone. Speaking with new tongues is trying to cover for what Peter said in The Acts which never worked for John the Baptist why would it work for Peter? "Then Peter said unto them, Repent, and be baptized every one of you in the name of Jesus Christ for the remission of sins, and ye shall receive the gift of the Holy Ghost." The Acts 2:38

Speaking with new tongues and the fire mentioned in the second chapter of The Acts gives me pause. All of these verses at the last chapter of Mark have no biblical validity but 19 is the exception "So then after the Lord had spoken unto them, he was received up into heaven, and set on the right hand of God." St Mark 16:19

"I indeed baptize you with water unto repentance: but he that cometh after me is mightier than I, whose shoes I am not worthy to bear: he shall baptize you with the Holy Ghost, AND WITH FIRE:" St Matthew 3:11 This is the only verse that I am aware of, that they got "fire", for the second chapter of Acts. It doesn't mean fire," literally" it means the new Word that Jesus was taught, that His Father wanted His son to say, and taught by the Holy Ghost when He was in the wilderness. It doesn't say how long Jesus was in the wilderness it only says He fasted forty days and nights. "And when he had fasted forty days and forty nights, he was afterward hungry." St Matthew 4:2 (The human side of Jesus)

Luke I have said is suspect he said "And behold, I send the promise of my Father upon you: but terry ye in the city of Jerusalem, until ye be endued with power from on high." Luke 24:49 The Acts second chapter, a sound from heaven? (a spirit making a sound) mighty wind, (a spirit a mighty wind) and it filled the house where they were sitting.? (A blob as a small dove filled the house? As in St Matthew) "And there appeared unto them cloven tongues like as of FIRE, and it sat upon each of them." The Acts 2:3 That is what Matthew said that the Holy Ghost, "lighting on him" but it never, it went in his mouth and down His throat as it did mine. The FIRE means the new gospel for this dispensation, or the new Word will spread over the earth as a fire if not then, but eventually it will happen before the second coming. St Matthew 3:11

In the rest of the second chapter of The Acts, Peter opened up, as if he knew something, and his main point was that they had received the promise of the Holy Ghost, and they made the mistake of asking Peter what shall we do'? Then Peter saved the day by telling them the same thing that John the Baptist preached (and lost his head) "Repent, and be baptized in (water) every one of you in the name of Jesus Christ for the remission of sins, and ye shall receive the gift of the Holy Ghost." The Acts 2:38 (Never mind that the Holy Ghost will not enter into a filthy body, you have to be born again first, or receive a replacement of your heart, from God first)

It reads that, that day three thousand souls were added, still having their sin in their heart, plus the original disobedience from Adam? Some churches would die for that verse; The Acts 2:38.

There is one thing that seems certain, those that were fooling with the bible sense Jesus left, tried to connect what Paul and Peter said with the Gospels of what Jesus spoke. "For John truly baptized with water; but ye shall be baptized with the Holy Ghost not many days hence." The Acts 1:5 Did they think of this in Acts first or was Luke first? "And behold I send the promise of my Father upon you: but tarry ye in the city of Jerusalem, until ye be endued with power from on high." Luke 24:49 The only thing that is wrong is, a person's body must be clean, before the Holy Ghost will enter it, and tongues has nothing to do with the Holy Ghost.

Because fire was mentioned in St Matthew they wrote that in The Acts 'cloven tongues like as of fire, and it sat upon each of them.' I wonder what did set on each of them it just mentioned, as of fire? Do we see lights (as in Paul's conversion or fire, or whatever sat on them, in the churches today?) I have heard a lot of blabber as it reads "And they were all filled with the Holy Ghost, and began to speak with other tongues as the Spirit gave them tterance." The Acts 2 4

It was the Holy Ghost that taught Jesus, "the will of God" in the wilderness, and when God was satisfied that Jesus knew the Gospel, He had angels minister unto him or revel His graduation. This all happened to me, but it took two years after I received the Holy Ghost, in the mouth as Jesus did, after He was baptized by John the Baptist. An Angel appeared that I saw toward the ceiling 11 Jan. 1970 at 11a m in a Sunday school class in San Pedro, California. It is explained in the book.

It reads in St John unless a person receives the Spirit (Holy Ghost) they can't enter into the kingdom of God. It is the new Spirit in Ezekiel. It is like a dove or blob that entered the mouth of Jesus, "it never lighting on Him" as it reads in St Matthew It is known as him or he the teacher of the Words of Jesus or Gospel, and it will be with a person for eternity. Ezekiel 36:26-27 : St Matthew 3:16 ; St John 14:15-26

But what does Peter say about it, in Peter 1 "Elect according to the foreknowledge of God the Father, through sanctification of the Spirit, unto obedience and sprinkling of the blood of Jesus Christ: Grace unto you, and peace be multiplied." 1 Peter 1:2 Any truth would have scared Peter to death. According to Peter, the elect has knowledge of God being set apart by the Spirit. It keeps the money coming in, regular attendance, food brought to the church, more food brought in, janitor happy, and more food brought in. That is what Peter said the Spirit produces (obedience), and only God knows what he is writing about the sprinkling of blood of Jesus Christ: (peace be multiplied unto you) For those that become saved there is no joy. I know the preachers will tell you if you have no joy you're not saved. My Bible tells me ye shall be sorrowful, but your sorrow shall be turned into joy. (At the end time) It is the world that shall rejoice, and superficial peace will be multiplied. St John 16:20

"Who are kept by the power of God through faith unto salvation ready to be revealed in the last time." 1Peter 1:5 12/1/1968 at 9pm it was revealed to me through the power of God, physically, that He was on the throne. I don't know what he means by it will be revealed at the last day, 'salvation?' It reads when a person is born again they will enter the kingdom of God, but still be here on this earth.

. "Whom having not seen, ye love:" 8 (when I was born again I felt my heart being removed and then replaced. I saw and felt the blob 'Spirit or Holy Ghost' go in my mouth. An angel was revealed to me in a Sunday school class.) Love has nothing to do with a person becoming righteous which is the requirement of God, it reads seek ye first His righteousness. "But seek ye first the kingdom of God, and His righteousness--- " St Matthew 6:33

"But as he which hath called you is holy, so be ye holy in all manner of conversation; " 15 (Yes Jesus is holy, and I found out salvation is physical) so be ye holy in all manner of conversation;?" "Because it is written, be ye holy, for I am holy." 16 (The reference of this verse is not in the Bible) To me it is saying be nice, and there are a lot of nice people sitting in the a-men corner agreeing with the pastor. Jesus said be perfect as your Father is perfect St Matthew 5:48

There is no way biblically, that living a holy life will get a person anywhere. It says that in the Bible but it is not true.

"And if ye call on the Father, who without respect of persons judgeth according to every man's work,---".1 Peter 1:17 So, be nice and feed the poor that will give them something to eat, that is as far as it goes, your work has nothing to do with being saved.

";---that your faith and hope, might be in God." 21 When I was physically saved I don't need any hope or faith, I knew at that time there is a God. In the Islam faith they hope Allah likes them, but they won't know for sure until they die.

"Seeing ye have purified your souls (how does this come about?) In obeying the truth through the Spirit (which you have never received) unto unfeigned (genuine) love of the brethren, see that ye love one another with a pure heart fervently." 22 (Which church are the brethren in?) (You haven't received a pure heart so how can this be?) My heart was removed and replaced by God, now that is a pure heart. Ezekiel 36:26 "Being born again, not of corruptible seed, but of incorruptible, by the word of God---." 23 In St John it reads unless your born again and receive the Spirit you cannot enter into the kingdom of God. The Word of God or washing of the word, has nothing to do with being born again, because it is physical. Nicodemus said it was physical as the birth of a child. I will tell you it is physical.

"And this is the word which by the gospel is preached unto you." 25 (What Paul said was that (my) Gospel Is preached unto you)

"As newborn babes, (let's see, you have listened to the sinner's prayer spoken by the pastor, now what do I do?) Desire the sincere milk of the Word, that you may grow thereby." 1 Peter 2:2 I never needed to grow, at 9pm 12/1/1968 I was redeemed, in one or two minutes. Even Luke said, "But if I with the finger of God (power) cast out devils, (born again by the spirit of God) no doubt the kingdom of God is come upon you." Luke 11:20

"---and he that believeth on him shall not be confounded." 6 (My concordance says it means disappointed, I can't by that) confounded means, "be confused." How many churches do you count that are confused? The sad part is they don't even know they are confused, because what they preach is in the Bible, but Paul was the advocate for Satan.

"Which in time past were not a people, but are now the people of God: (which church) which had not obtained mercy, (I'm not sure how mercy got in here) but now have obtained mercy." 10 That is true God was kind in giving us Jesus but no place have I read where Peter nor Paul understood how to become righteous, to enter into the kingdom of heaven.

"---abstain from fleshly lusts, which war against the soul:" 1 Peter 2:11 In Ezekiel all my filthiness was removed in about two minutes, and all my idols or the things that doesn't have anything to do with God. Ezekiel 36:25 In other words, everything that I do must be done in moderation with no sin, and other things in moderation. Doing nothing that might harm the body, and doing my utmost to maintain a healthy clean body for the Lords work.

"Honor all men, Love the brotherhood, fear God, honor the king." 17 Which is it whom do we honor than, men or God? In St John It reads they honor one another, and seek not the honor that cometh from God only? St John 5:44

"Servants, be subject to your masters with all fear;" 1 Peter 2:18 (If you think I'm going to follow preachers into hell your crazy) A person can judge righteously or biblically. I was saved physically so as it reads, "Judge not according to the appearance, but judge righteous judgment." St John 7:24 "Ye judge after the flesh; I judge no man." 8:15 (According to human ideas) "Thou hypocrite, first cast out the beam out of thine own eye; and then shalt thou see clearly to cast out the mote out of thy brother's eye."St Matthew 7:5

"Who did no sin, neither was guile found in his mouth:" 1 Peter 2:22 " (Jesus) The original sin of Adam must only come down through the male. Jesus was born of Marry impregnated by the Spirit of Genesis, and not the Holy Ghost as it reads in St Matthew. A person will be condemned by what comes out of their mouth. "Not that which goeth into the mouth defileth a man: but that which cometh out of the mouth, this defileth a man." St Matthew 15:11

"Who his own self bear our sins in his own body on the tree, that we, being dead to sins, should live unto righteousness: by whose stripes ye were healed." 1 peter 2:24 (The original sin of Adam and your accumulative sin is in your own body that a person must get rid of, Jesus, could not bear our sin in His body for us) "that we, being dead to sins," (unless your born again a person is not dead to sins) "should live unto righteousness:" (a person cannot live a righteous life unless they have been given a new heart and a new Spirit first as in Ezekiel 36:26-27) "by whose stripes ye were healed." (His stripes that He received has nothing to do with salvation only his death)

"For ye were as sheep going astray; but are now returned unto the Shepherd and Bishop of your souls." 25 (This smells too much like the Catholic faith, when a man can't do one thing for man.)

"Wives---being in subjection unto their own husbands: 3:5 (This is hard for me to believe what about single women or a man that tells five wives, this is the only way to paradise) I never knew that it was in the KJB of 1611 that unmarried women should work for God. (Nuns) "---The unmarried women careth for the things of the Lord, that she may be holy both in body and in spirit:" 1 Corinthians 7:34

"Finally, be ye all of one mind, having compassion one of another, love as brethren, be pitiful, be courteous:" 1 Peter 3:8 "For I am come to set a man at variance against his father, and the daughter against her mother, and the daughter-in-law against her mother-in-law." St Matthew 10:35 "And a man's foes shall be they of his own household." 36 After my dad and mother got a divorce, he blamed her for ruining his life. That was all I ever heard him say about it. Understanding my dad a person needed to know verses in the Bible. "For if a man know not, how to rule his own house, how shall he take care of the Church of God?" 1 Timothy 3:5 I was twelve when they divorced and he was drunk from then on as much as possible. He was a carpenter, and one time my boss asked me if I was the son of Mike? I told him I was, and he said that he had to lay him off one time, because he had a whisky bottle in his tool box.

"For the eyes of the Lord are over the righteous, and his ears are open unto their prayers, but the face of the Lord is against them that do evil."

1 Peter 3:12 Is he saying be nice, they are the only ones God cares about, and live a life as close as you can to being righteous? The Lord wants those that are doing evil, into His kingdom? Who did he say He came to save, those that think they are righteous or them that do evil. Who did Jesus sit with in St Matthew, wasn't it, Publicans and sinners' St Matthew 9:10 "And when the Pharisees saw it, they said unto his disciples, why eateth your Master with publicans and sinners?" 11 "But when Jesus heard that, he said unto them, They that be whole (think they are righteous) need not a physician, (saved) but they that are sick." 12 When I was seeking salvation there was no doubt in my mind, that I was a sinner that needed a savior, and what got me on this path was I wondered if religion was real? At that time in the sixties the country was in turmoil.

"And who is he that will harm you, if ye be followers of that which is good?" 1 Peter 3:13, Is he saying be nice? A person can't possibly do good, and live with God in His kingdom.

"But sanctify the lord God in your hearts: and be ready always to give an answer to every man that asketh you a reason of the hope that is in you with meekness and fear:" 15 (I'm not sure "why the s" is on hearts.) Salvation is up close and personal, and I know it reads that a person is suppose to hang-in-their-together, and smell each other's socks. I'm not a member of any church but have no doubt that I will live with God in His kingdom. St John 3:3-5 and Ezekiel 36:26-27

"For Christ also hath once suffered for sins,---" 18 Jesus died that we might become righteous that a person must believe in one of the works that he did, that is the only connection that He had between the cross and mankind. "If I do not the works of my Father, believe me not. But if I do, though ye believe not me, believe the works: that ye may know and believe that the Father is in me, and I in him." St John 10:37-38 What that does is trigger the Spirit of Genesis to give a person a new heart where there is no doubt of the existence of God, as it reads. Ye may know (beyond any doubt) that the Father (in heaven) is in me, and I in him, or they have the same goals. "Believe me that I am in the Father, and the Father in me: or else believe me for the very works' sake." St John 14:11 I believed in my heart that I could heal my mother, "one of the works of healing, that Jesus did."

"By which also he went and preached unto the spirits in prison;" 19 (I don't believe this verse at all or he is referring to the people in prison which is a strange word to use) Too get out of their sell they become Christians in their eyes, and that is what they are told.

"In the days of Noah ---eight souls were saved by water." 20 If I were to write this verse I believe I would use the word, "a boat." The water killed everybody but the eight souls in the boat, but the preachers say the Bible (which one) is infallible.

"The like figure (maybe Jesus) whereunto even baptism (in water) doth also now save us." 21 Baptism in water has nothing to do with saving anybody but Peter said it did in The Acts. "Then Peter said unto them, Repent, and be baptized every one of you in the name of Jesus Christ for the remission of sins, and ye shall receive the gift of the Holy Ghost." The Acts 2:38 The Holy Ghost comes from God, in heaven or as John said, "from above" man can do nothing to receive it. Then Peter said "not the putting away of the filth of the flesh, ??? but by the resurrection of Jesus Christ." 21 Sin is in the heart, my heart that I was born with was removed, and I received a new heart as it reads in Ezekiel "I will take away the stony heart out of your flesh, and I will give you a heart of flesh." (From God) Ezekiel 36:26 "Then will I sprinkle clean water (not HTO but the new heart "born again") upon you, and ye shall be clean: from all your filthiness, and from all your idols, (football in moderation) will I cleanse you." 25

"Who is gone into heaven, and is on the right hand of God;" 1 Peter 3:22 (Jesus) (God did say He gave all judgment to the Son) But God never relinquished all power to Jesus as it reads. "Angels and authorities, and powers, being made subject unto him." 22 "For the Father judgeth no man, but hath committed all judgment unto the Son." St John 5:22 Jesus was not God.

"---For he that hath suffered in the flesh hath ceased from sin;" 1 Peter 4:1 (what is Peter writing about?) My Dad almost beat me to death when I was 3 or 4, did that take care of my sin for the rest of my life?

"That he no longer should live the rest of his time in the flesh to the lusts of men, but to the will of God?" 1 Peter 3:2

"For this cause was the gospel preached also to them that are dead, that they might be judged according to men in the flesh, but live according to God in the spirit." 6 What does the dead have to do with the living? I recognize babble when I see it. (Live according to God in the spirit?) If you haven't received the new Spirit or Holy Ghost how can you live, according to God in the Spirit? Blabbering in tongues is not the Holy Ghost

"But the end of all things is at hand: be ye therefore sober, and watch unto prayer." 7 Would it have made a difference if Noah got down on his knees? "And above all things have fervent charity among yourselves: for charity shall cover the multitude of sins." 1 Peter 4:8 Jesus said a person must be born again and receive the Holy Ghost to enter into the kingdom of God. I see—you can work your way into the kingdom of God according to Peter by giving money.

"As every man hath received the gift, even so minister the same one to another, as good stewards of the manifold grace of God." 10 (It is too bad Peter never mentioned which church and what is the gift that he is writing about?) In The Acts Peter called the Holy Ghost a gift, but which gift is it, the one Jesus received when He was baptized by John or as Peter put it? They began to speak in other tongues? The Acts2:4 Do we want to believe Jesus or Peter? We are to minister the same (gift) one to another. The only problem is man has nothing to do with the Holy Ghost, when it comes from God, only after a person is born again and his body is clean.

"---as though some strange thing happened unto you:" 12 Peter, it did happen to me it is called salvation, redemption or transformation, and it is too bad it never happened to you.

"Then opened he their understanding that they might understand the scriptures." St Luke 24:45 The reference goes to The Acts "The heart of a women, was opened unto the things which were spoken of Paul." The Acts 16:14 I don't believe St Luke, How could Peter have spoken in The Acts, if he understood the salvation plan, which he didn't. The Acts 2:38 Paul never understood the true Gospel either.

"And when the chief Shepherd shall appear, ye shall receive a crown of glory that fadeth not away." 1 Peter 5:4 I have already received the crown of glory, and don't have to wait until Jesus appears (again) I'm ready to leave now. Jesus left in bodily form as the witnesses say. After being born again and receiving the Holy Spirit a person will enter into the kingdom of God and never leave the earth. St John 3:3-5

"Likewise, ye younger, submit yourselves unto the elder." (When salvation is between God and yourself, I'm not going to submit to nobody) "Yea all of you be subject one to another, and be clothed with humility:

for God resisteth the proud, and giveth grace to the humble." 5 God gives grace physically, to the sinner and hates those that believe they are righteous according to the Gospel.

"Humble yourselves therefore under the mighty hand of God, that he may exalt you in due time." 6 The night before I was saved on a Saturday night I took a women home to her house and had sex with her. The next night God saved me, it must have been my time. How can you humble yourself when you don't know God exist? I was a sinner that needed a savior.

"Casting all your care upon him; for he careth for you." 7 Love has nothing to do with achieving the righteousness of God, and that is why Jesus died on the cross. In Genesis it reads it grieved God in His heart that He made man on the earth. Genesis 6:6 Does this sound like He careth for you? He does, but in a different way that the preachers put it, of love.

"Be sober, be vigilant because your adversary the devil (might get you) as a roaring lion, walketh about, seeking whom he may devour:" 8 At the end of Jesus time in the wilderness it reads He saw angels that ministered unto him. St Matthew 4:11 It was the same with me I saw an Angel in a Sunday school class. After that, I don't ever believe it reads anymore about Satan bothering Jesus, and it is the same with me after two years, after I received the Holy Ghost spending time in the wilderness. "Ye shall drink indeed of my cup, and be baptized with the baptism that I am baptized with:" St Matthew 20:23 The same things that happened to me or Jesus will happen to you.

"But the God of all grace, who hath called us unto his eternal glory, by Christ Jesus, after ye have suffered a while, (it will) make you perfect, stablish, (stabilize) strengthen, settle you." 10 I'm not sure what Peter is trying to say. I can certainly understand where preachers get the grace bit. It was by the grace of God that He gave mankind Jesus for righteousness sake.

"To him be glory and dominion forever and ever." A'-men." 11 God can take care of himself.

"By Silvanus, a faithful brother; unto you, as I suppose, I have written briefly, exhorting, and testifying that this is the true grace of God wherein (ye) stand." I'm afraid it is where Peter stood, leave me out of it. 12

The second epistle of Peter

"Simon Peter, a servant and apostle of Jesus Christ, to them that have obtained like precious faith with us through the righteousness of God and our Savior Jesus Christ:" 1 Peter 1:1 (to them that have obtained like precious faith (with us?) In St Matthew it reads go by what came out of the mouth of Jesus. Peter has shown over and over again he doesn't have a clue about how a person achieves righteousness. It is the sin of Adam that a person must get rid of obtaining a new heart and a new Spirit, not only Adam's sin but your accumulative sin.

"Grace and peace be multiplied unto you, through the knowledge of God, and of Jesus our Lord." 2 I found out physically, with my senses, the knowledge of God.

. There is no such thing as growing in grace.

"Knowing this first, that no prophecy of the scripture is of any private interpretation." 20 That is not what the Bible says. Paul and Peter came, "on their own" without the sanction of God. "I am come in my Father's name, and ye receive me not: (Jesus) if another shall come in his own name, him ye will receive." St John 5:43 (Believe, Paul) From The Acts –Jude is of a private interpretation, and not of God from Paul and his disciples.

"For the prophecy came not in old time by the will of men: but holy men of God spake as they were moved by the Holy Ghost." 11 Peter 1:21 It was the Spirit of Genesis, and not the Holy Ghost because the Holy Ghost is only for those that are born again first, for this dispensation, it has nothing to do with it before the time of Jesus. In the time of Jesus it was only for Him, when He was baptized by John as the teacher from God, of what He was to do and say. For the pilgrims (that is us) it wasn't to be until after Jesus went to His Father in heaven. "Nevertheless I tell you the truth; It is expedient for you that I go away: for if I go (not) away, the Comforter (Holy Ghost) will not come unto you; but if I depart, I will send him unto you." St John 16:7 (There is another chapter on 11 Peter chapter 6)

Chapter 4

Timothy's Travesty

The First Epistle of Paul the Apostle to Timothy

"Paul, an apostle of Jesus Christ by the commandment of God our Savior, and Lord Jesus Christ, which is our hope;" 1 Timothy 1:1 (They touched on all the basses here) I was saved physically, what is it that I am hoping for? "I am come in my Father's name, and ye receive me not: (Jesus) if another shall come in his own name, him (Paul) ye will receive, (Believe) St John 5:43

"----that they teach no other doctrine," 3 Paul never knew the true doctrine. 'unless your born again from above, and have received the new Spirit, (Holy Ghost in the mouth) a person cannot enter into the kingdom of God.' St John 3:3-5 There is no such thing as teaching the doctrine of salvation, John said it comes from heaven, and I found out that was true. "--- A man can receive nothing, except it be given him from heaven." St John 3:27

"Now the end (goal) of the commandment is charity out of a pure heart, and of a good conscience, and of faith unfeigned:" 1 Timothy 1:5 (unpretended) They never received a different heart than what they were born with, so how could they have a pure heart, one from God? Charity is the love of God for man or man for his fellow men. God couldn't very well have said hate your fellow man, but in Genesis It reads it "grieved God in His heart, that he had made man on the earth". Genesis 6:6 "Blessed are the pure in heart: for they shall see God." St Matthew 5:8 On this earth a person will only see the power of God, in the form of a Spirit that replaces your heart, a light did that for me. .

(false prophets) "Desiring to be teachers of the law;" (No Paul, you should be teachers of the Word that Jesus gave us from His Father.) understanding neither, (that is true) what they say, nor whereof they affirm." 1 Timothy 1:7(teach) I was taught the commandments of God after I received the Holy Ghost, but they wouldn't know anything about that, and remaining in the wilderness for two years. The same as Jesus, He received the Holy Ghost in His mouth on His first breath, coming out of the water of John's baptism. He went in the wilderness, for instruction by the New Spirit, and to be tempted by the Devil. St Matthew 4:1-11

"Knowing this, that the law is not made for a righteous man, but the lawless and disobedient,----." 9 "For verily I say unto you, That many prophets and righteous men have desired to see those things which ye see, and have not seen them; and to hear those things which ye hear, and have not heard them." St Matthew 13:17 "But blessed are your eyes, for they see: and your ears for they hear." St Matthew 13:16 I was given a new heart (from a light, 'power' from God) and a new Spirit (in my mouth) in Ezekiel. The law of the Old Testament ended with John the Baptist, but Jesus gave us the new Word for this dispensation. "For all the prophets and the law prophesied until John." St Matthew 11:13

"According to the glorious gospel of the blessed God, which was committed to my trust." 1 Timothy 1:11 (If you can believe that) The Gospel is condemnation of mankind, how can it be glorious? It is extremely sad, I have read the last chapter. Who was, "my" trust? Paul, Peter, and Timothy Etc. Jesus said they were on their own in St John 5:43, and comparing with what they said, has nothing to do with what Jesus spoke.

Paul said Jesus put him in the ministry; 12 Paul came on his own with Satan who enabled him. St John 5:43

"Who was before a blasphemer, and a persecutor, and injurious: but I had obtained mercy, because I did it ignorantly in unbelief." 13 I can understand the ignorantly part. At his so-called conversion Paul never got rid of the sin of Adam plus his accumulative sin, that is why it is necessary to be given a new heart. Adam and Eve was changed physically, from being perfect, and a person must be made perfect back again, as they were before ordained too live with God in His kingdom. "Be ye therefore perfect, even as your Father which is in heaven is perfect." St Matthew 5:48 All of mankind is in that category of being ignorant in unbelief, and Paul never did change because he never did receive redemption.

"And the grace of our Lord was exceeding abundant with faith and love which is in Christ Jesus." 1 Timothy 1:14 None of this rant means anything. The belief in one of the works that Jesus did in your heart, triggers, or the catalyst for the Spirit, to give a person a new heart for righteousness sake. It has nothing to do with faith and love. "Believe me that I am in the Father, and the Father in me; or else believe me for the very works' sake." St John 14:11

,"---Christ Jesus (Paul means God) came into the world to save sinners; of whom I am chief." 15 It reads that Paul was there when Stephen was stoned, I don't believe he threw any, but he saw that it was useless to stone all the sinners, he decided with the help of Satan, to contaminate the Word, and that has worked out very well for him.

"Howbeit for this cause I obtained mercy, that in me first Jesus Christ might show forth all long-suffering, for a pattern to them which should hereafter, believe on him to life everlasting." 16 If it were only true, it sounds good, and that is what St John tells us but it shouldn't be in the Bible. St John 3:16

Paul said he delivered Hy-me-ne'-us and Alexander unto Satan, that they may learn not to blaspheme. 20 It doesn't bother God or Jesus assuming he is writing about swearing, so why is it bothering Paul? It is not good to blaspheme the Holy Ghost because you need it, to become saved, on the street they would say it is the only game in town. "Wherefore I say unto you, all manner of sin and blasphemy shall be forgiven unto men: but the blasphemy against the Holy Ghost shall not be forgiven unto men." "And whosoever speaketh a word against the Son of man, it shall be forgiven him: but whosoever speaketh against the Holy Ghost, it shall not be forgiven him, neither in this world, neither in the world to come." St Matthew 12:31-32 Do you think any mortal man, can deliver another person to Satan?

Paul exhorts to prayer

"Exhort (Pray) therefore, that, first of all supplications, prayers, intercessions, and giving of thanks, be made for all men;" 1 Timothy 2:1 "For this is good and acceptable in the sight of God our Savior;" 3 "Who will have all men to be saved, and to come unto the knowledge of the truth." 4 "For there is one God, and one mediator between God and man, the man (Son) Christ Jesus;" 5 "Whereunto I am ordained a preacher, and an apostle, (I speak the truth in Christ, and lie not;) a teacher of the Gentiles in faith and verity." 7 'Truth' "I will therefore that men pray everywhere, lifting up holy hands, without wrath and doubting." 8 I wish that was all there was to it?

"But when ye pray, use not vain repetitions, as the heathen do: for they think that they shall be heard for their much speaking." St Matthew 6:7 "Be not ye therefore like unto them: for your Father knoweth what things ye have need of before ye ask him." 8 What about St John, "No man can come to me, (that I have not chosen) except the Father which hath sent me draw him: and I will raise him up at the last day:" St John 6:44 I'm not sure where preachers get that God is Jesus, and the Holy Ghost is God, it is separate except Paul again wrote Christ Jesus which to me he means God?: Lucifer wanted to be like God, could he be like God without an advocate? Isaiah 14:14 Then Paul said he speaks the truth and lie not but St John says Paul came on his own, and how could the Gospels be the same, he never had them to read nor did he ever meet Jesus. St John 5:43

'Lucifer said he would be in the mount (all) the congregation (Churches).' Isaiah 14:13 That is why I don't go to any church. "Hereafter I will not talk much with you: for the, "prince of this world" cometh and hath nothing in me." St John 14:30 Satan is a spirit, that needed an advocate, which was Paul.

! Timothy it Is about woman. How can they learn anything when the Gospel of salvation has been with-held from the church? 1 Timothy 2: 9 through 15 " ---for the meat offering and the drink offering is with holden from the house of your god." Joel 1:13 In St John, it is about being born again and receiving the Holy Ghost using meat and drink offerings in allegorical form. St John 6:31-58 People can't seem to handle the truth, they just want to live, be lied to, and die. That is why few will find the way.

Haven't men lied to women enough, it is your soul that you must look out for, Before the end time I hope the true church will be revealed before Jesus returns the second time. The sad thing is men follow Paul's gospel, and don't realize that he was not of God but was on his own, it is the worst situation of all. If you sent your Son to die on the cross for mankind, and they 'preach' another gospel wouldn't you withhold the Spirit of redemption from the churches? The Jehovah's Witnesses believe it is so bad not calling God Yahweh, when they have no problem with Paul? Does that make any sense to you? Paul wrote half of the New Testament in the KJB of 1611, and comparing the two halves it is unmistakably different.

Salvation is physical, I don't think God cares what a person's apparel is, and good works isn't the answer for true salvation.

"This is a true saying, If a man desire the office of a bishop, (preacher) he desireth a good work." 1 Timothy 3:1 That is what is wrong with the religious community people only desire to be a leader of a church. My Dad was one of those, but in St Matthew it reads "But seek ye first the kingdom of God, (born again and receive the new Spirit St John 3:5) and His righteousness; and all these things shall be added unto you." St Matthew 6:33 Afterward whatever God's desire for your life, will be given to you.

(rules of being a preacher) "One that ruleth well his own house, having his children in subjection with all gravity;" (stoic= free from emotion) 4"For if a man know not how to rule his own house, how shall he take care of the church of God?" 1 Timothy 3:5 My dad said my brother was acting up, and he quit preaching one time, took him outside gave him a spanking, and he came back in, and finished his sermon. Before he was called to preach he almost beat me to death. He was having sex on the couch, I was on the floor, and the size of his penis impressed me. Mine was smaller than that, so I was checking out the neighbor boy, when my mother saw me. Mom said she was going to tell dad when he came home from work. When dad came home he beat me with tree branches, coming at me twice, I couldn't breathe the first time, I don't know how close I came to die. Afterward he was called to preach. After a divorce, I'm sure dad believed, that verse in Timothy, and stayed drunk most of the time for forty years, I was twelve years old.

"Even so must their wives be grave, not slanderers, sober, faithful in all things." 1 Timothy 3:11 Neither one of my parents ever received the righteousness of God, so my mother had a hysterectomy when we lived on the first farm. Dad had gone to Kansas City, working a deferred job on the railroad, instead of going in to World War 11. I was five years old, too young to go to school. Every time the neighbor came to the house I had to go outside, and play with the frogs. My mother taught Sunday school, and I asked her if she ever read the Bible, I was five years old.

Whatever you want to call them, bishop, preacher, pope, deacon, elder, mu-la, evangelist, pastor, etc. if they have not received the righteousness that comes from God only, the life they live will be in vain.

"But if I tarry long, that thou mayestI know you will behave thy self in the house of God, which is the church of the living God, the pillar and ground of the truth." 1 Timothy 3:15 (Which church) I was saved, at a gasoline service station it should give a person some indication on what God thinks of the churches.

"And without controversy great is the mystery of godliness:---"16 Let's count how many churches there are, and it reads they are without controversy? Controversy= a discussion of a question in which opposing opinions clash. "God was manifest in the flesh," wasn't that Jesus the Son. "And the Word (that was from the beginning Genesis 1:1) was made flesh," (apparent to the senses) and dwelt among us, (and we beheld his glory, the glory as of the only begotten of the Father,) full of grace (from God) and truth." St John 1:14 One of the few verses that has the word Grace in it is St John "For the law was given by Moses, but grace and truth came by Jesus Christ." St John 1:17 It was by the grace of His Father God, that He gave us Jesus. "For I have not spoken of myself; but the Father which sent me, he gave me a commandment, what I should say, and what I should speak."St John 12:49 Grace ends here at this time in history with Jesus being born.

When Jesus spent His time in the wilderness, after He received the Holy Ghost in the mouth, during the baptism of John the Baptist, there were two things going on. He was being taught from the Holy Ghost the commandments that God wanted Jesus to do, and say. The devil was trying to get Jesus too worship him. St Matthew 4:1-11

"Then the devil leaveth him, and, behold, angels came, and ministered unto him." St Matthew 4:11 This happened to me after two years, and it only says Jesus fasted 40 days, it doesn't say how long he was in the wilderness. In a Sunday school class in San Pedro, California, a protestant church, at the end of the class I looked up toward the ceiling and there was an angel, with an extremely white robe with no head, feet, or hands. I blurted out, 'The day of judgment is coming.' The devil never bothered me or Jesus again after that.

Predictions of apostasy
An abandoning of what one believed

"Now the Spirit speaketh expressly, that in the latter times some shall depart from the faith, giving heed to seducing spirits, and doctrines of devils;" 1 Timothy 4:1 That is what people should do is depart from Paul and Timothy's faith, because it is false doctrine. That is why God has removed His Spirit from all the churches. "Gird yourselves, and lament, ye priests: howl, ye ministers of the altar: come, lie all night in sackcloth, ye ministers of my God: the meat offering and the drink offering is withholden from the house of your god." 'God' Joel 1:13 99% Of preachers, preach what Paul said, and there are no comparison with the Gospels of St John, Matthew, and Mark.

I read 80% of people wouldn't even think of maybe their parents were wrong, in the faith, in whatever they believed, and were brought up in.

"For herefore we both labor (Paul and Timothy) and suffer reproach, (rebuke) because we trust in the living God, who is the Saviour of all Men, especially of those that believe." 10 (We are back to St John 3:16) Some of Paul's disciples, asked him if he believed what he was saying? Have you ever tried to change a person's mind? They will tell you don't bother me with the facts or the truth.

How many in Noah's day were trusting in the living God? It only reads that Noah was perfect in his generation, what about the other seven, food for thought?

"These things command and teach." 11 Whatever Paul, Peter, and Timothy speak, teach? When my mother sent me my King James Bible of 1611, every time I started to read in The Acts, God put a nauseous feeling on me, until I finally saw that there was something wrong with The Acts –Jude. Then when I read how Paul was saved it left no doubt that he was a false prophet.

"Neglect not the gift that is in thee, which was given thee by prophecy, with the laying on of the hands of the presbytery."1 Timothy 4:14 (Is that the way it's done the laying on of the hands, I thought anything a person needs comes from God, and I found out that is true.) "---A man can receive nothing, except it be given him from heaven." St John 3:27 (here is the biggest problem in the churches) "Ye do err, not knowing the scriptures, nor the power of God." St Matthew 22"29 The preachers tell their congregations, how powerful God is but that is as far as it gets.

"Take heed unto thyself, and unto the doctrine; (of Paul, Peter, and Timothy) continue in them: for in doing this thou shalt both save thyself, and them that hear thee." 16 Does Jesus words, count for anything, He was only the Son of God? I found out His Word is true, finding verses that verified what happened to me, in the king James Bible of 1611, is the explanations of St John, which is in true allegorical form of the salvation experience. Ezekiel never wrote it in sequence that it must occur. As the old timers said he got the cart before the horse. Ezekiel 36:26-25-27

"But if any provide not for his own, and especially for those of his own house, he hath denied the faith, and is worse than an infidel." 1 Timothy 5:8 Because salvation is between God and yourself, and physical, I'm not going to say this verse is important, but interesting. After my dad almost beat me to death, he was called to preach. He quit a deferred railroad job and bought a farm in Seneca, Missouri. It was too much hill then what a person could farm, he was going to live on his preachers' salary of $6.00 or less a week. He went to Kansas City and got back on the railroad, after he got a letter from the Army in World War 11. When the war ended he quit again, as he said, "He couldn't stand prosperity." Because we were on two farms we did have things to eat, mostly because of my mother's hard work. My brother did most of the farm work and dad laid in the shade, reading his Bible. All my shoes came from either my brother or Salvation Army. My sister and moms dresses came from flour sacks that she sewed together. Honey and molasses were used for sugar. We only took a bath on Saturday evening, for the Sunday service, all five of us in a galvanized tub, with hot water heated on the cook stove, put in as needed the smallest person first. I was the only one that always bathed in clean water. Dad always turned the engine of the Model A off, at the top of the hill and started it at the bottom, by letting out the clutch after putting it in gear, a trusty model A

Ford. After the divorce dad always sent me $5.00 for Christmas, the judge said Mom filed for the divorce, so he never needed to pay alimony.

"----keep thyself pure." 22 How is he going to do that, when he has not gotten rid of the original sin of Adam? "Drink no longer water? But use a little wine for thy stomach's sake and thine often infirmities." 23 A child of God with often infirmities, I thought Islam, and the Qur'an had all the peculiarities. Evidently the winos are the only ones that got it right. Mohammad said drinking Camel urine is a purification, of your body, so go buy a Camel.

"Some men's sins are open beforehand going before to judgment; and some men they follow after."24 That is true. I believe there is going to be a rapture of the saints, and they have had all their sins forgiven with a body that is ready, to live with God in His kingdom. They have gotten rid of the original sin of Adam by removing their heart, and replacing it. It reads that those born again, and have received the Spirit has entered into the kingdom of God in St John. It is hard for me to believe that Jesus stayed in the same form as He left, because I'm sure God is a Spirit, so I might have to have one more change of my body to live in His kingdom.

"If any man teach otherwise, and consent not to wholesome words, even the words of our Lord Jesus Christ, and to the doctrine which is according to godliness." 6"3 'Thanks Timothy, Jesus was only the Son of God,' "and to the doctrine which is according to godliness;" (be nice and pray all the time.?)

"For the love of money is the root of all evil: (it is amazing how Satan knew what the last days would be like) which while some coveted after, they have erred from the faith, and pierced themselves through with many sorrows."1 Timothy 6:10 It is worse than that God has removed the plan of salvation from their church. "---for the meat offering and the drink offering is withholden from the house of your God." (god) Joel 1:13 (I tried to write and tell the mega preachers the fallacy of their ways, but all people do is, remove the money sent to them from the envelopes.) "and pierced themselves through with many sorrows." (That is going to come later, and it will be too late if they stay on the track they are on)

The good fight of faith

I call it playing church. "But thou, O man of God flee these things; and follow after righteousness, godliness, faith, love, patience, meekness." 1 Timothy 6:11 "Fight the good fight of faith, lay hold on eternal life, whereunto thou art also called, and hast professed a good profession before many witnesses." 12 The more witnesses the more money that comes in.

"I give thee (preachers) charge in the sight of God, who quickeneth all things,---" 13 Joel the first chapter it says that God is not in the churches so He is not working with the preachers, they are on their own the same way Paul was. "I am come in my Father's name, and ye receive me not: (Jesus) if another shall come in his own name, him (Paul) ye will receive." (believe) St John 5:43 "Ye are of your father the devil, and the lusts of your father ye will do. He was a murderer from the beginning, and abode not in the truth, because there is no truth in him. When he speaketh a lie, he speaketh of his own: (preachers) for he is a liar, and the father of it." ST John 8:44

"Who only hath immortality, dwelling in the light which no man can approach unto: whom no man hath seen, nor can see: to whom be honor and power everlasting." 16 When I received the new heart it was a light (Spirit) from heaven that did the work. When I saw a blob of light come through the windshield, of a Ford, the Holy Ghost, and went in my mouth, did that light count? When I saw an Angel ,"in brilliant white adornment" in the Sunday School Class, and I blurted out, "the day of judgment is coming," did that count?

"Laying up in store for themselves a good foundation, 'against the time to come' that they may lay hold on eternal life." 19 According to this verse you can work your way to eternal life, feed the poor, pray for the sick, collect the money, be a witness, collect the money, be nice, collect the money, do good works, and collect the money. Jesus said ; "Verily, verily, I say unto thee, except a man be born of water (3rd verse born again) and of the Spirit, (Holy Ghost) he cannot enter into the kingdom of God." St John 3:5 and Ezekiel 36:26-25-27

"Which some professing have erred (made mistakes) concerning the faith. Grace be with thee." 21 There are more people then I can count have erred' grace has nothing to do with salvation. Doesn't it read few will find the way'? During the two months that I was seeking salvation I had more than one chance, to follow the established church doctrine but never did, I knew I was a sinner that needed a savior. Now you only have to raise your hand connected to your arm, to receive the sinner's prayer for salvation, and (as told) at the same time the Spirit.

Profess= to make an open declaration, to lay claim, to declare one's belief, pretend. When I was saved it was physical, I never professed anything but I did make an open declaration in a church building, of going forward, and at the time I thought that was needed?

11 Timothy
Chapter 3
The coming apostasy (abandon what one believed in as a faith)

"This know also, that in the last days perilous times shall come." 11 Timothy 3:1

It proves that it is Satan that knows what is going to be like for man, Jesus was more into things that will happen to the earth, and planets but the first thing He said was, "take heed that no man deceive you." St Matthew 24:4 Even Paul.

"For men shall be lovers of their own selves," (only think of themselves, Isn't tattoos a sign of liking yourself, and taking a photo of oneself, covetous, (greedy or desire something that another person has) boasters, (to talk about oneself) proud, blasphemers, disobedient to parents, unthankful, unholy, without natural affection, trucebreakers, false accusers, incontinent, fierce, (MMA) despisers of those that are good, traitors, heady, (reckless and tending to affect the head, like pot and alcohol) high minded, lovers of pleasures more than lovers of God, having a form of godliness, but denying the power thereof, a martyr gets 72 virgins. From such turn away." 11 Timothy 2 through 5 "Ye do err not knowing the scriptures, nor the power of God." St Matthew 22:29

"For of this sort are they which creep into houses, and lead captive silly women laden with sins, led away with diverse lusts," 6 Who did Jesus say He was going to save? The sinner; St Matthew 9:13

"Ever learning, and never able to come to the knowledge of the truth." 7 Isn't that a picture of the churches, and religious organizations today?

Usually the Sunday School class teaching books, they come from the organization, and there is nothing in them to disrupt their church doctrine.

"Three shepherds also I cut off in one month: and my soul loathed them, and their soul also abhorred me." Zechariah 11:8 Paul of TBN (Bands) and Billy, (Beauty) with a third shepherd, Paul of The Acts, God looks on the heart to know this, that they abhorred Him. That was how He knew what was in Satan's heart in Isaiah 14:13.

Wouldn't Paul of the Acts be one of the three I believe he is. "Woe to the idol shepherd that leaveth the flock---!" Zechariah 11:17 Paul created his own gospel with his own disciples, so Jesus, wouldn't be a part of his ministry. The last of the verse reads "and his arm shall be clean dried up, (no effect toward the gospel of being truth) "and his right eye shall be utterly darkened." (Blinded with his disciples, that Paul created) Not everybody is blind. "But blessed are your eyes, for they see: and your ears for they hear." St Matthew 13:16 My ears, tell me immediately, if what I hear is false doctrine.

The second shepherd was called Beauty that must be Billy that most preachers try and emulate today, and his main verse for salvation is in St John which shouldn't be in the Bible. He went all over the world pretending to know something, but never received God's righteousness that a person must receive first. "But seek ye first the kingdom of God, and his righteousness.;" St Matthew 6:33 Does it make any common sense to go down in the front, and get his literature, and go back to your drunken friends. You are suppose to be born again, and transformed to a child of God, your friends you had before are no more. That is, if truly saved as I was, with the new heart and new Spirit. My good friend on the last ship was knocking on my front door, and because I wasn't into wild women, beer, dancing or the night life, I never opened the door.

The third shepherd was called Bands that must be Paul of T B N Trinity Broadcast Net-work, bands are a part of the mechanism that runs a television network. The preachers are back slappers with generally the same message of what Paul wrote of faith, grace, walk in righteous, or work out your own salvation. "How can ye believe, which receive honor one of another, and seek not (the preachers will tell you, I'm saved, happy rich and on my way) the honor that cometh from God only." St John 5:44 The person that they all believe in is in St John you can't fool God. "I am come in my Father's name, and ye receive me not: (Jesus) if another shall come in his own name, him (Paul) ye will receive." (believe) St John 5:43 (Paul was the Devil's advocate as in Isaiah 14:14) "I will ascend above the heights of the clouds; (churches) I will be like the most High." (God) "---I (Lucifer) will sit also upon the mount (all) of the congregation." (Churches and religious organizations) Isaiah 14:13-14

"Now as Jannes and Jambres withstood Moses, so do these also resist the truth: men of corrupt minds' reprobate (without good sense or even common sense) concerning the truth." 11 Timothy 3:8 "And the disciples came, and said unto him, Why speakest thou unto them in parables?" St Matthew 13:10 "He answered and said unto them, because it is given unto you to know the mysteries of the kingdom of heaven, (physically saved) but to them it is not given." 11 (Unsaved as Paul and his disciples were)

"But evil men and seducers, shall wax worse and worse, deceiving, and being deceived." 11 Timothy 3:13 (Those that follow Paul, Peter, Timothy, The Qur'an etc. don't have a clue, that they are deceived)

"And that from a child thou hast known the holy scriptures, which are able to make thee unto salvation through faith which is in Christ Jesus." 15 80% of children, I read, believe whatever their parents believe, it could be worse than that. 'Knowing the scriptures through faith' has nothing to do with being redeemed or saved.

(The big one) "All scripture is given by inspiration of God, and is profitable for doctrine, for reproof, (or reprove to express disapproval, does man have the knowledge to do this) "for correction," (does man have the where-with-all to correct the Gospels?) "for instruction in righteousness:" 16 (now the truth comes out, it is physical a person cannot be instructed in righteousness) "---Work out your own salvation with fear and trembling." Philippians 2:12 Is that Biblical, that you can work out your own salvation? False doctrine is certainly profitable that is correct. Luke said go by all the Bible but Jesus said go by what came out of Jesus mouth. You hear this all the time, he or she is a, 'Man of God.' "That the man of God, may be perfect, thoroughly furnished (prepared) unto all good works." 11 Timothy 3:17 How can this be, when in their heart they still have the original sin of Adam, and their accumulative sin. People are doing good works in vain.

"For the time will come when they will not endure sound doctrine; but after their own lusts shall they heap to themselves teachers, having itching ears;" 11 Timothy 4:3 (wanting to hear certain pleasing ideas) "And they shall turn away their ears from the truth, and shall be turned unto fables." 4 (Isn't that the truth). A fable is a fictitious story meant to teach a moral lesson. It is almost nonexistent to hear a biblical verse mentioned in a sermon today. "How can ye believe, which receive honor one of another, and seek not the honor that cometh from God only?" St John 5:44 In most churches the congregations likes men that are not to churchy, a Baptist Church in town took two years to find a (suitable preacher that wasn't too churchy).

Because Satan instigated or inspired what Paul wrote, he certainly knows what the last days are going to be like.

"Only Luke is with me, Take Mark, and bring him with thee: for he is profitable, (or is it useful, according to the mega churches they like profitable) "to me for the ministry." 4:11 What they need, is His righteousness first.

(there are three separate people) "And the devil (do we question who that is) that deceived them was cast into the Lake of fire and brimstone, where the beast (wouldn't that be the anti-Christ) and the false prophet are." Revelation 20:10 Wouldn't that be Paul, I don't know of any other person it would fit, he had such a profound detriment to the Word that Jesus spoke, from His Father in heaven. Most Preachers will tell you the false prophet is going to come, one of these days, but in this verse the false prophet is in the lake of fire and brimstone already. I'll let you figure out why the beast is in the fire already? Most preachers will tell you the beast is the anti-Christ and will be on the earth someday.

CHAPTER 5

JOHN

The First epistle of John

With Paul, Peter, and Timothy in the book I thought it would suffice, but John seems to be in a different league.

What got my attention was the commentary at the beginning it reads. The fourth Gospel and the epistles of John are very similar in style, subject matter, and vocabulary. This epistle cannot be separated from the author of the fourth Gospel. Watch me. I believe an entirely different John wrote these epistles because the Gospel of John is written in more of an allegorical form.

"And these things write we unto you, that your joy may be full." 1;4 "Verily, verily, I say unto you, that ye shall weep and lament, but the world shall rejoice: and ye shall be sorrowful, but your sorrow, shall be turned into joy." St John 16:20 (Your last day, or the end time)

"---God is light, and in him is no darkness at all." (Sinfulness) 5

"If we say that we have fellowship with him, and walk in darkness, we lie, and do not the truth:" 6 There are millions of people that believe they have the truth, and some would even die for their belief, doctrine or church, but they walk in darkness.

"---and the blood of Jesus Christ his Son cleanseth us from all sin????" 7 A person must believe on one of the works that Jesus did, I believed that

I could heal my mother, "Believe me that I am in the father, and the Father in me: or else believe me for the very works 'sake." St John 14:11 (It triggers the Spirit of Genesis to give a person a new heart) Believe is a condition or catalyst for the Spirit to act. Than we have the problem of a person must be born again, and receive the Holy Ghost physically. St John 3:3-5 with the explanation in Ezekiel 36:26-25-27 (The blood of Jesus respectfully, has nothing to do with cleansing anybody from sin) "A new heart also will I give you, and a new Spirit will I put within you." Ezekiel 36:26-27

"If we say that we have no sin, we deceive ourselves, and the truth is not in us." 8 The original sin of Adam plus the accumulative sin of a person must be physically removed, given a new heart where sin is located. I don't have the same heart that I was born with in my body, so I can say that I have no sin, but perfect as God is perfect and righteous. "Be ye therefore perfect, even as your Father which is in heaven is perfect." St Matthew 5:48 "But seek ye first the kingdom of God, and his righteousness." St Matthew 6:33 Where does it say go to a divinity college first? My heart is thirty years younger than my body.

"If we confess our sins, he is faithful and just to forgive us our sins, and to cleanse us from all unrighteousness." 9 It is impossible to do this, which I have heard this statement all my life. A person would have to have a better memory than an elephant. It happened to me physically. The bottom line is receiving the Holy Ghost that is when you become righteous. It teaches you the commandments or statutes of God. "And I will put my Spirit (Holy Ghost) within you, and cause you to walk in my statutes, and ye shall keep my judgments, 'and do them." Ezekiel 36:27 Two years I was in training.

"If we say that we have not sinned, we make him a liar, and his word is not in us." 10 That is not true because when Adam sinned or disobeyed God, everybody sense then, has sinned and need salvation for His righteousness; physically.

That is a person that believe they are righteous, which Jesus said He never came to save, but I'm not sure what he means by his word is not in us. It reads in Jeremiah; "---I will put my law in their inward parts, and write it in their hearts; and will be their God, and they shall be my people" Jeremiah 31:33 It is the same as when the Ten Commandments, were written on the stone. That is what happened when my heart that I was born with was removed and replaced.

"And he is the propitiation (reconciliation) for our sins: and not for ours only, But also for the sins of the whole world?" 1 John 2:2 What about being one of the chosen, and drawn by the Father. "No man can come to me, except the Father which hath sent me draw him: and I will raise him up the last day." St John 6:44 "So the last shall be first, and the first last: for many be called, but few chosen." St Matthew 20:16 (if you are one of the called, and you get a tattoo would God still consider you one of the chosen to be saved?) "And except that the Lord had shortened those days, no flesh should be saved: but for the elect's sake, whom he hath chosen, he hath shortened the days." St Mark 13:20 To believe that Jesus took the sins of the whole world can get a person in trouble when salvation is on a personal level.

"And hereby we do know that we know him, if we keep his commandments." 1 John 2:3 No, I was born again, and received the New Spirit or Holy Ghost, that is what makes me keep His commandments. I would ask John, were you born again, and did you receive the Spirit physically? There is no way that a person can walk in God's righteousness, if you don't become redeemed or transformed first. It reads seek ye first the kingdom of God and his righteousness.

"He that saith he abideth in him ought himself also so to walk, even as he walked." 6 That is a stretch, you do whatsoever the Spirit (Holy Ghost) commands a person to do, but you have to receive it first. A person can't walk as He walked without it.

"---the darkness is past,---" 8 (where did Satan go if the darkness is past?)" In Isaiah it reads Satan is doing very well, it reads he is in (all) the congregations. 14:13 Satan has contaminated the bible that everybody preaches from, 'with Paul as his advocate.' "I am come in my Father's name, and ye receive me not: (Jesus) if another shall come in his own name, him ye will receive. (Believe; Paul) St John 5:43

"I write unto you, little children, because your sins are forgiven you for his name's sake." 1 John 2:12 John what about St John "---Except a man be born of water (3rd verse born again) and of the Spirit, he cannot enter into the kingdom of God." St John 3:3-5 His name has nothing to do with your sin.

"---But he that doeth the will of God abideth for ever." 17 Without receiving His righteousness or will first, you abide or live only until you die. People can't seem to handle the truth, they just want to live be lied to and die.

"Little children, it is the last time: and as ye have heard that an-ti-Christ shall come, even now are there many an-ti-Christ, whereby we know that it is the last time." (Days) 18 This was written over 2,018 years ago. John should come back now and count the religious organizations that they started. When Jesus was asked when the end time will come, He said, "Take heed that no man, deceive you in St Matthew "---Tell us when shall these things be? And what shall be the sign of thy coming, and of the end of the world?":3 "And Jesus answered and said unto them, Take heed that no man deceive you." 4 To name, just a few deceivers, Paul, Peter, Timothy, John, James, Jake, Billy, TBN, Muhammad, Joyce and Buda.

Which church is John referring to? "They went out from us, but they were not of us; for if they had been of us, they would no doubt have continued with us: but they went out, that they might be made manifest that they were not all of us." 1 John 2:19 The verse, must have kept him up all night, to get the uses, in the right place.

"Who is a liar but he that denieth that Jesus is the Christ? He is an, an-ti-christ, that denieth the Father AND the Son." 1 John 3:22 They probably wish AND was not between the Father and Son in this verse; there are a lot of an-ti-Christ, today. A verse that seems to really separate the two is found in St John "He that hath my commandments, (saved) and keepeth them, he it is that loveth me: and he that loveth me shall be loved of my Father, and I will love him, and will manifest myself to him." St John 14:21 (With the born again, and the Holy Ghost experiences) "But if I with the finger (Power) of God cast out devils, no doubt the kingdom of God is come upon you." Luke 11:20 I had a lot of devils, alcoholic, smoking, swearing, sex for sport, Adam's original sin, Etc., not realizing there was a God, Spirit, Holy Ghost and Jesus, finding that out physically when I was thirty one years old 12/1/1968 at 9pm. Preachers and others will tell you that God loves everybody, does He? "And it repented (grieved) the Lord that he had made man on the earth, and it grieved him at his heart." Genesis 6:6

"And this is the promise that he hath promised us, even eternal life." 1 John 2:25 (St John is the reference). "And this is life eternal, that they (might) know thee the only true God, and Jesus Christ, whom thou hast sent." St John17:3 'Might know thee' is a lot different than being promised eternal life. That is, being born again and receiving the Holy Ghost or Spirit is to know Him.

"But the anointing (Holy Ghost) which ye have received of him abideth in you, and ye need not that any man teach you: but as the same anointing teaches you of all things, and is truth, and is no lie, and even as it hath taught you, ye shall abide in him." 27 (but first a person must be born again to start the process of cleaning the body). It is true the Holy Ghost goes in your mouth as it did Jesus and me, without water baptism on my account. "---but ye know him, for he dwelleth with you, and shall be in you." St John 14:17 (No, he 'Holy Ghost' doesn't abide in you from birth you receive a new heart first from the Spirit in Genesis, and then the new Spirit (Holy Ghost) that I received physically) "Then Jesus said unto them, "Verily, verily, I say unto you, Except ye eat the flesh (new heart) of the Son of man, (Jesus) and drink his blood, (Holy Ghost) ye have no life in you." St John 6:53

"And now, little children, abide in him; (do the things that you think is right according to St John or is it Paul that when he shall appear, we may have confidence, and not be ashamed before him at his coming." 1 John 2:28 What about the notion that those saved, will depart this earth before the, day of judgment, it reads the elect's days shall be shortened. "And except those days should be shortened, there should no flesh be saved: but for the elect's sake those days (shall) be shortened." St Matthew 24:22 I believe God's use of, "should" here because there is a possibility that if enough people become saved, the end time destruction would not happen???There is a lot of difference between should and shall.

(It just isn't so his being righteous has nothing to do with your being righteous) "If ye know that he is righteous, (OK) ye know that everyone that doeth righteousness is born of him." 1 John 2:29 There are a lot of good people, by appearance, doeth righteous things but sorry to say it is going to be in vain. "Not everyone that saith unto me, Lord, Lord, shall enter into the kingdom of heaven; but he that doeth the will of my Father which is in heaven." St Matthew 7:21 "Many will say to me in that day, Lord, Lord, have we not prophesied (preached) in thy name? And in thy name done many wonderful works?" 22 "And then will I profess unto them, I never knew you: depart from me ye that work iniquity." 23 What comes out of the mouth defile the person.

"Behold, what manner of love the Father hath bestowed upon us,---" (He never bestowed any love upon us, love has nothing to do with God being righteous, that is why Jesus died for our sins, it was because mankind could achieve the righteousness of God) "that we should be called the sons of God: therefore the world knoweth us not, because it knew him not." 1 John 3:1 (Only one verse recorded in the Gospels of sons of God that is in St John "But as many as received him, to them gave he (them) power (Spirit in Genesis) to become the sons of God," St John 1:12 (somebody that never knew the salvation experience wrote) "even to them that believe on his name:" (St John 3:16 should not be in the Bible) Usually, instead of sons of God it will read child or children of God in the Gospels. With Satan in the media, publishing, and all the churches the chances are pretty slim, to get any truth out to the public.

"And every man that hath this hope in him purifieth himself even as he is pure?" 1 John 3:3 How can a person purify their self, did I miss something?. "John answered and said, A man can receive nothing, except it be given him from heaven." St John 3:27 I found out that, is true.

"And we know that he was manifested to take away our sins; and in him is no sin." 5 But a person must believe on one of the works that Jesus did, and it is the Spirit of Genesis that gives a person the new heart, and it removes a person's sin, the original sin of Adam plus your accumulative sin. The sin of Adam must come through the generations by the man, because Jesus was born of Mary.

"Whosoever abideth in him sinneth not: whosoever sinneth hath not seen him, neither known him." (That is true they come under the protection of the Son, and that is another reason, for Jesus to give his life on the cross) I quit sin because of the disgusting habits that they were, and it is a requirement of God. "Whosoever sinneth hath not seen him, neither known him." 6 (That is true they don't even know that God exists, why worry be happy) It reads that a person will see the kingdom of God or a part of God. St John 3:3 and Ezekiel 36"26

"Little children, let no man deceive you:" (That was the first thing that came out of the mouth of Jesus when they asked what shall be the sign of thy coming, and of the end of the world) St Matthew 24:3 "he that doeth righteousness is righteous, even as he is righteous." 7 (Any Tom, Dick, Harry, and Judy, can live a righteous life, it has nothing to do with God's righteousness.)

"He that commit sin is of the devil; for the devil sinneth from the beginning. For this purpose the Son of God was manifest, that he (might) destroy the works of the devil." 1 John 3:8 Jesus doesn't have anything to do with the works of the devil except for salvation of the individual in believing of one of the works that Jesus did. St John 14:11

"We know that we have passed from death unto life, because we love the brethren. He that loveth not his brother abideth in death." John 3:14 (NUTTS) A person can love brethren, and it has nothing to do with passing from death unto life. Which Church brethren is he speaking about?

Trying the spirits

"---Hereby know ye the Spirit of God: Every spirit (assuming a person) that confesseth that Jesus Christ is come in the flesh is of God:" 1 John 4:2 (Which is not true; a person must be born again and receive the Holy Ghost or Spirit physically to enter into the kingdom of God St John 3:3-5 or Ezekiel 36:26 - 27)

God is love

"Beloved, let us love one another: for love is of God; and every one that loveth is born of God; and knoweth God." 1 John 4:7 (This is about as far from the truth as a person can get) "It grieved God in His heart that He made man on the earth." Genesis 6:6 Love of one another has nothing to do with receiving God's righteousness. "But seek ye first the kingdom of God, and his righteousness: and all these things shall be added unto you." St Matthew 6:33

(I hate to break your bubble but God is not into love as the preachers suggest). "He that loveth not, knoweth not God; for God is love." 8 It is because of the righteousness of God that Jesus died on the cross, and a person must become righteous to live with God in His kingdom, love has nothing to do with that. In the book of Leviticus the sacrifices was all about maintaining God's righteousness.

"No man, hath seen God, at any time." 12 (I felt the power of God, (Spirit) I saw a light filled with power isn't that close to seeing Him, receiving a new heart, and His Spirit the Holy Ghost, I saw the blob, (as a dove) go in my mouth, and an angel of God one time, blurting out, "the day of judgment is coming." Does all that count for anything? "And Jesus when he was baptized, went up straightway (immediately) out of the water, and, lo, the heavens were opened unto him, and he saw the Spirit of God descending like a dove, and lighting upon him:" St Matthew 3:16 (It went in His mouth that is a mistake) "Not that any man hath seen the Father, save (except) he which is of God, he hath seen the Father." St John 6:46 "At that day ye shall know that I am in my Father, and ye in me, and I in you." St John 14:20 12/1/1968 at 9pm "---but ye know him; for he dwelleth with you, and shall be in you." St John 14:17 "Therefore, behold, I am against the prophets, saith the Lord, that steal my words everyone from his neighbor." Jeremiah 23:30 "How can ye believe, which receive honor one of another, (That steal my words everyone from his neighbor) and seek not the honor that cometh from God only?" St John 5:44

"Hereby know we that we dwell in him, and he in us, because he hath given us of his Spirit." 1 John 4:13 (The only way a person can receive his Spirit is to be given a new heart first.) A person can't receive, the spirit, "during the sinner's prayer" your body must be clean first.

"---the Father sent the Son to be the Savior of the world." 14 That is true, (In Leviticus the sacrifices were physical, and so is salvation physical as in Ezekiel 36:26-27)

"Whosoever shall confess that Jesus is the Son of God, God dwelleth in him, and he in God." 1 John 4:15 (That is the first biggest lie on planet earth, but sadly that is what the preachers preach, because it is in the Bible but I know better) It is the Spirit or Holy Ghost, and not God for those that receive it, 'that dwelleth in us for eternity.' St John 14:16 (New heart, or born again) that he (Spirit or Holy Ghost the other Comforter) may abide with you forever;" St John 14:16

"And we have known and believed the love that God hath to us. God is love: and he that dwelleth in love dwelleth in God, and God in him." 1 John 4:16 It is the second biggest lie on planet earth, and it is not God but the Holy Spirit (not God) that dwells in man.

"There is no fear in love;but perfect love caseth out fear; because fear hath torment. He that feareth is not made perfect in love." 18 (It is righteousness that makes a person perfect as God is perfect, and love has nothing to do with that, or being fearful) "Be ye therefore perfect, even as your Father which is in heaven is perfect." St Matthew 5:48 A person must be made perfect as Adam was perfect, before the original sin came into the world.

"For this is the love of God, that we keep his commandments: and His commandments are not grievous." (hard to obey) 1 John 5:3 The preacher's commandments are easy to obey, from The Acts –Jude, but they are not the true commandments of God. 'The true commandments are difficult.' Being born again and receiving the Holy Ghost they are the beginning of the commandments of God. Then there is the problem of being drawn and one of the chosen, but a person doesn't have a clue unless they receive it, sorry to say. "He answered and said unto them, because it is given unto you to know the mysteries of the kingdom of heaven, but to them it is not given." St Matthew 13:11

"For whatsoever is born of God overcometh the world: and this is the victory that overcometh the world, even our faith." 1 John 5:4 (Does faith, have anything to do with receiving His commandments or being born again of God?) I think not, as far as I am concerned faith is pie in the sky along with the, "gospel of grace, or hope " as I heard yesterday. The creation of the heavens and the earth does not have anything to do with faith grace, or hope it is matter and energy. Matter=what a thing is made of; whatever occupies space and is perceptible to the senses in some way: (I felt, and saw the light, "power of God" removing and replacing my heart.) I saw the Spirit (like a dove in St Matthew just before it entered my mouth) Energy=capacity for action, effective power, in physics, the capacity for doing work and overcoming resistance. Replacing my heart was my first death and it reads I will not be hurt of the second death. "He that hath an ear, (not stuck in the mud) let him hear what the Spirit saith unto the churches; He that overcometh (from the false doctrine of the churches) shall not be hurt of the second death." Revelation 2:11

"This is he that came by water and blood, (born the same way man is) even Jesus Christ; not by water only, but by water and blood, And it is the Spirit (blood) that beareth witness, because the Spirit is truth." 1 John

5:6 (It wasn't until just before His ministry at thirty years old, that Jesus received the Spirit or Holy Ghost in the mouth, and then went into the wilderness to receive instruction from the Spirit and tempted by the devil.) St Matthew 3:16 and 4:1-11

"For there are three that bear record in heaven, the Father, the Word," (made flesh the Son of God Jesus) and the Holy Ghost: and these three are one." 7 "And the Word was made flesh, and dwelt among us, (and we beheld his glory, the glory as the only begotten of the Father,) full of grace and truth." St John 1:14 The Holy Ghost is inside a person it occurs after they are born again, or receive a new heart as in Ezekiel. A new heart also, will I give you, (thirty days later I received the new Spirit or Holy Ghost) "And I will put my Spirit (within) you, and cause you to walk in my statutes, and ye shall keep my judgments, and do them." Ezekiel 36"26-27 So I don't know how the Holy Ghost is in heaven as one of the three? Why is it dangerous to blasphemy the Holy Ghost but alright to blasphemy Jesus or God? With this in mind, if they are the same wouldn't it be dangerous to blasphemy Jesus and God in St Matthew "Wherefore I say unto you, all manner of sin and blasphemy shall be forgiven unto men: but the blasphemy against the Holy Ghost shall not be forgiven unto men. And whosoever speaketh a word against the Son of man, (Jesus) it shall be forgiven him: but whosoever speaketh against the Holy Ghost, it shall not be forgiven him, neither in this world, neither in the world to come." St Matthew 12:31-32 "No man can come to me, except the Father which hath sent me draw him: and I will raise him up at the last day." St John 6:44 The Holy Ghost when it is received in a person's body, how could it be in heaven? It is the other Spirit of Genesis 1:2 that is in heaven.

The false doctrine; "and these three are one." When two people get married the KJB of 1611 say they are one also, but I have always counted two. Why is it safe to blasphemy God and Jesus, but leave the Holy Ghost alone? Because it is the only method to receive salvation, after your born again that is the next step, with me it was thirty days later that I received the Holy Ghost or Spirit. The Holy Ghost as the verse implies, is in God? I don't think so. "Nevertheless I tell you the truth; It is expedient for you that I go away: for if I go (not) away, the Comforter will not come unto you; but if I depart, I will send him unto you." St John 16:7

"He that hath the Son hath life; and he that hath not the Son of God hath not life." 1 John 5:12 "---the bread that I will give is my flesh, which I will give for the life of the world." St John 6:51 (I have a feeling John doesn't mean this) It means the new heart or being born again is the beginning of being transformed. Those that haven't received the Holy Ghost hath not life.

"And we know that we are of God, and the whole world lieth in wickedness." 19 (How many? It reads few will find the way) "Because strait is the gate, and narrow is the way, which leadeth unto life, and few there be that find It." St Matthew 7:14

"And we know that the Son of God is come, and hath given us an understanding, that we may know him that is true, and we are in him that is true, even in his Son Jesus Christ. This is the true God, and eternal life." 1 John 5:20 It is false; it seems to say superficially we may know him, (Jesus) and have eternal life. If you would ask anyone in a bar or on the street, "do you believe Jesus lived" they would tell you yes. Do they have eternal life?

"And we are in him." That could be true because of the 6th chapter of St John "I (Jesus) am the bread of life." St John 6:48 "I am the living bread which came down from heaven: if any man, eat of this bread, he shall live forever: and the bread that I will give is my flesh, which I will give for the life of the world." 51 "---Except ye eat the flesh of the Son of man, (born again or new heart) and drink his blood, (Holy Ghost or Spirit in the mouth) ye have no life in you." 53" Whoso eateth my flesh, and drinketh my blood, hath eternal life; and I will raise him up at the last day." 54 "For my flesh is meat indeed, and my blood is drink indeed." 55 "He that eateth my flesh, and drinketh my blood, dwelleth in me, and I in him." 56 "As the living Father hath sent me, and I live by the Father: so he that eateth me, even he shall live by me." 57 "This is that bread which came down from heaven: not as your fathers did eat man'-na and are dead: he that eateth of this bread shall live forever." 58 It is about being born again and receiving the Spirit as in Ezekiel 36:26 and 27 receiving the new heart and new Spirit. I have been told, it is speaking of the sacraments, the cracker and juice or wine, which is not true.

If, this John is writing about these verses from the Gospel of St John, "then it is true" that we are in him."

The above verses are truly allegorical, but Ezekiel gave the explanation of St John 3: but never got the verses in sequence, that they must occur as I have written in other parts of the book. Ezekiel 36:26-25-27

The second epistle of John

"For many deceivers are entered into the world, who confess not, that Jesus Christ is come in the flesh. This is a deceiver and an an'-ti-Christ." 11 John 1:7 If a person went down to the nearest bar, and asked the patrons, "before the band started" if they believe Jesus came in the flesh? Your chances of getting a, "No" answer would be slim. It is only in other religions that confess that Jesus Christ never came in the flesh, for instance Islam doesn't believe in the divinity of Jesus, but that He was a prophet but not divine. Most of the churches mention Jesus, as if He came in the flesh, but that has nothing to do with salvation.

"If there come any unto you, and bring not (this) doctrine, receive him not into your house, neither bid him Godspeed:" 10 (The doctrine of Paul, Peter and their disciples?) They never knew the true doctrine, it reads in St John unless a person is born again and receive the

Spirit (Holy Ghost) they can't enter into the kingdom of God, and that is the true doctrine but a parable. The problem is in St Matthew "---it is given unto you to know the mysteries of the kingdom of heaven, but to them (unsaved) it is not given." St Matthew 13:11

"Having many things to write unto you, I would not write with paper and ink: but I trust to come unto you, and speak face to face that our joy may be full." 12 "Verily, verily, I say unto you, that ye shall weep and lament, but the world shall rejoice: and ye shall be sorrowful, but your sorrow shall be turned into joy." St John 16;20 I am sorrowful for the condition of the religious community, but my sorrow shall turn into joy at the last day. Eventually they must have gotten some paper and ink. When my boss in construction wanted me to build something I liked them to write it down on paper.

The Third epistle of John

"The elder, unto the well beloved Gai'-us, whom I love in the truth." 111 John 1:1 Now days, a person is introduced as a, "Man of God" like they know one, when they see one. "How can ye believe, which receive honor one of another, and seek not the honor that cometh from God only?" St John 5:44 In my day they called them back slappers, and TBN and SBN is a good example of back slappers..

"Beloved I wish above all things that thou mayest prosper----."2 One preacher asked for 1,000 people to give $1,000 dollars he wasn't bashful at all, to spread (his) gospel. Another preacher wanted the congregation to buy him a 67 million dollar jet plane to spread (his) gospel. In one sermon he was making fun of the way an elderly person walks, they were suppose to say they are," righteous" and old age won't come on you, a natural phenomenon.

"I have no greater joy then that my children walk in truth."4 Who's truth? Lucifer said he would be over the mount (all) the congregation (churches) in Isaiah. Last night a preacher on T V went from 13 to 14 "I will exalt my throne above the stars of God (to) I will ascend above the heights of the clouds; I will be like the most High." He conveniently left out "I will sit also upon the mount (all) of the congregation," (churches). Who would think, that Lucifer is inside the churches?

The sad part is did those that wrote, "The Acts –Jude" did they know that what they said was not the truth. I believe in their heart they thought they had the truth, just as it is today in the different denominations, and or religions around the world. Common sense should tell a person there is something wrong. With one God how can there be so many different religions?

Your children are, "on their own" it sounds good what preachers tell you but there is no reason to believe it, but most of what they say is in the Bible, can it get any worse than that. It reads as soon as a baby is born they start speaking lies. Having the baby baptized in water is a waste of time. Some people believe if that is done, they have nothing to worry about.

"Beloved, follow not that which is evil, but that which is good. He that doeth good is of God: but he that doeth evil hath not seen God." 11 I have seen the power of God (12/1/1968 at 9pm the night I received the new heart I quit sin, and it never entered my mind to sin again. But because I play league pool in bars, and drink water, I know many that, "play Christian" would call me a sinner with no hope.

CHAPTER 6

THE SECOND EPISTLE OF PETER

False prophets and teachers

Peter, the one that said John the Baptist was right when John said he was wrong, and for us to follow Jesus. Peter said that we need water baptism to be saved. The Acts 2:38

"But there were false prophets also among the people, even as there shall be false teachers among you, who privily (secretly) shall bring in damnable heresies, even denying the Lord that bought them and bring upon themselves swift destruction." 11 Peter 2:1 It would be hard to find anybody in the U S that wouldn't tell you in the bar or church that Jesus never existed, "and bring upon themselves, swift destruction." I don't believe God does this there wouldn't be any one left on the earth today. "That ye may be the children of your Father which is in heaven: for he maketh his sun to rise on the evil and on the good, and sendeth rain on the just and on the unjust." St Matthew 5:45 It reads that the, sun to rise." That would really ruin a person's day if the earth was stationary and the sun orbited around it. When a plane leaves Salt Lake City and flies to Miami, Florida the minute the plane leaves the ground Miami moved. What is the Algebraic formula, for landing at their airport? Not everybody believes the Earth goes around the Sun, I have read that in Russia they believe the Sun rotates around the Earth, with it stationary.

"And many shall follow their pernicious (evil) ways; by reason of whom the way of truth shall be evil spoken of." 11 Peter 2:2 Peter never knew what the Gospel of Jesus was about, so he was the one that was spreading lies.

"Which have forsaken the right way, and are gone astray, following the way of Ba'-laam the son of Bo'-sor, who loved the wages of unrighteousness;" 11 Peter 2:15 When a person receives a new heart, with their sins forgiven, and the new Spirit, for once in their life they don't have the desire to sin any more, I see no reason that they would want to go astray. With the new Spirit inside of your body would it be possible for a person to go to hell, I don't think so. If you are not of Jesus you are a child of Satan. St John 8: 44 "Ye are of your father the devil, and the lusts of your father ye will do,---" St John 8:44

"For it had been better for them not to have known the way of righteousness, then, after they have known it, to turn from the holy commandment delivered unto them." 11 Peter 2:21 From The Acts through Jude nothing seems to tell me that the writers knew the way of righteousness, of removing and replacing a person's heart to get rid of the original sin of Adam plus a person's accumulative sin, and receiving the Holy Ghost which is the only way to the kingdom of God. Receiving the new heart is not enough either, by its self, too be saved they need to receive the Holy Ghost.

"That ye may be mindful of the words which were spoken before by the holy prophets, and of the commandment of us the apostles of the Lord and savior:" 3:2 (Paul) The prophets of the Old Testament had very little to say about the new Word, of the New Testament Gospels of St Matthew, John, and Mark. It reads the law and the prophets ended with John the Baptist. "For all the prophets and the law prophesied until John." St Matthew 11:13 (There are a few verses that gives a more clear understanding, of the New Word but that is all. What Jesus spoke will stand on its own as far as salvation goes, but more difficult to understand because Jesus spoke allegorically or in parables.) "---And of the commandment of us the apostles of the Lord and Savior:?" 11 Peter 3:2 The true commandments come from the Holy Ghost which is found in the Gospels, or Jesus Christ, out of His mouth. None of the verses from The Acts through Jude has anything to do with God. It reads Paul will come on his own after I leave, and what about Peter? St John 5:43 Peter never did show me that he knew what Jesus was about.

"Knowing this first, that there shall come in the last days scoffers, walking after their own lusts," 3:3 These kinds of statements or verses are extremely harmful to Elijah. It reads he will come in the last day. "Behold, I will send you Elijah the prophet before the coming of the great and dreadful day of the Lord:" Malachi 4:5 Peter is saying don't listen to Elijah he is walking after his own lusts.

"Whereby the world that then was, being overflowed with water, perished:" 6 Most of the people and animals perished, see how God loves you? All but Noah plus seven people, in his boat, that God told him to build, and a few animals were saved.

"But beloved, be not ignorant of this one thing, that one day is with the Lord as a thousand years, and a thousand years as one day." 8 Does this sound like something I need to know? A lot of people have used this verse to figure out when Jesus is going to return, and so far none have been right. It reads God is the only one that knows when the end time will occur. A person would think that God would have brought in the end time during World War 11, when the millions of Jews were being slaughtered but I believe, He has a time table that can't be broken. "For verily I say unto you, Till heaven and earth pass, one jot or one tittle shall in no wise pass from the law, till all be fulfilled." St Matthew 5"18 Verily I say unto you, This generation shall not pass, till all things be fulfilled." 24:34

"---not willing that any should perish, but that all should come to repentance." 11 Peter 3:9 Is this verse biblical? I think not, what about being one of the chosen or a person must be drawn by God to be saved. "No man can come to me, except the Father which hath sent me draw him: and I will raise him up at the last day." St John 5:44 What about many are called but few chosen? What if your name is written down as one of the called, does God have to draw you to Him? What if God doesn't like tattoos or you have messed up your life in some other way, will you still be one of the chosen and drawn? It is something to think about. I haven't heard one preacher say anything about not getting a tattoo, and they are beyond number. Your body whose is it? Jesus said His body is a temple, would that mean God owns your body? Are you defacing God's body?

"But the day of the Lord will come as a thief in the night; in the which the heavens shall pass away with a great noise, and the elements shall melt with fervent heat, the earth also and the works that are therein shall be burned up." 11 Peter 3:10 St Matthew and Mark never mentioned this happening suddenly, and they had a lot to say about the end of days. "Seeing then that all these things shall be dissolved, (made liquid or melt) what manner of persons (s) ought ye to be in all holy conversation (manner of life?) and godliness." 11 My Bible tells me that while the tribulation is going on, the elect will be removed from the earth. "And except those days should be shortened, there should no flesh be saved: but for the elect's sake those days shall be shortened." St Matthew 24:22 Peter asks what manner of life will you be? My body was made perfect physically as Jesus said it shall be of being born again, and having received the Holy Ghost, I'm in the kingdom of heaven already I don't need to be scrutinized or fudged at the last day.

"---be diligent that ye may be found of him in peace, without spot, and blameless." 14 It can't happen if a person has the original sin of Adam, in your heart, it must be removed first, as it is called being born again. "And account (consider) that the long suffering of our Lord is salvation: even as our beloved brother Paul also according to the wisdom given unto him hath written unto you;" 11 Peter 3:15 His ultimate sacrifice for the righteousness of God, that through Him, a person might become saved. You have to believe on one of the works that Jesus did I believed, I might be able to heal my mother. Paul has nothing to do with salvation. St John 10:37-38 and 14:11

The long suffering of our Lord had nothing to do with salvation, for individuals.

??? "Even as our beloved brother Paul also according to the wisdom given unto him hath written unto you:" (3:15 above) It reads Paul came on his own accord, without anything to do with God. "I am come in my Father's name, and ye receive me not: (Jesus) if another shall come in his own name, (Paul) ye will receive." (Believe) St John 5:43

"As also in all his (Paul's) epistles, speaking in them of these things; (the same things as Peter) in which are some things hard to be understood," 16 (yes, Peter and Paul give it to us as truth) "Which they that are unlearned and unstable wrest, (believe) as they do also the other scriptures, (like the Gospels of Jesus) unto their own destruction." 11 Peter 3:16

It speaks of Peter's and Paul's way is the only way to salvation. "Don't be led away, with the error of the wicked. Be steadfast in your belief." 17 Which church has the right doctrine that Jesus died for? I read 80% of people wouldn't give it a second thought that their parents could be wrong going to church or otherwise.

"But grow in grace, and in the knowledge of our Lord and saviour Jesus Christ, To him be glory both now and forever." 11 Peter 3:18 'Grow in grace,' is one of the favorites among the preachers, which is false doctrine. At best that keeps the money coming in.

Salvation is a personal matter between God and man, but Peter and Paul said the only way, were to go to church and grow in grace. In about one or two minutes I was born again and it only took thirty days for the entirety of my salvation experience to be completed, after receiving the Holy Ghost, but there was one more thing that I experienced later. I'm not sure if it were necessary, I believe I was given the 'Tree of Life' to live forever.

In comparing Peter and Paul with what Jesus said there is no comparison that works. Thomas Jefferson figured it out with his own intelligence, he said Paul was the first corrupter of the doctrines of Jesus. He might have been wrong in that, Peter never did understand the Word that Jesus conveyed either. If he did he wouldn't have said Peter's salvation plan. "Then Peter said unto them, Repent, and be baptized (in water) every one of you in the name of Jesus Christ for the remission of sins, and ye shall receive the gift of the Holy Ghost," The Acts 2:38 It is completely contrary to the Gospels. It wasn't much different then what John the Baptist did, and John said his way was not the right way. "I indeed baptize you with water unto repentance: but he (Jesus) that cometh after me is mightier than I, whose shoes I am not worthy to bear: he shall baptize you with the Holy Ghost (Spirit) and with fire:" ST Matthew 3:11 (new Gospel) "He (Jesus) must increase, but I (John) must decrease." St John 3:30 (John the Baptist) answered and said, "A man can receive nothing, except it be given him from heaven," St John 3:27 "He that rejecteth me, and receiveth not my words, hath one that judgeth him: the word that I have

SPOKEN, the same shall judge him in the last day." St John 12:48 "For I have not SPOKEN of myself: but the Father (God) which sent me, he gave me a commandment, what I should SAY, and what I should SPEAK." 49 "And I know that his commandment is life everlasting: whatsoever I SPEAK therefore, even as the Father said unto me, so I SPEAK." 50 "---It is written, "Man shall not live by bread alone, but by every word that proceedeth out of the MOUTH of God." St Matthew 4:4 (Jesus His Son) Did anything that Paul said, "come out of the mouth of God?" There is a choice Jesus or Paul? Peter said go by what they both said. I don't study anything from The Acts –Jude, and nothing that I have accidently read or heard of, compares with the Gospel. Luke wrote "---That man shall not live by bread alone, but by every word of God." Luke 4:4 (The whole Bible) Paul said, every word comes from God.

Paul and Peter they like to use Jesus Christ with the emphasis on Christ, I believe that is where people associate Christ with being God in the flesh. The trinity than according to them, all three are one, "'which I don't believe.' I believe God created the other three, and they are separate helpers in the creation of the earth etc., and the salvation of man. The Bible reads a husband and wife are one, but the last time I counted them, they were two individuals, that are suppose to have the same goals.

Salvation or redemption has become cheapened, that is true, it is why I was saved at a gasoline service station, and received the Holy Ghost in a 1959 Ford on the way to work. I believe I came close to receiving the Holy Ghost in a protestant church but they couldn't find my name on their program. At the beginning of a Sunday service the preacher said turn to page --- and the congregation started singing. With the song book open at the page there was a force that knocked the song book to the floor, and with no control I started walking toward the front of the church, raising both arms. The preacher and a deacon were pushing their fingers in my sides when I came to my senses at the front of the church. I went back to my seat. It was the next morning going to work, in a Ford car, that I received the Holy Ghost or Spirit, it came through the windshield, and went in my mouth, the same way Jesus received it, when He was baptized by John on His first breath. That is why it reads, "straight-way He came out of the water." A vision was put on me, to get my mouth open.

A true seeker will find truth and hold on to it passionately, whatever the consequences according to the Islam faith. Most of the time they hold on to what is untrue that is the problem. Jesus knew He was the Son of God, and would be with His Father after the crucifixion that was why He could go to the cross without any reservation. The problem is finding the truth. It reads in Proverbs "There is a way which seemeth right unto a man; but the end thereof are the ways of death." Proverbs 14:12 "The simple believeth every word: but the prudent man looketh well to his going." 15 That must be why the preachers wave the Bible around as it is, in its entirety the infallible word of God, without err, "as they say. "The simple (again) inherit folly; but the prudent are crowned with knowledge." 18 (They inherit folly from each other) "How can ye believe, which receive honor one of another, and seek not the honor that cometh from God only?" St John 5:44

Chapter 7

Galatians

"Paul an apostle, (not of men, neither by man, but by Jesus Christ, and God the Father, who raised him from the dead;") Galatians 1:1 (He means spiritual death ?) "I am come in my Father's name, and ye receive me not: (Jesus) if another shall come in his own name, him (Paul) ye will receive." (Believe) St John 5:43 The preachers that I know of preaches about what Paul and his disciples said, but according to Isaiah it is Satan that is in all the churches.

"And all the brethren, (people) which are with me, unto the churches of Galatia:" 2

"Grace be to you and peace from God the Father, and from our Lord Jesus Christ:" 3 (He covered most all the bases here except faith, believeth, be nice, water-dunk, etc.)

What if grace only means one thing, from God to man? God made it possible that he created Jesus, and by God's grace through Jesus, man could achieve righteousness, if they played their cards right or were one of the chosen and drawn. I looked up grace in my concordance, and in the gospels of St John, Matthew, and Mark John is using it in three verses St John 1:14 "And the Word was made flesh, and dwelt among us, (and we beheld his glory, the glory as of the only begotten of the Father,) full of grace and truth." St John 1:14 (It is Jesus that is full of the grace of God and truth) "For the law was given by Moses, but grace and truth came by Jesus Christ." 17 (It is for mankind to achieve righteousness, by being saved, to live with God in His kingdom) "And of His fullness have all we received, and grace (God's grace) for grace." 16 That man can become righteous. His fullness means a person has received His (new heart) (new Spirit "Holy Ghost"), and fasted three days and nights. It is the beginning of getting your body clean, for the Spirit to enter your mouth.

After Jesus received the Spirit in the mouth He went in the wilderness to be tempted by the Devil, and it was here He learned from that Spirit or Holy Ghost the statutes of God "For I have not spoken of myself; but the Father which sent me, (by His grace) he gave me a commandment, what I should say, and what I should speak." St John 12:49 I was in the wilderness two years, and as Jesus saw an Angel so did I at the end of that time. It only says that Jesus fasted forty days and nights, it doesn't say how long He was in the wilderness."Then the devil leaveth him, and, behold, angels came and ministered unto him." St Matthew 4:11 The angel I saw was in a Sunday school class toward the ceiling, and I blurted out, 'he day of judgment is coming.'

"Who gave himself for our sins, that he might deliver us from this present evil world, according to the will of God and our Father." 4 A person must be born again and receive the Spirit to be delivered from evil, but the evilness of mankind is still in the world, until the end time, and from the time of Adam for this dispensation.

"But though we or an angel from heaven, preach any other gospel unto you than that which we have preached unto you, let him be accursed." 8 The gospel that Paul preached, is not the Gospel, and it is hard to believe that the Angel Moroni' gave the gold tablets to Joseph Smith of the Latter day Saints, that they were from God. There is one thing about the Mormon bible that bothers me, and that is the amount of material that is in it. One of my renters left their Mormon bible when they vacated the apartment.

It is amazing to me of all the books from The Acts –Jude how consistent or repetitive the verses are. If that doesn't prove that Lucifer is behind what is written down, I don't know what to tell you. The authors never had at that time, any written material to go by. It reads that God saw in Lucifer's heart that he would sit upon the mount (all) the congregation. (Churches and religious organizations) Isaiah 14:13

"But when it pleased God, who separated me from my mother's womb, and called me by his grace," 15 Paul was on his own without God. St John 5:43

"Now the things which I write unto you, behold, before God, I lie not." 20 "And the devil that deceived them was cast into the lake of fire and brimstone, where the beast (anti-Christ) and the false prophet (Paul) are, and shall be tormented day and night forever and ever." Revelation 20:10 I can't think of any other person that has devastated the Gospel that Jesus died for, other than Paul as much. After I was saved, every time I started reading The Acts, God put a feeling of nausea on me until after I figured out there was something wrong with the Bible from The Acts –Jude. When I read about Paul's conversion, "it left no doubt" that Paul was never saved or redeemed. "---Ye do err, not knowing the scriptures, nor the power of God." St Matthew 22:29 "To Receive the new heart', and the new Spirit', it took the power of God to be saved or redeemed." Ezekiel 36:26-27 I have heard the preachers say that the false prophet hasn't came yet, but it reads Paul is already in the lake of fire in Revelation 20:10

"I am crucified with Christ: nevertheless I live, yet not I, but Christ liveth in me: and the life which I now live in the flesh I live by the faith of the Son of God, who loved me, and gave himself for me." Galatians 2:20 Jesus gave himself that through him mankind could be transformed into righteousness, and love has nothing to do with it. It is the Spirit or Holy Ghost that a person receives, and it will be with you for eternity, Christ doesn't live in anybody it is the Holy Ghost that lives in you, if you have received it. It hints that Paul died, but I physically died when my heart was removed, "clinically by the standards" I must have died, and in Revelation it reads that, I won't be hurt of the second death. If I won't be hurt of the second death, doesn't a person need a first death?

"Know ye therefore that they which are of faith, the same are the children of Abraham." 3:7 I'm not sure how Abraham got in here? "----In thee shall all nations be blessed." 8 It reads in Revelation, all nations will be deceived. "---for by thy sorceries were all nations deceived." Revelation 18: 23 "And the great dragon was cast out, that old serpent, called the Devil, and Satan, which deceiveth the whole world: he was cast out into the earth, and his angels were cast out with him." Revelation 12:9

"But the scripture hath concluded all under sin, that the promise by faith of Jesus might be given to them that believe." Galatians 3:22 (faith has nothing to do with salvation, when the earth was made a person doesn't walk on faith it was physically put together the same with salvation) It is true all under sin because of Adam, and it is true about believe BUT you have to believe in your heart, it triggers the Spirit in Genesis to act or a catalyst to act. I believed that perhaps I could heal my mother. "Believe me that I am in the Father, and the Father in me: OR ELSE BELIEVE ME FOR THE VERY WORKS' SAKE." St John 14"11 It was the Spirit of Genesis that removed my heart that I was born with and gave me my new heart as in "A new heart also will I give you---." Ezekiel 36:26 It happened at a gasoline service station after I left a protestant church. Joel 1:13 "-----for the meat offering and the drink offering is withholden from the house of your god." It means salvation cannot be achieved in the church you attend, and I believe it is because the preachers preach Paul 98% of the time if they use the Bible at all.

"Wherefore the law was our school-master to bring us unto Christ, that we might be justified by faith." Galatians3:24 The laws of Leviticus were physical sacrifices, so salvation is physical, and has nothing to do with being justified by faith for this dispensation.

"For ye are all the children of God, by faith in Christ Jesus." Galatians 3:26 Jesus answered and said unto him (Nicodemus) "Verily, verily, I say unto thee, except a man be born again, he cannot see the kingdom of God." St John 3:3 (See the power of God) "Jesus answered, Verily, verily, I say unto thee, except a man be born of water (born again 3rd verse) and of the Spirit, he cannot enter into the kingdom of God." St John3:5 (The Spirit or Holy Ghost, receiving it is the only way to the kingdom of God) Born again=the new heart. Spirit=the new Spirit or Holy Ghost in Ezekiel 36:26--27

Faith, grace, hope, walk in righteousness, work it out, be nice, be charitable, pray without ceasing. The Acts – Jude, Etc has nothing to do with entering the kingdom of God.

"For as many of you as have been baptized into Christ have put on Christ." 27 Water baptism has nothing to do with salvation. "Then Peter said unto them, Repent, and be baptized (water) every one of you in the name of Jesus Christ for the remission of sins, and ye shall receive the gift of the Holy Ghost." The Acts 2:38 (Before the Holy Ghost will enter your body it must have the sin of Adam removed, (new heart) to clean your body after a three day fast. It reads in those days you will fast. "----but the days will come, when the bridegroom (Jesus) shall be taken from them, and then shall they fast." St Matthew 9:15 God made me fast twice, after receiving the new heart and thirty days later the Holy Ghost, three days and nights each time. It means that when He goes back to the Father after crucifixion, you will fast, after receiving the new heart and Holy Ghost.

"There is neither, Jew nor Greek, there is neither bond nor free, there is neither male nor female: for ye are all one in Christ Jesus." 28 (If, you are not transformed or saved, it reads; few will find the way) "Because strait is the gate and narrow is the way, which leadeth unto life, and few there be that find it." St Matthew 7"14 I can't believe the verse, the Jew has always been the apple of God's eye.

"But when the fullness of the time was come, God sent forth his Son, (conceived by the Spirit of Genesis) made of a woman, (evidently sin only comes through the male from generation to generation) made under the law," 4:4 (the law had nothing to do with Jesus, except He was prophesied to come when the time was right)

"And because ye are sons, God has sent forth the Spirit of his Son into your hearts, crying, Abba, Father." 6 The Spirit or Holy Ghost is a separate being that is not that much associated with Jesus, that a person receives for eternity. In the Gospels we are called a child or children of God most of the time. I'm not sure what the Spirit of his Son into your heart is? The preachers will tell you that you receive the Spirit at the time of the sinner's prayer?

"Wherefore thou art no more a servant, (possibly to the Devil) but a son; and IF a son, (born again and received the Holy Ghost) an heir of God through Christ?" 7

"My little children of whom I travail (suffer pangs) in birth again until Christ be formed in you," 19 (A preacher today, can't do one thing, except perhaps preach a sermon it is up to God to give him salvation from above). "John answered and said, A man can receive nothing, except it be given him from heaven." St John 3:27 It is the Holy Ghost the second Spirit, not Christ that is formed inside you, it went in my mouth and down my throat.

"Now we brethren, as Isaac was, are the children of promise." 28 Anything promised to give a basis for expecting something. Because I was physically saved, I'm not a child of promise for anything.

"Behold, I Paul say unto you, that if ye be circumcised, Christ shall profit you nothing." 5:2 "For I testify again to every man that is circumcised, that he is debtor to do the whole law."3 Is Paul saying there is no hope of salvation if you are circumcised? "Christ is become of no effect unto you, whosoever of you are justified by the law; ye have fallen from grace?" 4 That is true the Pharisees and Sadducees were under the law, and Jesus never spent time trying to change their mind. I was never circumcised I must be a true gentile.

"For we (Paul) through the Spirit wait for the hope of righteousness by faith" 5 On 12/1/1968 at 9 pm and 12/30/1968 at 6:30 am I was physically saved (born again) and received the (Holy Ghost,) respectively. I'm not waiting for anything, and hope for nothing.

"For in Jesus Christ neither circumcision availeth any thing, nor uncircumcision; but faith which worketh by love." Galatians 5:6 "It grieved God in His heart, that He made man on the earth." Genesis 6:6 Faith, Grace, Hope, and Love, as preached, has nothing to do with God's righteousness for mankind to live with Him for all eternity.

"A little leaven leaveneth the whole lump."9 From The Acts –Jude I would call that a lot of leaven. At the time of being born again there is no sin left, to contaminate your body.

The Galatians, it sounds like they never believed Paul's rant.

"This I say then, Walk in the Spirit, and ye shall not fulfill the lust of the flesh." 16 The New Spirit goes in your mouth, resides inside of you for an eternity, and beyond this life on planet earth. It gets rid of any, 'lust of the flesh. "And Jesus when he was baptized, went up straightway (Immediately) out of the water and, lo, the heavens were opened unto him, and he saw the Spirit of God (Holy Ghost) descending like a dove, (a blob) and lighting upon him:" St Matthew 3:16 It went in Jesus mouth that is why it mentions straightway out of the water. This same thing happened to me except, instead of water baptism a vision was put on me to get my mouth open. "---ye shall drink indeed of my cup, and be baptized with the baptism that I am baptized with:" St Matthew 20:23 A person can't just Walk in the Spirit, it is impossible before they are saved first.

"For the flesh lusteth against the Spirit, and the Spirit against the flesh:---". 17 After I was saved I had no desire of doing those sinful things that I once did from the age of fourteen or fifteen. I stole cigarette packages out of my mother's boy friend's car, and drink whisky with eggnog at a Christmas party, for the green house employees where I worked. It was the beginning of being drunk most of the time for seventeen years.

"But if ye be led of the Spirit, ye are not under the law." 18 But a person must receive the new Spirit or Holy Ghost, and I have seen nothing, from The Acts –Jude that indicates that they received it.

"Bear ye one another's burdens, and so fulfill the law of Christ." 6:2 The false doctrine and burdens in this world are too great. All I have to do is try to give people the true Gospel, I don't have to be successful, and according to the standards of today I'm a failure, according to the mega churches. That is all Jesus had to do was present the truth. "And because I tell you the truth, ye believe me not." St John 8:45 Paul never knew what the truth was.

"For if a man think himself to be something, when he is nothing, he deceiveth himself." 3 (Speak for yourself) God has always chosen special people throughout history. "Behold, I will send you Elijah the prophet before the coming of the great and dreadful day of the Lord:" Malachi 4:5 So I think I'm special, and I don't deceive myself.

"For every man shall bear his own burden" 5 It isn't much but it is the truth.

"Be not deceived;--." 7 In regard to the Gospel of Christ, I can't think of anybody, not deceived. When they asked Jesus about the end time that is what He said in St Matthew "----Take heed that no man deceive you." St Matthew 24:4 "For many shall come in my name, saying I am Christ; and shall deceive many." 5 "But in the days of Noah were, so shall also the coming of the Son of man be." St Matthew 24:37 There were eight people on Noah's boat, it can't get any sadder than that, all of mankind and most of the animals were destroyed.

"For he that soweth to the flesh shall of the flesh reap corruption; but he that soweth to the Spirit shall of the Spirit reap life everlasting." 8 I sow to the Spirit or Holy Ghost that I received thirty days after being born again, the savior, the teacher, and before I was saved physically I sowed to the flesh.

"And let us not be weary in well doing for in due season we shall reap, if we faint not." 9 If a person is transformed, redeemed, born again and received the Spirit or Holy Ghost, or saved, and graduated into His kingdom, once saved always saved.

Chapter 8

James

"If any of you lack wisdom, let him ask of God, that giveth to all men liberally, and upbraideth (does not scold) not; and it shall be given him." James 1:5 "But let him ask in faith---." 6 What does this have to do with St Matthew? "---Why speakest thou unto them in parables?" St Matthew 13:10 Because it is given unto you to know the mysteries of the kingdom of heaven, but to them it is not given." 11 When redeemed, that is when you will understand the mysteries, so you can ask God for wisdom until your blue in the face and no wisdom will come your way, true wisdom of the understanding the allegorical or parable kind.

"Blessed is the man that endureth (is having trials) temptation: (sin) for when he is tried, he shall (no doubt) receive the crown of life, which the Lord hath promised to them that love him." 12 Jesus died because of the righteousness of God, that has nothing to do with love. If we want to call it the crown of life, it is receiving the Holy Ghost after a person is born again. It is the only way to the kingdom of God. St John 3:5

"Wherefore lay apart all filthiness and superfluity of naughtiness, and receive with meekness the engrafted word, which is able to save your souls." 21 Without getting rid of your accumulative sin, and disobedient sin of Adam, "in your heart" that happens when a person is born again only. "Then will I sprinkle clean water upon you, (born again) and ye shall be clean: from all your filthiness, and from all your idols, will I cleanse you." Ezekiel 36:25

"If any man among you, seem to be religious, and bridleth not his tongue, but deceiveth his own heart, this man's religion is vain." 26 The Acts through Jude is false doctrine, they seem to need to slap each other's back deceiving their own heart. They must realize with all the different churches, and doctrines there is something wrong. "How can ye believe which receive honor one of another, and seek not the honor that cometh from God only?" St John 5:44

"Pure religion and undefiled before God and the Father Is this, to visit the fatherless and widows in their affliction, and to keep themselves unspotted from the world." 27 What about unless you are born again and receive the Spirit, you will not enter into the kingdom of God? St "---I say unto thee, Except a man be born of water (born again 3rd verse receive a new heart) and of the Spirit, (new Spirit) he cannot enter into the kingdom of God." St John 3:5 Pure religion is this; to visit the fatherless and widows. Does that make any sense to you?

"And ye have respect to him that weareth the gay clothing, and say unto him, sit thou here in a good place; and say to the poor, Stand thou there, or sit here under my footstool:" James 2:3

The difference in church, between a man in a suit, wife and three kids, and a poor single man they are treated differently ? Automatically the family is going to heaven, and the poor man needs worked on. "Are ye not then partial in yourselves, and are become judges of evil thoughts?" 4 James seems to believe that love is where salvation is at in James 2:5&8.

Faith that works

James is saying that works is more important than faith alone. Neither one has anything to do with becoming righteous or saved, that requires a person to be physically redeemed. Can either one make a person righteous as God is righteous? When Adam disobeyed God he was physically changed, and a person must become the same as Adam was, when he was created without sin of any kind in the heart. To enter into the kingdom of God a person must be born again, and receive a new Spirit as explained in this book. James 2:14-26

"For in many things we offend all. If any man offend not in word, (give no offense) the same is a perfect man, and able to bridle the whole body." 3;2 How can a person believe this came from God when you compare the Gospels with what is said from The Acts through Jude. John the Baptist said, and I found it to be true. "A man can receive nothing, except it be given him from heaven." St John 3:27 and Ezekiel 36: 26-27

True and false wisdom

The Holy Ghost, after a person receives it, is where the wisdom comes from, that a person needs because it comes from God. It enters your mouth and will be with you for eternity. "But the Comforter which is the Holy Ghost, whom the Father will send in my name, (he; a New Spirit) shall teach you all things, and bring all things to your remembrance, whatsoever I have said unto you." St John 14:26 "And I will pray the Father, and he shall give you another (born again; first) Comforter, (Holy Ghost) that (he; the other Spirit) may abide with you forever." 16 "Even the Spirit of truth; whom the world cannot receive, (Paul and James) because it seeth him not, neither knoweth him: but ye know him; for he dwelleth with you, and shall be in you." 17

"Submit your selves therefore to God, Resist the Devil', and he will flee from you." 4:7 It is too bad that James doesn't have a clue. After Jesus received the Holy Ghost in the mouth He spent time in the wilderness, it reads He fasted forty days, and it doesn't say how long He was there, with me it was two years. The devil never bothered Him again as I discovered, going through the same things as Jesus did. St Matthew 4:1-11 It is impossible to just submit yourself to God.

"Draw nigh to God, and he will draw neigh to you? Cleanse your hands, ye sinners; and purify your hearts, ye double minded." 8 A person on their own can't purify their heart it takes God to do that physically. James should look in the mirror to see a (two faced hypocrite) St "-----Who then can be saved?" St Matthew 19:25 "But Jesus beheld them, (understood what they were thinking) and said unto them, with men this is impossible but with God all things are possible." 26

"Humble yourselves in the sight of the Lord, and he shall lift you up." James 4:10 It is only the Holy Ghost inside of you that can lift you up." Whatever, that means.

"There is one lawgiver, who is able to save and (or) to destroy: who art thou that judgest another?" 4:12 The author judges what he hears. The beam has been removed from my eye, I'm going to judge, what I see and hear, a person can judge, if it is biblical or not. "Judge not according to the appearance, (what comes out of their mouth) but judge righteous judgment." St John 7:24 James, I find you and your colleagues are teaching false doctrine, according to the Gospels that Jesus died for.

I have never studied The Acts –Jude and I see a lot of catch phrases that the preachers use, I never did know where they came from like, "---If the Lord will, we shall live, and do this, or that." 4:15 "Therefore to him that knoweth to do good, and doeth it not, to him it is sin." 17

That is a drastic statement, over the top, according to that, nobody would be in the kingdom of God. It must be why people think they are working toward living in the kingdom of God.

"Be ye also patient; stablish (strengthen) your heart-s for the coming of the Lord draweth nigh." 5:8 It means congregate, pray a lot, give money, fast, wash each other's feet, give money, pat each other's back, eat food, give money, give to the needy, say a-men to reverberate the preacher, eat food, and give money, sign up for the cruise to Alaska, eat, give to our missionaries preaching St John 3:16, and Mable, is down on her luck. Etc. I found a true statement. "Grudge not one against another, brethren, lest ye be condemned: behold, the judge standeth before the door." 9 That is correct Jesus is not inside.

"Is any among you afflicted? (in trouble) Let him pray. Is any merry? Let him sing psalms." 13 The last time I sang to some kids, they went home.

"Is any sick among you? Let him call for the elders of the church; and let them pray over him, anointing him with oil in the name of the Lord:"14 My Dad had a barrel of olive oil, and to my knowledge it never did anybody any good. What is true is they are all sick. I don't go to any church. A study done on the subject, they never found one person that was ever healed by being prayed for. I personally have seen a lot of action with no results.

"And the prayer of faith shall save the sick, and the Lord shall raise him up; and if he have committed sins, they shall be forgiven him." 15 I'm not sure how faith got in hear, "man can't do anything without God," and that would come from above. I was saved or redeemed 12/1/1968 at 9pm. I believe if I haven't led a perfect life afterward, 'through the blood of Jesus,' God the Father can't see my discrepancies, so that He remains righteous.

"Confess your faults one to another, and pray one for another, that ye may be healed. The effectual fervent prayer of a righteous man availeth much." 5:16 God said He knows what you need, so why asked him that much. God hates people that believe they are righteous. "But thou, when thou prayest, enter into thy closet, and when thou hast shut thy door, pray to the Father which is in secret; and thy Father which seeth in secret; shall reward thee openly." St Matthew 6:6 "But when ye pray, use not vain repetitions, as the heathen do: for they think that they shall be heard for their much speaking." 6:7 "Be not ye therefore like unto them: for your Father knoweth what things ye have need of before ye ask him." 8 "For verily I say unto you, That many (false) prophets and righteous men have desired to see those things which ye see, and have not seen them; and to hear those things which ye hear, and have not heard them." St Matthew 13:17 "But blessed are your eyes, for they see: and your ears, for they hear." 16 .

"Brethren, if any of you do err from the truth, and one? Convert him;" 19 'Which church? The problem is, man can't convert a person. It took the power of God (the Spirit in Genesis 1:2) to give me a new heart and a new Spirit. John said it can only happen from above, and that is what I found out to be true. "---A man can receive nothing except it be given him from heaven." St John 3:27

CHAPTER 9

1CORINTHIANS

"Paul, called to be an apostle of Jesus Christ through the will of God, and Sos'-the-nes our brother." 1 Corinthians 1:1 In St John it reads Paul was on his own without God. St John 5:43 "Hereafter I will not talk much with you: for the prince (Lucifer) of this world cometh, and hath nothing in me." St John 14:30 Who was Sos'-the-nes our brother? "For thou hast said in thine heart, (Lucifer) I will ascend into heaven, I will exalt my throne above the stars of God: I will sit also upon the mount (all) of the congregation, (Churches) in the sides of the north." (America) Isaiah 14:13 "I will ascend above the heights of the clouds; I will be like the most High." 14 (God) Paul was the advocate for Lucifer.

"-----with all that in every place call upon the name of Jesus Christ our Lord, both theirs and ours:" 1 Corinthians 1:2 There must be two different Lords?

"I think my God always on your behalf, for the grace of God which is given you by Jesus Christ." 4 That is true,' it is only by the grace of God that He sent Jesus so we could become redeemed.

"Even as the testimony of Christ was confirmed in you:" 6 No, a person must receive the New heart when they are born again, and it took me about a month to receive the Holy Ghost which is the other Spirit, that is the confirmation that I received. Ezekiel 36:26-27

"God is faithful, by whom ye were called unto the fellowship of his Son Jesus Christ our Lord." 9 Salvation is more then to just have fellowship it is a physical matter. Fellowship is companionship or friendly association of a group of people with the same interests. That is true in the church and religious organizations' today, they have a superficial interest in their wellbeing, just don't get to churchy. " And then will I profess unto them, I never knew you: depart from me, ye that work iniquity." St Matthew 7:23

"Now I beseech you, brethren, by the name of our Lord Jesus Christ, that ye all speak the same thing, and that there be no division among you; but that ye be perfectly joined together in the same mind and in the same judgment." 10 It sounds like pie in the sky to me with all the different religious organizations on the earth.

"Now this I say, that every one of you saith, I am of Paul; (that's the truth then and now) And I of A-pol'los; (Islam?) And I of Ce'-phas; (Hindu?) And I of Christ." 12 Which one makes any common sense as being the true worshipers of Jesus that will live with God in His kingdom for eternity?

"Is Christ divided?" (Yes) was Paul crucified for you? Or were ye baptized in the name of Paul?" 13 It seems like, in most churches, that is the case, when they go by what he said 99% of the time.

"For the preaching of the cross is to them that perish foolishness; but unto us which are saved it is the power of God."18 Both of the Spirits show the power of God. The first Spirit the born again experience receiving a new heart, and the Holy Ghost a Spirit, that is referred to as a He, being given a New Spirit in Ezekiel 36:26-27. That seems to be what we have today only the mention of the cross, not believing that redemption is physical.

"---hath not God made foolish the wisdom of this world?" 20 I run into this all the time on the social networks, people try and use their wisdom, in relationship to God.

"---it pleased God by the foolishness of preaching to save them that believe." 21 The problem is, a man is limited to what they can accomplish, when redemption comes from above, and there is more to believe then to just believe.

"And I brethren, when I came to you, came not with excellency of speech or of wisdom, declaring you the testimony of God." 1 Corinthians

2:1 That is true out of the three nonfiction books working on the fourth, the editors never believed me, so they tried to do as poor a job as they could get away with. But that doesn't deter me in my quest to get the truth out to mankind. I know I'm not an author, but have a message.

"For I determined not to know anything among you, save Jesus Christ, and him crucified." 2:2 That is true about me, but Paul never knew anything about being born again by the Spirit of God, and receiving the Holy Ghost in the mouth, but the preachers can't get enough of Paul. It is the Holy Ghost that teaches a person the commandments of God. When Jesus received what God wanted Him to know He saw an angel in St Matthew; "Then the devil leaveth him, and, behold angels came and ministered unto him." St Matthew 4:11 The same thing happened to me but two years later, and it doesn't say how long Jesus was in the wilderness it only reads He fasted forty days and forty nights.

"But we speak the wisdom of God in a mystery, even the hidden wisdom, which God ordained before the world unto our glory:"7 Paul never understood the wisdom of God or the truth of God he was never redeemed. They are the only people that understand the mysteries.

"He answered and said unto them, because it is given unto you to know the mysteries, of the kingdom of heaven, but to them it is not given." St Matthew 13:11 If you would ask a preacher if they knew the mysteries, they would tell you they did. A person can't find the mysteries from The Act – Jude.

"---For had they known it, (hidden wisdom) they would not have crucified the Lord of glory." 8 That is why Jesus spoke in parables He had to get to the cross, and that was the plan of God that He die on the cross, there was no other way.

"Eye hath not seen, nor ear heard, neither have entered into the heart of man, the things which God hath prepared for them that love him." 9 That is not true, because when your born again and receive the Holy Ghost physically a person has their heart replaced and given a new Spirit about thirty days later, as given in this book, love has nothing to do with being redeemed. "But blessed are your eyes, for they see: and your ears for they hear." St Matthew 13:16 Speak for yourself Paul, which you have done in half of the New Testament. A person must believe in one of the works that Jesus did, while He was on the earth. It triggers the Spirit in Genesis 1:2 to give a person a new heart, and that has nothing to do with love from God too man, nor from man to God. "Believe me that I am in the Father, and the Father in me: or else believe me for the very works' sake." St John 14:11

"But God hath revealed them unto us by his Spirit ---."10 There is no record that Paul ever received His Spirit in the mouth or the New Heart. It is not His Spirit but the Holy Ghost the second Spirit becomes your New Spirit. "Even the Spirit of truth; whom the world cannot receive, (nor Paul) because it seeth him not, (I saw it just before it entered my mouth) neither knoweth him: but ye know him; (Holy Ghost) for he dwelleth with you, and shall be in you." St John 14:17

"Now we have received, not the spirit of the world, (The spirit of the world a person is born with, and it must be replaced) "but the Spirit which is of God; that we might know the things that are freely given to us of God." 12 That is true but your body must be clean before the Spirit of God will enter into it, as a start, replacing the heart. That is true but it wasn't free It took me two years that I was in the wilderness being tempted by Satan, and learning the statutes of God. "And I will put my Spirit within you, and cause you to walk in my statutes, and ye shall keep my judgments, and do them." Ezekiel 36:27

"And I brethren, could not speak unto you as unto spiritual, but as unto carnal, even as unto babes in Christ." 3:1 Paul never knew spiritual, nor was he aware of the truth in the Gospels. He never met Jesus nor was the Gospels in print before he started his rant. "I have fed you with milk, and not with meat:---."2 I have to tell it like it is explaining the truth, there can't be milk for some and meat for others. That is why it reads greater things you will do. At that time they never understood Jesus and the parables, so it was easy for Him, but difficult when a person knows the true Word of God. To overcome what people has been told for 2,018 years is hard to overcome.

"---and every man shall receive his own reward according to his own labor." 3'8 A person can't work their way into the kingdom of God so I don't know how you receive your reward according to his own labor, salvation was physical from above? "John answered and said, A man can receive nothing, except it be given him from heaven." St John 3:27 That is a true statement, but find me a preacher, that will tell you that. "----Ye do err, not knowing the scriptures, nor the power of God." St Matthew 22:29

"----Who can be saved?" St Matthew 19:25 "---With men this is impossible; but with God all things are possible." 26

"Know ye not that ye are, the 'temple of God' and that the Spirit of God dwelleth in you?" 16 That is true but if you haven't received it in the mouth the Spirit of God is not in you as Paul put it, you are carnal. Jesus received it in the mouth when He was baptized by John, and it reads that a person will receive it the same way. "Ye shall drink indeed of my cup, and be baptized with the baptism that I am baptized with:" St Matthew 20:23 It never 'lighting on Him' as it reads in St Matthew 3:16.

"If any man defile the temple of God, (your body) him shall God destroy; for the temple of God is holy, which temple ye are?" 1 Corinthians 3:17 The preacher's don't mention this in their sermons they are too busy collecting the money. Now, 80% of their congregation would walk out if they said anything against tattoos or defacing your body. .

"For who maketh thee to differ from another---?" 4:7 God, (the two Spirits) because I was born again and received the Holy Ghost, that seems to make me different from mankind. "And except those days should be shortened, there should no flesh be saved: but for the elect's sake those days shall be shortened." St Matthew 24:22

"Wherefore I beseech you, be ye followers of me." 4:16 "For the kingdom of God is not in word, but in power." 4:20 Yes Paul that is true it is too bad that you like Satan, have no real power nor have ever felt the power with your senses all you have is words. That is where the trouble is, most all the preachers are following what Paul and his disciples said.

"To deliver such a one unto Satan for the destruction of the flesh," (Satan has no power for the destruction of the flesh, the original sin is in the heart that a person must get rid of.) "that the spirit may be saved in the day of the Lord Jesus." 5:5 I'm in the kingdom of God at this time because I was born again 12/1/1968 at 9pm, and Holy Ghost 12/30/1968 at 6:30 am.

"Purge out therefore the old leaven, that ye may be a new lump---." 7 A person can't purge out the leaven, it takes the Spirit in Genesis to do that from above. "John answered and said, a man can receive nothing, except it be given him from heaven." St John 3:27 I found out that is true.

"I wrote unto you in an epistle not to company with fornicators:" 1 Corinthians 5:9 Jesus ate with the fornicators' He liked that rather than eat with half baked Christians. "And when the scribes and Pharisees saw him eat with publicans and sinners, they said unto his disciples, how is it that he eateth and drinketh with publicans and sinners?" St Mark 2:16 "---I came not to call the righteous, but sinners to repentance,---." St Mark 2:17 Too be redeemed or saved.

"Flee fornication, every sin that a man doeth is without the body; but he that committeth fornication sinneth against his own body."1 Corinthians 6:18 "---for out of the abundance of the heart the mouth speaketh." St Matthew 12:34 "For by thy words thou shalt be justified, and by thy words thou shalt be condemned." 37 When a person is preaching Paul, isn't it coming out of their mouth from the heart, according to the scriptures in the KJB of 1611? What? Know ye not that your body is the temple of the Holy Ghost which is in you, which you have of God, and ye are not your own?" 1 Corinthians 6:19 Your body is not the temple of the Holy Ghost unless you receive it after the replacement of the heart that you were born with, after it becomes clean. The Holy Ghost will not dwell in a filthy body. "Ye shall be clean: from all your filthiness, and from all your idols, will I cleanse you." Ezekiel 36:25 "My Father giveth you the true bread from heaven; St John 6:32 This is the bread which cometh down from heaven, that a man may eat thereof, and not die. 50 Whoso eateth my flesh, (born again) and drinketh my blood, (Holy Ghost) hath eternal life; and I will raise him up at the last day. 54 For my flesh is meat indeed, and my blood is drink indeed 55 ---he that eateth of this bread shall live forever." 58

"For ye are bought with a price: therefore glorify God in your body, and in your spirit, which are God's." 1 Corinthians 6:20 The preachers say that Jesus bore or bare the sin of mankind when He died on the cross, and that the spirit is inside of you, healing, righteousness, also He went to hell for mankind? Etc. What if He never did any of these things?

"There is difference also between a wife and a virgin. The unmarried women careth for the things of the Lord, that she may be holy both in body and in spirit:----." 7"34 I have often wondered about the nuns in the Catholic Church, I always assumed it was in there bible, it never occurred to me it was in the KJB of 1611.Unless they are born again and receive the Holy Spirit or Holy Ghost in the mouth physically, they will not enter into the kingdom of God as I have explained in this book. Nobody can work their way into being holy. "For whosoever shall do the will of my

Father which is in heaven, the same is my brother, my sister, and mother." St Matthew 12:50 Mary was not blessed as Luke said she was.

"And if any man think that he knoweth any thing, he knoweth nothing yet as he ought to know." 1 Corinthians 8:2 Look in the mirror Paul, I have no way of knowing how the preachers think that Paul's half of the Bible could be like the Gospels, when at that time nothing was written down and it reads go by what came out of the mouth of Jesus. In Luke it reads, go by all of the Bible, which would include what Paul said, but in St Matthew it said go by what came out of the mouth of Jesus. Jesus was not God. St Matthew and Luke 4:4

"But if any man love God, the same is known (recognized) of him." 3 Love has nothing to do with making a person righteous, and without becoming righteous, a person will not enter into the kingdom of God. "But seek ye first the kingdom of God, and his righteousness: and all these things shall be added unto you." St Matthew 6:33

"---there is none other God but one." 4 That is true, the spirit of Genesis, Holy Ghost, and Jesus were not Gods but His helpers, but if you don't believe in one of the miracles that Jesus his Son performed there is no hope for you. St John 14:11 "Believe me that I am in the Father, and the Father in me, or ELSE believe me for the very works' sake." St John 14:11 Or 10; 37-38 as told in this book.

Paul got it right in 6 there is one God the Father, of whom are all things (were made), and one Jesus His Son that (through Him we get our salvation.. "Verily, verily I say unto you, He that entereth not by the door into the sheepfold, but climbeth up some other way, the same is a thief and a robber." St John 10:1 The Acts –Jude is false teaching, and not by the door.

"And through thy knowledge shall the weak brother perish, for whom Christ died?" 1 Corinthians 8:11 That could be true' I believe they call it collateral damage. It seems to say Jesus died for everybody which according to the Gospels He never died for everybody, there is the matter of being one of the chosen and drawn, before they can be saved.

"But when ye sin so against the brethren, and wound their weak conscience, ye sin against Christ." 8:12 Every person is on their own, if they make heaven or hell.

"Am I not an apostle? Am I not free? Have I not seen Jesus Christ our Lord? Are not ye my work in the Lord? 9:1 No, Paul you never saw Jesus, you said a light shined round about your body, and there was no power shown., Paul those that follow you will have the same cell in hell.

---who (is it that) feedeth a flock, and eateth not of the milk, (money) of the flock? 7 There certainly isn't anybody that I know of that does that.

"---woe is unto me, if I preach not the gospel?" 16 How many woes are there, when someone writes half of the New Testament of rant, that doesn't come from God?

"---he that ploweth should plow in hope---." 10 When physically redeemed a person doesn't have to hope for anything.

"To the weak became I as weak, that I might gain the weak;" 22 The old timers said, you don't have to wallow with the hogs. Paul never knew the Gospel of Jesus in the first place. "I am made all things to all men; that I might by all means save some." 22 The Bible reads; it is only God that can save a person. John said it comes from above, which I found out to be true.

"Wherefore, my dearly beloved, flee (avoid) from idolatry." 1 Corinthians 10:14 (Excessive devotion to or reverence for some person or thing) " I speak as to wise men; judge ye (think over) what I say."15 It reads more than once that people, should go by what Paul said, or his disciples, that he is the only one with the Gospel, so avoid idolatry.

"The cup of blessing, which we bless, is it not the communion of the body of Christ? The bread which we break, is it not the communion of the body of Christ? 1 Corinthians 16 No; "But I (Jesus) say unto you, I will not drink henceforth of the fruit of the vine, until that day when I drink it new with you (saved) in my Father's kingdom." St Matthew 26:29

"But I say, that the things which the Gentiles sacrifice, they sacrifice to devils, and not to God: and I would not that ye should have fellowship with devils." 20 He is alive and well in the churches, and religious organizations all over the earth.

"Give none (no occasion to take offense) offense, (feeling hurt) neither to the Jews, nor to the Gentiles, nor to the church of God:" 32 Coddle, treat tenderly, and pamper the congregation, that will get them ready for judgment day. A Person can judge righteously, so which church or religious organization is Paul referring too? 'All of the churches or just the Church of God?'

"Even as I please all men in all things, not seeking mine own profit, (money) but the profit of many that they may be saved." 33 The sinner's prayer is not the answer. It reads salvation comes from above. There is no money in the truth so far as I can ascertain.

"Be ye followers of me, even as I also am of Christ." 11:1 "Flee from idolatry." 10:14 Jesus said there would be a man that would come after he left that people would believe. St John 5:43

3 "But I would have you know, that the head of every man is Christ; the head of the women is the man; and the head of Christ is God." 1 Corinthians 11:3, The Holy Ghost who God created gave Jesus what to say and do when He was in the wilderness, and it came from the His Father. With me; salvation was between God and me, it is hard to believe that the head of the women is the man. "For I have not spoken of myself; but the Father which sent me, he gave me a commandment, what I should say, and what I should speak." St John 12:49

"Every man praying or prophesying, having his head covered, dishonoreth his head." 11:4 Do you really believe God is concerned with your head?

Paul said the sacrament is: "this do in remembrance of me." Verses 24 through 27 Is dealing with the sacrament, and some churches have made it the backbone of their doctrine. In St Matthew it reads that Jesus would not, "drink henceforth of this fruit of the vine, until that day when I drink it new with you in my Father's kingdom." St Matthew 26:29 "For he that eateth and drinketh unworthily, eateth and drinketh damnation to himself, not discerning the Lord's body." 1 Corinthians 11:29 "For this cause many are weak and sickly among you, and many sleep." 30 If this verse were true according to my salvation, no one would be living on the earth. . .

"And if any man hunger, let him eat at home;" 34 several verses suggest this, but now days food is half of the experience of going to church.

Prophecy superior to tongues

"Follow after charity, and desire spiritual gifts, (There are no such things as spiritual gifts) but rather that ye may prophesy." 1 Corinthians 14:1 "For he that speaketh in an unknown tongue speaketh not unto men, but unto

God: for no man understandeth, him; howbeit in the spirit he speaketh mysteries. 2 "Now when this was noised abroad, (unknown tongues) the multitude came together', and were confounded, because every man heard them speak in his own language." The Acts 2:6 (There is no such thing as speaking in an unknown tongue as being from the Holy Ghost. The Holy Ghost is a Spirit that went in Jesus mouth and mine, after a vision was put on me going to work in a 1959 Ford Thunderbird about 6:30am on a Monday morning. "And they were all filled with the Holy Ghost', and began to speak with other tongues, as the Spirit gave them utterance," The Acts 2:4 which is a lie, to put it mildly.

"Moreover, brethren, I declare unto you the gospel which I preached unto you, which also ye have received, and wherein ye stand:" ! Corinthians 15:1 "By which also ye are saved, if ye keep in memory what I preached unto you, unless ye have believed in vain." 2 St John 3:3-5 If you are born again, and have received His Spirit, if not, you cannot enter into the kingdom of God, ye have believed in vain as the verse says.

"For I delivered unto you first of all that, which I also received, (When did you receive anything Paul, that was of God?) "How that Christ died for our sins according to the scriptures;" 3 "And that he was buried, and that he rose again the third day according to the scriptures." 4 (That is true but a person needs to be physically saved or redeemed in which Paul missed out on.)

"For I am the least of the apostles, that am not meet (worthy) to be called an apostle, because I persecuted the church of God." 9 'I would say if anything, you are a False Prophet', and the true church was not established yet to be persecuted.

"But by the grace of God (Satan) I am what I am: and his (Satan's) grace which was bestowed upon me was not in vain: but I labored more abundantly than they all: yet not I but the grace of God (Satan) which was with me." 10 "For thou hast said in thine heart, (Satan) I will ascend into heaven, I will exalt my throne above the stars of God: I will sit also upon the mount (all) of the congregation, (churches) in the sides of the north." Isaiah 14:13 "I (Satan) will ascend above the heights of the clouds; I (Satan) will be like the most High." 14 Didn't Satan need an Advocate such as Paul, as Jesus was to God to be like him? St John 5:43

"Therefore whether it were I or they? So we preach, and so ye believed." 15:11 It is too bad that salvation is physical. (I or they) I'm not sure about 'they'.

"For as in Adam all die, even so in Christ shall all be made alive." 22 There are two Spirits that assures a person of redemption or to be made alive. The first Spirit is triggered by believing in one of the works that Jesus did, it gives a person a new heart. After your body is clean the other Spirit called the Holy Ghost comes in your body in the mouth as Jesus received it. So it is two Spirits and not Christ but it is the belief in one of His works' that saves a person. St John 14: 11

"Awake to righteousness, and sin not; for some have not the knowledge of God; I speak this to your shame." 1 Corinthians 15:34 Is Paul saying live a holy life, and not sin that will get a person into the kingdom of God. The knowledge of God is physical by the two Spirits, and other places in this book, there are many without the knowledge of God.

"Now this I say brethren, (which church) that flesh and blood cannot inherit the kingdom of God;---" 50 (If a person is born again and have received the Holy Ghost physically it says that they will enter into the kingdom of God) They are flesh and blood, but remain on the earth. "Behold, I show you a mystery; We shall not all sleep, but we shall all be changed," 51 "In a moment, in the twinkling of an eye, at the last trump: for the trumpet shall sound, and the dead shall be raised incorruptible, and we shall be changed." 52 When a person receives a new heart, and about thirty days later a new Spirit, they have already been changed. "For this corruptible must put on incorruption, and this mortal must put on immortality." 53 That is true for me, but Paul it's too late for you, before Jesus comes back,. Ezekiel 36:26-27

11 Corinthians

"For we must all appear before the judgment seat of Christ; that every one may receive the things done in his body, according to that he hath done, whether it be good or bad." 5:10 "Let both grow together until the harvest: and in the time of harvest I will say to the reapers, gather ye together first the tares, and bind them in bundles to burn them: but gather the wheat into my barn." St Matthew 13:30 There is a separation of the tares and wheat, why would, "all have to appear before the judgment seat of Christ? I am already made perfect with the new heart and the new Spirit physically or made righteous, and ready to go live, with God in His kingdom. The preachers will tell you Jesus dying on the cross did it all, "went to hell and even took our sickness on our behalf, etc."For he hath made him to sin for us, who knew no sin; that we might be made the righteousness of God in him." 11 Corinthians 5:21 The two other Spirits what were they, for if Jesus did it all?

"---behold, now is the accepted time; behold, now is the day of salvation." 6:2 Sorry Paul, but salvation comes to a person in two different days. With me those days were thirty days apart.

The attributes of ministers according to Paul' " pureness, of knowledge, (Paul's rant of course) by longsuffering, by kindness, by the Holy Ghost, (speaking in tongues). By Love unfeigned, (genuine true love, love, and more love) "---yet making many rich:" 11 Corinthians 4;5;6;10

"Be ye not unequally yoked together with unbelievers---." 14 Jesus preferred to eat with publicans and sinners, rather than half baked Christians. "Two women shall be grinding at the mill; the one shall be taken, and the other left" St Matthew 24:41 Luke (Had a different slant, I have mentioned before, he can get a person in trouble) "I tell you, in that night there shall be two men in one bed; the one shall be taken, and the other shall be left." Luke 17:34 "---for ye are the temple of the living God; as God hath said, I will dwell in them, and walk in them; and I will be their God, and they shall be my people." 11 Corinthians 6:16 It is not God but the Holy Ghost that dwells in man. "And I will pray the Father, and he shall give you another Comforter, (Holy Ghost) that he may abide with you forever." St John 14"16 "Even the Spirit of truth; whom the world cannot receive, because it seeth him not, neither knoweth him: but ye know him; for he dwelleth with you, and shall be in you." 17

"Having therefore these promises clearly beloved, let us cleanse ourselves from all filthiness of the flesh and Spirit, perfecting holiness in the fear of God." 11 Corinthians 7:1 It can't be done as long as man has the same heart that they are born with in their body. When Adam sinned it changed his heart, and the Spirit will remove the heart you were born with, giving a new heart from God and about thirty days later a New Spirit, the Holy Ghost. " A new heart also will I give you: and I will take away the stony heart out of your flesh, and I will give you a heart of flesh." (from God) Ezekiel 36:26 And a new Spirit (Holy Ghost) will I put within you: And I will put my Spirit within you, and cause you to walk in my statutes, and ye shall keep my judgments, and do them." 27

"Receive us; we have wronged no man, we have corrupted no man, we have defrauded no man." 7:2 Paul you have done all three to your fellow man, because they believe you.

"Great is my boldness of speech toward you, great is my glorying of you: I am filled with comfort, I am exceeding joyful in all our tribulation." 4 "Verily, verily, I say unto you, that ye shall weep and lament, but the world shall rejoice: and ye shall be sorrowful, but your sorrow shall be turned into joy." ST John 16:20 When this life is over with you will have joy.

"Nevertheless God, that comforteth those that are cast down, comforted us by the coming of Titus;" 11 Corinthians 7:6 "And not by his coming only, but by the consolation wherewith he was comforted in you, when he told us your earnest desire, your mourning, your fervent mind toward me (Paul) so that I rejoiced the more." 7 It sounds like Titus made Paul happy. Paul used the names of different people a lot, which never does make any sense to me, Silvanus, Stephanas, Fortunatus, Achaicus, Aquila, Priscilla, Apollos, Crispus, Gaius, Chloe and Sosthenes, to name a few. "Therefore we were comforted in your comfort: yea, and exceedingly the more joyed we for the joy of Titus, because his spirit was refreshed by you all." 13

"For if I have boasted anything to him (Titus) of you, I am not ashamed; but as we spake all things to you in truth, even so our boasting, which I made before Titus, is found a truth." 14 "And his inward affection is more abundant toward you, whilst he remembereth the obedience of you all, how with fear and trembling ye received him." 15 (Titus?)

"Insomuch that we desired Titus, that as he had began, so he would also finish in you the same grace also." 11 Corinthians 8:6 Grace has nothing to do with man it was the grace of God that He sent Jesus for the salvation of man, and that is as far as grace goes. "Therefore as ye abound in everything, in faith, (faith has nothing to do with receiving the righteousness of God) and utterance, (tongues has nothing to do with the Holy Ghost) and knowledge, and in all diligence, and in your love to us,

(Love has nothing to do with righteousness) that ye abound in this grace also." 7 "But thinks be to God, which put the same earnest care into the heart, of Titus for you." 16 The Spirit (of Genesis) replaces the Heart in your body it doesn't put anything in the heart of Titus, for you that you need, that is helpful for your salvation.

"Whether any do inquire of Titus, he is my partner and fellow helper concerning you:---." 23 That clears that up.

"---God loveth a cheerful giver:" 9:7 "And by their prayer for you, which long after you for the exceeding grace of God in you." 14 Grace of God is not in you.

Paul said he is preaching the gospel of Christ: 10:14 How could that be, when the Gospels weren't written down, when Paul was preaching?

"Are they ministers of Christ? (No) (I speak as a fool) I am more; in labors more abundant, ---." 11 Corinthians 11:23 These are some of the hardships that Paul said he went through. 27 "Beside those things that are without, (coming from outside the church) that which cometh upon me daily, the care of (all) the churches." 28 "Who is weak, and I am not weak? Who is offended, and I burn (hurt) not?" 29 Yes, Paul you journeyed in perils, and was killed, and it has been proven especially this day and age 72 virgins are worth dying for, even, when it is a farce also.

"The grace of the Lord Jesus Christ, and the love of God, and the communion of the Holy Ghost, be with you all. A'men." 11 Corinthians 13:14 Communion is a group of people of the same religious faith. Now days, we have a lot of 'groups'. The Holy Ghost is an individual, up close and personal Spirit, that dwells inside of a person's body after they are born again. I received it thirty days afterward it is not with you as it is presented today.

Chapter 10

Jesus

Jesus was the Word from the beginning of time, and the Word was with God. "And the Word was made flesh, and dwelt among us. And we beheld His glory, the glory as of the only begotten of the Father, full of grace and truth." St John 1:14 I don't believe man can understand this fully. I have heard that a person can find Jesus in every book in the Bible, is it Jesus or God I believe they are separate, and not equal, there is only one God it was God the Father, the creator, in the Old Testament.

It was the Spirit mentioned in Genesis that impregnated Mary who was a virgin, not knowing any man but espoused to Joseph. "In a dream an angel of the Lord appeared unto him saying, Joseph, thou son of David, fear not to take unto thee Mary thy wife: for that which is conceived in her is of the Holy Ghost". St Matthew 1:18 His name shall be called Jesus: for He shall save (his people) from their sins." 21 It wasn't the Holy Ghost mentioned in St Matthew 1:18 it was the Spirit in Genesis 1:2 that has been a helper to God from the beginning.

When Jesus was about thirty, God had given a job to John the Baptist of baptizing people in water. It wasn't the true salvation plan but God thought of it as being necessary for Jesus to receive the Spirit or Holy Ghost at the time He was baptized. That is why it reads immediately upon submersion He came up out of the water, and on His first breath the Spirit or Holy Ghost went in His mouth, and down his throat. John the Baptist had nothing to do with the true salvation or repentance, he was only a witness that Jesus received the Spirit. At the Day of Judgment, John will be there for a witness that Jesus received the Holy Ghost, and he came to save people from sin. As a way of explaining the phenomenon it reads that it was like a dove or blob. In the King James Bible of 1611 it says that, it "lighting on Him " but it never. Matthew 3:16 There are several names that the Spirit is given like Comforter, and it will abide with you forever when you receive it, and then it is called the Spirit of truth; whom the world cannot receive, because it see him (Spirit) not, neither knoweth Him: but ye know Him; for he dwelleth with you, and, "shall be in you." In general; John was the witness that Jesus was on the earth for the salvation of man. "The next day John seeth Jesus coming unto him, and saith, behold the Lamb of God, which taketh away the sin of the world." St John 1:29 (The chosen, and those that are drawn to God to be saved, it doesn't mean the entire world) "No man can come to me, except the Father which hath sent me draw him: and I will raise him up at the last day." St John 6:44

Shall be in you? Receive it? Jesus considered it as not being baptized in water but, of the new Spirit or Holy Ghost. It reads that you will drink indeed of my cup, or, the (Spirit) will go in your mouth, and then your baptized with the same baptism, that I (Jesus) was baptized with. Receiving the Holy Ghost has nothing to do with speaking in other tongues. Nor can it be given to a person when a preacher baptizes a person in water, or at the time of the sinner's prayer. John the Baptist said, "I indeed baptize you with water unto repentance: but he that cometh after me is mightier then I, whose shoes I am not worthy to bear: he shall baptize you with the Holy Ghost, and with fire." St Matthew 3:11 John also said, "a man can receive nothing, except it be given him from heaven." St John 3:27 Which I found out to be true.

It reads that a person must be born again. What does that mean? Jesus never needed to be born again but the Pilgrims need it first, before they can receive the Holy Ghost. What does that do for a person? It cleans the body, to get it ready to receive the Holy Spirit. Receiving the Holy Ghost is not an option it is a must, so a person can enter into the kingdom of God, the people that have been saved or transformed, from sinner to saint. A person can be in the kingdom of God, and never leave the earth surface.

Where is sin? It's in the heart. It reads out of the abundance of the heart the mouth speaks, so from the heart a person either brings forth good or evil things. Your words, you will either be justified or condemned. If the Lord cast out devils by the Spirit of God then the kingdom of God is come unto you. In other words you will know it when it occurs to you. It happened to me at 9pm 12/1/1968. In the beatitudes it reads blessed are the pure in heart: for they shall see God. It also reads that a person will be perfect even as your Father which is in heaven is perfect. St Matthew 5:8 and 48 Are the preachers safe, and those in the congregation listening to them? It reads out of the mouth your words condemn you?

With sin, and good or evil things in the heart, doesn't it make sense that a person must get rid of the heart that you were born with, to be perfect as God is. The two words born again means a lot of things to different people, but is there a true, "one and only meaning?" There is.

Jesus spoke in parables so we are back to square one, with born again in parable form. Ezekiel: never knew what he was writing down so he never got the verses in sequence of the actual occurrences that must take place. It is basically the salvation plan that I'm writing about now. Your body must be made clean before the Spirit will enter it, that is why the new heart was given to me first, with three days and nights fasting, It is the beginning of cleaning the body for the new Spirit or Holy Ghost, thirty days later entering the mouth. Instead of water, God put a vision on me, to get my mouth open. Ezekiel 36-25-27

I (Lord) will give you a new heart. It occurred to me when I believed in my heart, that I could heal my mother talking on a pay phone in Long Beach, California she was in Rapid City, South Dakota, after leaving a protestant churches alter call. God said it was a mystery, He wasn't lying to us. The mystery is found in three verses in St John. (there seems to be two kinds of people) "If I do not the works of the Father, believe me not." St John 10:37 "But if I do, though you believe not me, believe the works: (wasn't healing one of the works) that you may know, and believe, that the Father is in me, and I in him." 38 When you believe in your heart, it triggers or the catalysis for the Spirit to act. It is the Spirit (mentioned in Genesis 1:2) that takes away the heart a person is born with, and you receive a new heart from the Lord. St "Believe me that I am in the Father, and the Father in me: OR ELSE believe me for the very works' sake." St

John 14:11 Ezekiel put it this way; I (Spirit) will take away the stony heart (sinful, evil heart) out of your flesh, and I will give you a heart of flesh." Ezekiel 36:26 In other words God will literally remove your heart out of your flesh and put another one in it. What this does is, it starts the process of cleaning the body so you can receive the Spirit or Holy Ghost. I quit drinking, smoking, swearing, and started a fast that lasted three days and nights. Ezekiel put it this way "Then will I sprinkle clean water upon you, (not baptism in water but the removal of the heart) (born again) and you will be clean: from all your FILTHINESS, and from all your idols, will I cleanse you." Ezekiel 36:25

I have already written about receiving the Spirit or Holy Ghost, but Ezekiel put it this way. (I received it thirty days, after receiving the new heart.) "A new spirit will I put WITHIN you." 26 "And I will put my Spirit within you, and cause you to walk in my statutes, and you shall keep my judgments, and do them." 36:27 Instead of being baptized in water as Jesus was, God put a vision on me of a man that had left a church for the ministry, he seemed to be in trouble so I said out loud, "God help that BOY," and on the word boy the Spirit or Holy Ghost went into my mouth down my throat, going to work in a 1959 Ford Thunderbird, at about 6:30am 12/30/1968.

After Jesus received the Holy Ghost He went in the wilderness fasting forty days and nights, it doesn't say how long He was in the wilderness but He was tempted by Satan, and He received instruction from the Holy Ghost, the teacher of God. I went through the same things as Jesus, and it lasted two years. That is why it reads, "you will walk in my statutes, and you shall keep my judgments, and do them." Ezekiel 36:27 St Matthew 4:1-11

Jesus was the advocate for His Father God, in what He spoke and did. We find the verse in St John that it was the Father that taught Jesus what to say and do. (Holy Ghost the teacher) The other main thing was doing the miracles, for belief purposes, so a person could become saved as I said before, "triggering the Spirit to act." The main thing that God's Son had to do was give His life on the cross for those that are saved for their sins, not only the accumulative sin but the original disobedience of Adam. With Mary giving birth to Jesus, sin must only come down from generation to generation through the male lineage. That is why God only told Adam that he would surely die if he ate of the tree of the knowledge of good and evil. Eve knew of the danger, but Satan said she wouldn't die so she ate of it, and gave some to Adam. That is when the earth received the curse of God to this day.

Other verses in the Old Testament that deals with becoming righteous

"Behold the days come, saith the Lord, that I will make a new covenant with the house of Israel, and with the house of Judah:" Jeremiah 31:31 (Judah was not part of Israel but the fourth son of Jacob, couldn't we say it refers to the Gentiles) (God tells of the broken covenant in Egypt) God made several covenants with different groups, but it doesn't matter He said the covenant with Egypt was broke. 32 Are there two salvation plans after Jesus went to His Father in heaven? I think not. As I wrote above in Ezekiel this could be the last covenant that God makes until the end time with anybody. "But this shall be the covenant that I will make with the house of Israel; After those days, saith the Lord: (the end time) "I will put my law in their inward parts, and write it in their hearts;" (it reads 'in' their heart) "and I will be their God, and they shall be my people." Jeremiah 31:33 "---I will forgive their iniquity, and I will remember their sin no more. 34 In Ezekiel it Is about being given a new heart. 36:26 "He that eateth my flesh (receives a new heart from God), and drinketh my blood, (receives the new Spirit (Holy Ghost in the mouth) dwelleth in me, and I in him." St John 6:56

"The heart is deceitful above all things, and desperately wicked: who can know it?" Jeremiah 17:9 If a person has not been given a new heart they will never know until the end time that they have a wicked heart, but then it is going to be too late.

"For I will give them a heart to know me, that I am the Lord: and they shall be my people, and I will be their God: for they shall return unto me with their whole heart." Jeremiah 24:7 (I found out that God is real when I received my new heart)

"And I will give them one heart, and one way, that they may fear me forever, (even unto eternity) for the good of them, (the alternative has never sounded good to me) and of their children after them:" Jeremiah 39:29 (I have read 80% of people believe what their parents believe) " ---I will put my fear in their hearts, that they shall not depart from me." 40 I loved what we called the night life, and all it contained, but after I was saved it wasn't of God, so I quit.

Ezekiel 11: 19 "And I will give them one heart, (it reads a new heart in Ezekiel 36:26 which is more accurate?) and I will put a new spirit within you; and I will take the stony (sinful) heart out of their flesh, and will give them a heart of flesh (From God) (Jesus received the new Spirit in His mouth and it went down His throat when He came out of the water baptism, on His first breath, when He was baptized by John the Baptist.) St Matthew 3:16

"Blessed are the pure in heart: for they shall see God." St Matthew 5:8

In my concordance heart means one's entire emotional nature and understanding, which I disagree, in some cases it means a person's physical heart. When Adam disobeyed God it had an effect on his heart and spirit. I might be inhuman but I have had feelings that came from the heart. My half sister jumped out of a closet when my dad entered his trailer. He never said it hurt his head, he said it almost gave him a heart-attack.

Dose proverbs have hints of God's chosen?

Proverbs 6:18 "A heart that deviseth wicked imaginations, feet that be swift in running to mischief," Proverbs 6:18 "They that are of a froward (impudent=shameless or disrespectful) heart are abomination to the Lord:---" 11:20 "A man shall be commended according to his wisdom: but he that is of a perverse heart shall be despised." (has a sinful nature) 12:8 "There is a way which seemeth right unto a man; but the end thereof are the ways of death." 14:12 "The simple believeth every word: but the prudent man looketh well to his going." (carefully) 14:15

During my time in church as a child, at times I had felt the convictive spirit, and that was what I was looking for when I started back to church in 1968. Without that knowledge I might have went down to the front of a church prematurely. In the two months I was asked to raise my hand, and come forward but I felt like there was something wrong with it. Eventually I found out I was right, the sinner's prayer has nothing to do with being saved.

I am very aware that Jesus said love everybody, He couldn't very well say, go and hate everybody, remember Jesus spoke allegorically as well as in parables. What you read sometime is what mankind likes to hear, and Jesus knew mankind, His Father created them. It is part of the mysteries of keeping the truth away from people until they are saved. He said it was given unto you to know the mysteries but to them it is not given, to the unsaved. It reads that many prophets (false) and righteous (believe they're righteous) men have desired to see those things which ye see, and have not seen them; and to hear those things which ye hear, and have not heard them. "But blessed are your eyes, for they see: and your ears for they hear." St Matthew 13:16

The saved will know the mysteries. Jesus recognized that with what He was saying was in parable form, and it made it easy for Him, because those around Him never understood what He was talking about. "---I think thee, O Father, Lord of heaven and earth, because thou hast hid these things from the wise and prudent, and hast revealed them unto babes." St Matthew 11:25 "Even so, Father for so it seemed good in thy sight." 26 Does God love everybody? No. It grieved Him at His heart that He made man on the earth. Genesis 6:6 It is because of the righteousness of God that He sent His Son to die on the cross for our sins. "Love," as we hear so much about, has nothing to do with a person becoming righteous, to live with God in His kingdom.

"Blessed are the peacemakers:" Who are the peacemakers? (One preacher said they were the police) for they shall be called the children of God." St Matthew 5:9 As one Moslem said, don't fight with drones come down and fight. Is bombing Moslems the answer, and sending them to Paradise, "they like that." Martyrdom will get a Moslem, "by blowing himself up" 72 women, it sounds good to me, and they don't even have to go to hell for a a short time.

I was asked at the breakfast table, "what is the answer?" If it isn't bombs the conversion of the Moslem is the only answer that I see. If that doesn't work, I don't see any hope, and when it gets bad enough living on the earth than I see Jesus returning. That is what happened in Noah's day : "And God saw that the wickedness of man was great in the earth, and that every imagination of the thoughts of his heart was only evil continually." Genesis 6:5 "And it repented (grieved) the Lord that he had made man on the earth, and it grieved him at his heart." 6 "And the Lord said, I will destroy man whom I have created from the face of the earth; both man, and beast, and the creeping thing, and the fowls of the air; for it repenteth (grieved) Me that I have made them." 7 "But Noah found grace, in the eyes of the Lord." 8 "---Noah walked with God." 9 Of the seven others on the boat, it doesn't say anything about their relationship with God, so were they there to only replenish the earth after the flood? "But as the days of Noah were, so shall also the coming of the Son of man be." St Matthew 24:37

It goes on to say what will start happening at the end time that we should be concerned about in St Matthew 24 and St Mark 13.

"For then shall be great tribulation, such as was not since the beginning of the world to this time, nor ever shall be." St Matthew 24:21 "And except those days should be shortened, there should no flesh be saved: but for the elect's sake those days (shall) be shortened." 22

Why, "shall-should, be shortened?" When a person is transformed there is no doubt that they are a Child of God so they shall live with God in his kingdom. They have received the new heart, and received the new Spirit that makes them children of God for the sake of being righteous, so they can live with God in His kingdom. St John 3:3-5 "---Except a man be born again, he cannot (see the power) see the kingdom of God." St John 3:3 "---Except a man be born of water (born again 3rd verse) and of the Spirit, (Holy Ghost) he cannot enter into the kingdom of God. "A person must receive in their mouth a blob, which is the Spirit or Holy Ghost as Jesus received it in St Matthew 3:16. It was, "like a dove," and it never lighting on Him as it reads. St John 3:5 "Jesus answered, Verily, verily, (there is no other way) I say unto thee, except a man be born of water (born again verse 3): and of the Spirit, he cannot enter into the kingdom of God." St John 3:5 "That which is born of the flesh is flesh: and that which is born of the Spirit is spirit." 3:6

"I am the living bread which came down from heaven: if any man eat of this bread, he shall live forever: and the bread that I will give is my flesh, which I will give for the life of the world." St John 6:51 "Then Jesus said unto them, Verily, verily, (there is no other way) I say unto you, except ye eat the flesh of the Son of Man, (Born again) and drink his blood, (receive the Spirit 'Holy Ghost' in your mouth) ye have no life in you." 53 "Whoso eateth my flesh, and drinketh my blood, hath eternal life; and I will raise him up at the last day." 54 "For my flesh is meat indeed, and my blood is drink indeed." 55

In Joel 1:13 it is written that the meat offering and drink offering is withholden from the house of your God. (g) It is referring to verse 55 the salvation plan, and or God has removed the Spirit, for salvation from your church.

"Love," has nothing to do with salvation or receiving His righteousness. "For I say unto you, that except your righteousness shall exceed the righteousness of the scribes and Pharisees, ye shall in no case enter into the kingdom of heaven."St Matthew 5:20 "But seek ye first the kingdom of God, and His righteousness; and all these things shall be added unto you." St Matthew 6:33 (It is then, and only then, that you will find out if you are one of the chosen) "No man can come to me, except the Father which hath sent me draw him: and I will raise him up at the last day." St John 6:44

"For this is my blood of the new testament, which is shed for many for the remission of sins," St Matthew 6:28 The Bible is confusing in a lot of ways but Here Jesus had to say (many) but in another verse it reads few will find the way. "This is that bread which came down from heaven: not as your fathers did eat man'-na' and are dead: he that eateth of this bread shall live forever." St John 6:58 Jesus could be referring to the, 'tree of life' it reads that if you eat of it a person will live forever. In this book I explained that I received the 'tree of life'. When you say that when you eat bread, (the sacrament) it is the same as man'na but the preachers say salvation is grace, faith, walk in righteousness Etc.. Peter's baptism in water which is almost the same thing John the Baptist said, 'that never worked for John' does all this sound like it has anything to do with physically eating bread, for salvation? It reads unless your born again, and receive His Spirit a person will not enter into the kingdom of God. St John 3:3-5

"But I say unto you, I will not drink henceforth of this fruit of the vine, until that day when I drink it new with you (those that have been saved or the elect) in my Father's kingdom." St Matthew 26:29 The Sacrament is just to keep you interested, along with several other,'pies in the skies.'

In St Matthew 24: Should, is used, that gives God some wiggle room depending on the circumstances. 21 "For then shall be great tribulation, such as was not since the beginning of the world to this time, no, nor ever shall be." St Matthew 24:21 "And except those days should be shortened, there should no flesh be saved: but for the elect's sake those days shall be shortened." 22 It should happen on the earth, and with certainty one day those that become saved or redeemed they shall be brought up to live with God in His kingdom, that is why shall is used.

By receiving the Spirit or Holy Ghost it is the only game in town, as they say. It reads that it will come to you and be in you. "If ye love me, keep my commandments." St John 14:15 (I was on a short leash for thirty days after I received the new heart) 21 "He that hath my commandments, and keepeth them, he it is that loveth me: and he that loveth me shall be loved of my Father, (those that become saved the Father loves) and I will love, and will manifest myself to him." St John 14:21 (given the Holy Ghost) 16 "And I will pray the Father, and he shall give you another Comforter, (The new heart "born again" was the first comforter) that he may abide with you forever." 16 "Even the Spirit of truth; whom the world cannot receive, (unsaved) because it seeth him not, (Holy Ghost) neither knoweth him: but ye know him; for he dwelleth with you, and shall be in you."17 (shall be in you, it leaves no doubt that the Spirit has entered your mouth) 19 "Yet a little while, and the world seeth me no more; (when Jesus left it was the last time the world would see Him) but ye see me: (when I received the new heart I saw a light and feeling the power, of God, I never saw Him personally it was the Spirit, that did the work) because I live ye shall live also." 19 "At that day 12/1/1968 at 9pm ye shall know that I am in my Father, and ye in me, and I in you." 20 The preachers they change the light, that Paul said he saw, with the bodily form of Jesus. The Acts 9:1-18 "Yet a little while, and the world seeth me no more; but ye see me: because I live, ye shall live also." St John 14:19 A person sees Jesus when they are born again or at least the Spirit in Genesis 1:2.

St John 14:30 "Hereafter I will not talk much with you: for the prince of this world cometh (Satan and his helpers or advocates) and hath nothing in me." St John 14:30 Thomas Jefferson said that Paul was the first corrupter of the doctrine of Jesus. There have been many corrupters after Paul and Peter ranted.

Every Moslem (except those that die in Jihad will go to hell (for some period) It sounds like purgatory to me, and how to get out, isn't found in the KJB of 1611. With the new heart and new Spirit that I received, I believe that makes me eligible to live with God in His kingdom today, and tomorrow, I haven't left the earth.

Muslims believe that all prophets are without any sin, what about messengers? Muhammad said he was a messenger, that wasn't sure where he was going.

"He that rejecteth me, and receiveth not my words, hath one that judgeth him: the word that I have spoken, the same shall judge him in the last day." St John 12:48 "For I have not spoken of myself; but the Father which sent me, he gave me a commandment, what I should say, and what I should speak," 49 "And I know that his commandment is life everlasting: whatsoever I speak therefore, even as the Father said unto me, so I speak." 50 Does this read, after I leave a man called Paul and Muhammad will tell you how to get to the kingdom of heaven? Do you read that anyplace? There are a lot of verses in the Old Testament that has prophesy of the coming of Jesus, but I know of no verse that tells me Paul would come, and write half of the New Testament except in St John 5:43 in the New Testament.

Luke that traveled with Paul said in Luke It is written, "That man shall not live by bread alone, but by every word of God." (Every word of God) Wouldn't that be the entire Bible according to the preachers? St Matthew 4:4 said go by what came out of the mouth of God.(Jesus) St Matthew 4:4 I know that the bible is a mess but the King James Bible of 1611 is the best we have. I was physically saved and found verses in that Bible, 'afterward' to verify what happened to me is true. The only thing that it does is, give credence, for my piece of mind. The preachers wave the entire Bible around, and blurt out this is the true Word of God, infallible, without error, because it came from God, incapable of error, never wrong, reliable, every word God inspired because Paul said it was.

The Baptist say, that once a person is saved always saved. That is true if the heart your born with has been removed, replaced, and you have received the Holy Ghost. The Holy Ghost is in you forever, how could it go to hell in your body? "Yet a little while, and the world seeth me no more; but ye see me: because I live, ye shall live also." St John 14:19 "At that day ye shall know that I am in my Father, and ye in me, and I in you." 20 12/1/1968 at 9pm; and 12/30/1968 at 6:30 am as they say I was enlightened or given clarification of the one that made the heavens and the earth. Not only that, but I received the salvation experiences. It reads in St John "He that hath my commandments, (new heart, new Spirit etc) and keepeth them, (the new Spirit or Holy Ghost) he it is that loveth me: (Son) and he that loveth me shall be loved of my Father, and I will love him, and will manifest myself to him." St John 14:21 It reads here that God loves those that have physically been saved.

The preachers will tell you that God loves everybody. He killed all but eight during Noah's flood, and destroyed Sodom and Gomorrah. It reads the earth, is going to be almost destroyed, at the end time doesn't that mean also most of the people on the earth. "Immediately after the tribulation of those days shall the sun be darkened, and the moon shall not give her light, and the stars shall fall from heaven, and the powers of the heavens shall be shaken: St Matthew 24:29 We are writing about the love of God, that a person hears so much about, from the pulpit. "And it repented (grieved) the Lord that he had made man on the earth, and it grieved him at his heart." Genesis 6:6

Chapter 1; St Matthew
The generation of Jesus Christ

"So all the generations from Abraham to David are fourteen generations: and to David are fourteen generations; and from David until the carrying away into Babylon are fourteen generations; and from the carrying away into Babylon unto Christ are fourteen generations." St Matthew 1:17 "And Jacob begat Joseph the husband of Mary, of whom was born Jesus, who is called Christ." 16

Joseph was not the father of Jesus it was the Spirit of Genesis that was His father so how can we say, Jesus came from Abraham in the first place, and it reads Jesus was called Christ. No, an angel appeared unto Joseph in a dream, and said His name would be Jesus. The name used with Paul and his disciples most of the time, 'Jesus Christ' which I believe with them it means God. That fits in with Paul not of God but on his own, as in St John 5:43

qIn the beginning was the Word, and the Word was with God, (it would be great if it ended there) and the Word was God." St John 1:1 (Was it) 1:14 "And the Word was made flesh, and dwelt among us, (and we beheld his glory, the glory as of the only begotten of the Father.)" (Wouldn't that be Jesus the Son of God was made flesh) full of grace and truth." 14 "No man hath seen God at any time; the only begotten Son, which is in the bosom of the Father, (in close fellowship) he hath declared him." 18 This verse seems to say that Jesus Christ was not God, and that is what I believe. It reads; a married couple is one, the same as it reads Jesus and God are one, but I have always counted two.

"Blessed are the pure in heart: for they shall see God." St Matthew 5:8

"Ye are the salt of the earth: but if the salt have lost (his) savor, (strength) wherewith shall it be salted? It is thenceforth good for nothing, but to be cast out, and to be trodden under foot of men." 13 The Christians that are losing their heads are they Christians? Billy went all over the earth preaching St John 3:16 which shouldn't be in the KJB of 1611. The missionaries have been going all over the earth telling people how easy it is to become a Christian. The preachers are preaching the message that Paul, Peter, and their disciples wrote down of grace, faith, work it out, and walk in righteousness. Jesus said "But seek ye first the kingdom of God, and his righteousness;" St Matthew 6:33 Salvation is physical but in allegorical form, but it is true that without being born again, (new heart) and receiving a new Spirit (Holy Ghost) a person will not enter into the kingdom of God. St John 3:3-5

According to the verse the earth will be trodden under the foot of men. Those that think they know something, and don't, or those that are outside of the loop all together. Those that die that call themselves Christian, is it true, if they only believe in St John 3:16?

"Ye are the light of the world." St Matthew 5:13 It also reads few will find the way. I'm glad that I don't have to be successful but I must try, as a light to the world. It reads they never believed Jesus, why would I expect people to believe me? "And because I tell you the truth, ye believe me not." St John 8:45

"Whosoever therefore shall break one of these least commandments, and shall teach men so, he shall be called the least in the kingdom of heaven: but whosoever shall do and teach them, the same shall be called great In the kingdom of heaven." St Matthew 5:19 It is all about the kingdom of heaven, or God's domain, that is why He said those that enter into the kingdom of God are saved. St John 3:5

"For I say unto you, That except your righteousness, shall exceed the righteousness of the scribes and Pharisees, ye shall in no case enter into the kingdom of heaven." 20 Will Paul's righteousness get you to the kingdom of God? John the Baptist said "A man can receive nothing, except it be given him from heaven" St John 3:27 My redemption came from heaven, why should I believe there is some other way to be saved.

"Agree with thine adversary quickly, while thou art in the way with him;---" St Matthew 5:25 At the day of Judgment, it will take care of a lot of hurt, Jesus wants a person to stay out of trouble here on this earth

"Be ye therefore perfect, even as your Father which is in heaven is perfect." 48 Without physically receiving a new heart, and new Spirit, I have no way of knowing how a person can become perfect as it reads in 46-47 by being nice to everybody? 46 "For if ye love them which love you, what reward have you? Do not even the publicans the same?" 46

"Take heed that ye do not your alms before men, to be seen of them: otherwise ye have no reward of your Father which is in heaven." 6:1 In construction some people would only work when the boss showed up. They would be rested up, and ready to get after it. At times the person working would be laid off first, it worked for them, but according to this verse they won't get away with it.

"But when you pray, use not vain repetitions, as the heathen do: for they think that they shall be heard for their much speaking." 7

6:5 -15; Is about prayer (including the Lord's prayer) verse 8 "Be not ye therefore like unto them; for your Father knoweth what things ye have need of before ye ask him." 8 I have a tendency not to pray very much because of this verse, and let God handle what I need. Those that do this sort of thing it could be all in vain. Have you received His righteousness first, His redemption, His salvation, His commandments?

" Thy kingdom come, thy will be done in earth, as it is in heaven." 10 That is a mouth full, it reads they don't marry but are as the Angels. "And another of his disciples said unto him, Lord, suffer (let) me first to go and bury my father." 8:21 "But Jesus said unto him, follow me: and let the dead (who are they in this day and age) bury their dead." 22Those that bury a person what is the other common practice?

"---deliver us from evil:" 6:13 This verse goes over like water on a ducks back, but it fits in with other biblical verses. Who can deliver a person from the evil one? Since Adam disobeyed God man was changed, and the curse must be removed first, it is the beginning of deliverance of receiving a new heart. "And ye shall seek me, and find me, when ye shall search for me with all your heart." Jeremiah 29:13 When I started going to church at the age of 31 after several years of the night life I was wondering if, 'religion or God, were real?' After church I went to the local bars and dance halls for over two months, I went to several churches on Sunday night sitting on the back seat seeking God. In the scripture it reads seek me, and find me, (God) searching with all your heart. One night I felt the convictive Spirit that I was searching for, and went to the Alter. It wasn't until I left the church that I was saved at a gasoline service station. God has removed his saving Spirit, from the churches. Joel 1:13 "I am the door: by me if any man, enter in, he shall be saved, and shall go in and out, and find pasture." St John 10:9 In this verse It doesn't have God permanently inside controlling the church or why would it read those people will go in and out and find pasture. Every Sunday night God saw me coming to church seeking Him. Every night He saw me go out, without salvation until my special night on 12/1/1968 at 9pm.

"For thine is the kingdom, and the power and the glory, forever. Amen" St Matthew 6:13 It is God's kingdom, His commandments, His rules, His power, His glory, His Son for redemption, His eternity, His party forever. Amen.

"Moreover when ye fast, be not, as the hypocrites, of a sad countenance: for they disfigure their faces, that they may appear unto men to fast. Verily I say unto you, They have their reward." 16 "But thou, when thou fastest, anoint thine head, and wash thy face;" 17 "That thou appear not unto men to fast, but unto thy Father which is in secret: and thy Father, which seeth in secret, shall reward thee openly." 18 At the job where I worked twice I fasted, for three days and nights, probably not one of those around me knew I was fasting. St Matthew 9:15 (After Jesus leaves and goes to His Father in heaven) "---but the days will come, when the bridegroom shall be taken from them, and then shall they fast." St Matthew 9:15 I fasted when I received the new heart and thirty days later when I received the new Spirit or Holy Ghost. "Thou hypocrite, first cast out the beam out of thine own eye, and then shalt thou see clearly to cast out the mote out of thy brother's eye." St Matthew 7:5

Salvation is all about) A person's body that must be changed. "No man putteth a piece of new cloth unto an old garment, for that which is put in to fill it up taketh from the garment, and the rent is made worse." St Matthew 9:16 "Neither do men put new wine into old bottles: else the bottles break, and the wine runneth out, and the bottles perish: (Representing hell and separated from God) but they put new wine into new bottles, 'your body' (born again and receiving the Holy Ghost or Spirit) and both are preserved." 17 (The soul and the new Spirit preserved for all eternity)

In St Matthew It is about making people well, and that is what I believed in my heart that I could do perhaps make my mother well. It triggered the Spirit in Genesis to act, and it gave me my new heart. "Believe me that I am in the Father, and the Father in me: or else believe me for the very works' sake." St John 14:11 and 10:37-38

"And ye shall be hated of all men for my name's sake: but he that endurerth to the end shall be saved." St Matthew 10:22 Those that preach from The Acts –Jude it reads that Paul loved them, and they loved him. If a person preaches the truth, I guarantee that they won't love them. They will do everything possible to hinder the truth from being presented. Why not, if a person is not of God their father is the devil. Would the devil help a person spread the Gospel that Jesus died for? I'm even black balled from writing a letter to the editor in my home town. Would an editor working on getting a book published, do anything but collect their fee? I left a nonfiction book at a religious book store, and have never seen it on their shelf, but if you write lies they devote a four foot space for a single book. The book store is out of business now, did God have anything to do with that?

"And fear not therefore: for there is nothing covered, that shall not be revealed; and hid, that shall not be known." St Matthew 10:26 Jesus, with the blessing of God spoke in parables. That is what Elijah's job is, to explain the allegorical writing and parables to the people of the earth. With the back slappers preaching Paul, I couldn't tell you how this is going to take place.

"How can ye believe, which receive honor one of another, and seek not the honor that cometh from God only?" St John 5:44 Not everybody is blind to the truth. "But blessed are your eyes, for they see; and your ears, for they hear." St Matthew 13:16 It doesn't take me all day to hear false doctrine, and flee from it. The sad part is, I have to know what is occurring on the earth to try, and combat it.

When the leader of Jerusalem told the Jews to come home recently, I knew that was one of the Prophesies for the end time.

"And fear not them which kill the body, but are not able to kill the soul: but rather fear him (God) which is able to destroy both soul and body in hell." St Matthew 10:28

Not peace but a sword

St Matthew explains to us why the world is in such a mess. Why a person shouldn't expect any visitors when you go to a nursing home. Why a marriage turns' sour, and a person should put God first place in their life. "And a man's foes shall be they of his own household." St Matthew 10:36 "Think not that I am come to send peace on earth: I came not to send peace, but a sword." 10:34 "He that findeth his life shall lose it, and he that loseth his life for my sake shall find it." 39 What if that is true that a person must lose their life to become a child of God. In the transformation of the heart I was born with, and given a new heart from God by the standards that doctors go by, I must have died. If it doesn't mean this than in your life story, with money, a good Job, etc. from the cradle to the grave a person could be in trouble, and don't know it. When I was saved my business was going south, toward bankruptcy, in Long Beach, California.

Rewards

Any help given in the publicity of this book, will be given a prophets reward 10:40-42 "He that receiveth you receiveth me, and he that receiveth me receiveth him (God) that sent me." 10 40 "He that receiveth a prophet in the name of a prophet shall receive a prophet's reward; and he that receiveth a righteous man in the name of a righteous man shall receive a righteous man's reward." 41 "And whosoever shall give to drink unto one of these little ones a cup of cold water only in the name of a disciple, verily I say unto you, he shall in no wise lose his reward." 42

It is about John the Baptist "But what went ye out for to see? A man clothed in soft raiment? Behold, they that wear soft clothing are in kings' houses." (Churches) St Matthew 11:8 It reads seek ye first the kingdom of God and His righteousness, of being born again and receiving the Holy Ghost. Those that go from high school to a divinity college are they seeking a big church with lots of money or God?

"Verily I say unto you, Among them that are born of women there hath not risen a greater than John the Baptist: not withstanding he that is least in the kingdom of heaven is greater than he." 11 "And the same John had his raiment of camel's hair, and a leathern girdle about his loins, and his meat was locusts, and wild honey." St Matthew 3:4 I believe that God knew that John was going to be killed. He was only a witness that Jesus received the Holy Ghost, and his "repentant salvation plan" was not what God wanted.

"And from the days of John the Baptist until now the kingdom of heaven suffereth violence, and the violent take it by force." 11:12 Does this sound like God is in control of the earth? In Isaiah it reads Lucifer is in control not only of the earth but all the religions. According to this verse the violent are going to win, but the saints will be removed from the earth. "And except those days should be shortened, there should no flesh be saved: but for the elect's sake those days (shall) be shortened." St Matthew 24:22 It is hard to beat 72 virgin women or 72 select men by Jihad, of the Islam faith, but that is a earthly belief and not heavenly.

"For all the prophets and the law prophesied until John?" St Matthew 11:13 "Behold, I will send you Elijah the prophet before the coming of the great and dreadful day of the Lord:" Malachi 4:5 Did they forget about Elijah coming at the end time?

"And if ye will receive it, this is Elijah, which was for to come." 14 How could this be, Elijah when he was to come is at the end time, and they asked John if he was Elijah he said no twice. "And they asked him, What then? Art thou Elijah? And he saith, I am not. Art thou that prophet? And he answered, No." St John 1:21

"But I say unto you, that it shall be more tolerable for the land of Sodom, in the day of judgment than for thee." St Matthew 11:24 Because people are preaching from The Acts –Jude a false doctrine, and it has made God remove the spirit needed for salvation as in Joel "Gird yourselves and lament, ye priests: howl ye ministers of the alter, come, lie all night in sackcloth, ye ministers of my God: for the meat offering and drink offering is with holden from the house of your god." (G) Joel 1:13

Who is wise?

"At that time Jesus answered and said, I thank thee, O Father, Lord of heaven and earth, because thou hast hid these things from the wise and prudent, and hast revealed them unto babes." St Matthew 11:25 "Even so Father: for so it seemed good in thy sight." 26 "And the disciples came, and said unto him, Why speakest thou unto them in parables?" St Matthew 13:10 "He answered and said unto them, because it is given unto you to know the mysteries of the kingdom of heaven, but to them it is not given." 11 "Therefore speak I to them in parables: because they seeing see not; and hearing they hear not, neither do they understand." 13 "But blessed are your eyes, for they see: and your ears, for they hear." 16 "For verily I say unto you, that many (false) prophets and righteous men (those that believe they are righteous?) have desired to see those things which ye see, and have not seen them: and to hear those things which ye hear, and have not heard them."17

"All things are delivered unto me of my Father: and no man knoweth the Son, but the Father; neither knoweth any man the Father, save (except) the Son, and he to whomsoever the Son will reveal him." St Matthew 11:27 "No man can come to me, except the Father which hath sent me draw him: and I will raise him up at the last day." St John 5:44

"And I will pray (asked) the Father, and he shall give you another (after you're born again) Comforter, (Holy Ghost) that he may abide with you forever:" St John 14:16

Does God love everybody?

"He that hath my commandments, and keepeth them, he it is that loveth me: and he that loveth me shall be loved of my Father, and I will love him, and will manifest myself to him." St John 14:21 "But if I by the finger (power)of God cast out devils, no doubt the kingdom of God is come upon you." St Luke 11:20 St Matthew 6:33 "But seek ye first the kingdom of God, and his righteousness---:" St Matthew 6:33 "But if I cast out devils by the Spirit of God, (Spirit in Genesis) then the kingdom of God is come unto you." St Matthew 12:28

There are a lot of differences in the, "kingdom of God" and kingdom of heaven. God lives in the kingdom of heaven, and after you are born again and receive the Holy Ghost a person enters into the kingdom of God, which can be on this earth. In St John verse 3 you (see) the power of God St John 3:3, and in verse 5 you enter into the kingdom of God. Ezekiel 36:26-27

"---Every kingdom (church and religious organization) divided against itself is brought to desolation: and every city or house: divided against itself shall not stand?" St Matthew 12:25 This will happen at the end time if not today.

One of the ways that I use that makes common sense, when it comes to Jesus is God. The Holy Ghost or Spirit is not God. Why can a person blasphemy (swear) using God and Jesus name, but a person should be careful with the Holy Ghost or Spirit. The reason is the Spirit (Holy Ghost) is part of the salvation experience, as they say it is the only game in town. When I received the new heart I was not saved from hell yet, I had to receive the Holy Ghost to be saved or redeemed, and that came thirty days later. For thirty day I was on a short leash.

St Matthew 12:31 "Wherefore I say unto you, all manner of sin and blasphemy shall be forgiven unto men: but the blasphemy against the Holy Ghost shall not be forgiven unto men." St Matthew 12:31 "And whosoever speaketh a word against the Son of man, it shall be forgiven him: but whosoever speaketh against the Holy Ghost, it shall not be forgiven him, neither in this world, neither in the world to come."32

"O generation of vipers, how can ye, being evil, speak good things? For out of the abundance of the heart the mouth speaketh." 34 Some preachers can make a person believe they wrote the bible but they are speaking in vain, and the sad part is they don't have a clue. Their a-men corner doesn't have a clue. Thousands in the congregation don't have a clue. Most of the time their scripture they use, is from The Acts – Jude using Paul, Peter, or one of their disciples as a reference point if they use a reference. "For by thy words thou shalt be justified, and by thy words thou shalt be condemned." 37

"---An evil and adulterous generation seeketh after a sign; and there shall no sign be given to it, but the sign of the prophet Jonah:" 39 Jonah was three days inside the whale, and Jesus was in the grave three days. At Paul's conversion, it has Jesus speaking to him, according to the preachers, and after reading verse 39 is it biblical?

"For whosoever shall do the will of my Father which is in heaven, (born again and receive the Holy Spirit) the same is my brother, and sister, and mother." St Matthew 12:50 Luke is the only Gospel that said Mary was blessed. The first chapter of Luke is a night mare, the Holy Ghost the other Spirit, was only for Jesus to receive until after He went to His Father, after the crucifixion. "Nevertheless I tell you the truth: It is expedient for you that I go away; for if I go not away, the Comforter (Holy Ghost or Spirit) will not come unto you; but if I depart, I will send him unto you." St John 16:7 By receiving the Spirit after your body is clean is the only way to the kingdom of God. Even Marry according to verse 50 had to receive it in her lifetime, the Holy Ghost, after Jesus left.

"And the disciples came, and said unto him, Why speakest thou unto them in parables?" St Matthew 13:10 11 "He answered and said unto them, because it is given unto you to know the mysteries of the kingdom of heaven, but to them it is not given." 11 "And in them is fulfilled the prophecy of Isaiah, which saith, By hearing ye shall hear, and shall not understand; and seeing ye shall see, and shall not perceive:" 14 "for this people's heart is waxed gross, (callous=hardened, unfeeling; what are the chances of a carpenter from Wyoming getting a divinity college graduate to change their mind?) "And their ears are dull of hearing, and their eyes they have closed; lest at any time they should see with their eyes, and hear with their ears, and should understand with their heart, (receive a new heart) and should be converted, and I should heal them." 15 The preachers don't know they are sick. Should is used because shell means there is no doubt it would happen, and should is not that precise.

"But blessed are your eyes, for they see; and your ears, for they hear." 16 "For verily I say unto you, that many prophets (false) and righteous men (setting on the same seat or preached for fifty years) have desired to see those things which ye see, and have not seen them; and to hear those things which ye hear, and have not heard them."17

"But he that received the seed into stony places the same is he that hearth the word, and anon with joy receiveth it;" 20 "Yet hath he not root in himself, but dureth for a while : for when tribulation or persecution ariseth because of the word, by and by he is offended." 21 The problem with this verse is in Ezekiel "and I will take away the stony heart out of your flesh, and I will give you a heart of flesh" (From God) Ezekiel 36:26

The tares unsaved, and the wheat saved

"Let both grow together until the harvest: and in the time of harvest (end time) I will say to the reapers, Gather ye together first the tares, and bind them in bundles to burn them: but gather the wheat into my barn." St Matthew 13:30 Attending a church preaching Paul is difficult, I tried that. The preacher called for a foot washing when I knew his father was the devil I never showed up.

Mustard seed the least of all seed

Jeremiah 3:15 "And I will give you pastors according to mine heart, which shall feed you with knowledge and understanding." Jeremiah 3:15 "Gird yourselves, and lament, ye priests: howl, ye ministers of The Alter: come, lie all night in sackcloth, ye ministers of my God: for the meat offering and the drink offering (salvation and Holy Ghost) is withholden: (withheld) from the house of your God." (g) Joel 1:13 It doesn't sound like the pastors are preaching according to God's heart, but on their own as Paul was. St John 5:43 Joel 2:28 "And it shall come to pass afterward? (at the end time) that I will poor out my spirit upon all flesh;---." Joel 2:28 "And also upon he servants and upon the handmaids in those days will I pour out my spirit." 29 In Joel 1:13 Salvation is withheld, and 29 it is poured out? This might mean for the Jews in the last days, they will be given redemption as In Ezekiel 36:26-27. With one God, can there be more than one way to be saved? I don't think so.

Treasures new and old

"Then said he unto them, therefore every scribe which is instructed unto the kingdom of heaven is like unto a man that is a householder, which bringeth forth out of his treasure things new and old." St Matthew 13:52 The life that I lived before being saved are in my memory as my treasure to be used, and some time I wonder how I survived?

Jesus rejected at Nazareth

Jesus never knew what rejection is, speaking allegorically or in parables, until a person tries to explain what He said. That is when the rubber meets the road. "And they were offended in him. But Jesus said unto them, A prophet is not without honor, save (except) in his own country, and in his own house." St Matthew 13:57 I am rejected at every turn in the road, but why shouldn't I be, if people are not of God than their father is Satan. As the product of Satan than the media, and publishing, etc why would they help me in getting the truth out to the public?

John the Baptist beheaded

Peter said that salvation is brought about by being baptized in water, the same baptism as John's baptism. If it never worked for John why would it work for Peter? There are thousands of people that would die for that verse in The Acts. My uncle Leroy drove from Missouri to Wyoming with his sister, and "more than a friend." Before I could cross the road his, "more than a friend" and Leroy got back in the car and left, leaving the sister behind. She had to take a bus back to Missouri. It was quick, but Leroy and his brother Mike my dad, got into an argument over The Acts 2:38.

John said that he must decrease but the way of Jesus must increase. What is complicated with this sentence? If John had the salvation plan why was he beheaded? "I indeed baptize you with water unto repentance: but he that cometh after me is mightier than I, whose shoes I am not worthy to-bear: he shall baptize you with the Holy Ghost, and with fire:" (the new word) St Matthew 3:11 The only way to the kingdom of God is receiving the Holy Ghost, but first a person must receive a new heart to start the process of cleaning the body, and get rid of the original sin of Adam plus your accumulative sin sense birth. "The wicked are estranged from the womb: they go astray as soon as they be born, speaking lies." Psalm 58:3

The things that defile

"Ye hypocrites, well did Isaiah prophesy of you, saying," St Matthew 15:7 8 "This people draweth nigh unto me with their mouth, and honoreth me with their lips; but their heart is far from me." 8 If this isn't what we have in the churches today it would fool me. 9 "but in vain they do worship me, teaching for doctrines the commandments of men." 9 "How can ye believe, which receive honor one of another, and seek not the honor that cometh from God only?" St John 5:44 "Not that which goeth into the mouth defileth a man; but that which cometh out of the mouth, this defileth a man." St Matthew 15:11 "---Every plant, (Preacher) which my heavenly Father hath not planted, shall be rooted up." 13 "Let them alone: they be blind leaders of the blind, And if the blind lead the blind, both shall fall into the ditch." 14 To my knowledge Jesus never tried to change the mind of the religious leaders of his day. I gave a book to a preacher' he thumbed through it, and put it on the bottom shelf with his other religious books to sell. When a person is going to heaven 'according to them,' it can't get any better than that. Why should a divinity college graduate listen to a carpenter from Wyoming?

The leaven of the Pharisees and Sadducees

"Then Jesus said unto them, Take heed and beware of the leaven of the Pharisees and of the Sadducees." St Matthew 16:6 "For I say unto you, that except your righteousness shall exceed the righteousness of the scribes and Pharisees, ye shall in no case enter into the kingdom of heaven." St Matthew 5:20 "Jesus answered, Verily, verily, I say unto thee, Except a man be born of water (Born again 3rd verse) and of the Spirit, (Holy Ghost) he cannot enter into the kingdom of God." St John 3:5 "A new heart also will I give you, and a new Spirit will I put within you ---." Ezekiel 36:26 "Then understood they how that he bade them not beware of the leaven of bread, (earthly things) but of the doctrine, of the Pharisees and of the Sadducees." St Matthew 16:12

Peter's confession

"And I say also unto thee, that thou art Peter, and upon this rock I will build my church; and the gates of hell shall not prevail against it." St Matthew 16:18 The reason I question this verse is redemption or salvation, is a personal thing between God and yourself. It was Paul that stressed that people should congregate together, and he never did say which church or religious organization, not all doctrines are the same. "And I will give unto thee the keys of the kingdom of heaven; and whatsoever thou shalt bind on earth shall be bound in heaven: and whatsoever thou shalt loose on earth shall be loosed in heaven."19 The quickest way to explain this verse is it is not biblical. Scripture says that it is all up to God or Jesus, and the Spirit to become saved, man has nothing to do with it. "John answered and said, A man can receive nothing, except it be given him from heaven," St John 3:27 That is the way I received salvation from heaven with verses to prove it.

If Peter understood Jesus teaching would he have told those in The Acts to "Repent and be baptized (water) every one of you in the name of Jesus Christ for the remission of sins, and ye shall receive the gift of the Holy Ghost." The Acts 2:38

Peter never did show me that he knew what Jesus was about. 16:23 "But he turned, and said unto Peter, Get thee behind me Satan thou art an offense unto me: for thou savorest (understand) not the things that be of God, but those that be of men." St Matthew 16:23 "For whosoever will save his life shall lose it: and whosoever will lose his life for my sake shall find it." 25 In the transformation of receiving the new heart, clinically I died.

"For what is a man profited, if he shall gain the whole world, and lose his own soul? Or what shall a man give in exchange for his soul?" 26

The transfiguration chapter 17

The verses from St Matthew I find troubling? For one thing it was before Jesus had finished His ministry that He was transfigured, and it reads of the appearance of Moses and Elijah talking with Him. It shows Peter not understanding that a tabernacle or church building has nothing to do with a person being saved because it is personal and physical. After Jesus left,

Peter managed to get St Peters Basilica built with him as the first Pope, 'when I was saved at a gas station.' Moses had nothing to do with this dispensation so what was the reason for his appearance? Because it reads Elijah was to appear at the last day a lot of people believe he has already come and left. The Elijah or Elias of the Old Testament has nothing to do with the Elijah or Elias of the New Testament. We hear again from God; "This is my beloved Son, in whom I am well pleased; hear ye him.; 5 Who wants to believe that?

"And his disciples asked him, saying, why then say the scribes that Elijah must first come?" St Matthew 17:10 This is the same as it reads in Malachi that Elijah would come at the last days, to reveal the meaning of the allegorical or parables that Jesus spoke. "And Jesus answered and said unto them, Elijah truly shall first come, and restore all things." 11 (Why is this a reversal from the 12th verse?) "But I say unto you, That Elijah is come already, and they knew him not, but have done unto him whatsoever they listed. (Pleased) Likewise shall also the Son of man suffer of them." St Matthew 17:12 The last part is a true statement. Then we go against the other biblical verses in the rest of the Bible. "Then the (disciples) understood (did they) that he spake unto them of John the Baptist."13 How could John the Baptist be Elijah, when he lived at the same time in history as Jesus? It's been 2,018 years ago and Elijah was to come in the 11th verse, and at the last day, in Malachi 4:5?

They asked John if he was Elijah, and he said no twice in St John. In my KJB of 1611 nor my concordance, in the Cruden's Complete Concordance did they mention this verse in John as a reference, and I find that troubling. "And they asked him, (John the Baptist) who art thou Elijah? And he saith I am not. Art thou that prophet? And he answered, No." St John 1:21

Jesus explains greatness

St Matthew 18:3 "And said Verily I say unto you, Except ye be converted, (saved, or transformed, and have received the Holy Ghost or Spirit) and become as little children, (If there is anything that might be right, with Billy's ministry is going forward in a church in tears as a child might.) (except you do this) ye shall not enter into the kingdom of heaven." St Matthew 18:3 "Whosoever therefore shall humble himself as this little child, the same is greatest in the kingdom of heaven." 4 "And whoso shall receive one such little child in my name receiveth me."? 5 I went forward at the end of a protestant church service in tears, feeling the Spirit of conviction. It didn't bother me who was there I knew I was a sinner that needed salvation. Now days it is far from pathetic what the preachers tell those looking for salvation, that what they do is the truth.

Now days it seems, all you have to do is wave at the preacher just before the big prayer, but In Joel, it reads the Spirit of salvation has been removed from the church. That must be why I was saved at a gasoline service station, and received the Holy Ghost in my mouth in a 1959 Ford Thunderbird going to work in a manufacturing plant in Los Angeles, California.

The lost sheep

One sheep out of 100 goes astray. St Matthew 18:12 "And if so be that he find it, verily I say unto you, he rejoiceth more of that sheep, then of the ninety and nine which went not astray."13 Are these verses biblical? It is saying that 99 out of a hundred must be saved. All the other verses I read like few will find the way, or few will know the mysteries. "Even so it is not the will of your Father which is in heaven, that one of these little ones should perish." 14 'This verse is not biblical,' considering the people lost in Noah's day, or Sodom, or the end time. Then there is the problem of being chosen, and drawn. I haven't read of anything nice about it. "Many will say to me in that day, Lord, Lord, have we not prophesied (preached) in thy name?" "And in thy name have cast out devils? And in thy name done many wonderful works?" St Matthew 7:22 "And then will I profess unto them, I never knew you: depart from me, ye that work iniquity." 23

Jesus explains the obligation of brotherhood

"Verily I say unto you, "Whatsoever ye shall bind on earth shall be bound in heaven: and whatsoever ye shall loose on earth shall be loosed in heaven." St Matthew 18:18 I'm not sure how man got such a responsibility, when God or Jesus along with the Spirit, and Holy Ghost is the only way to the kingdom of God. "---Who then can be saved?" St Matthew 19:25 "But Jesus beheld them, and said unto them, With men this is impossible; but with God all things are possible." 26 "John answered and said, A man can receive nothing except it be given him from heaven." St John 3:27 I found out this verse is true in Ezekiel 36:26-25-27 "For where two or three are gathered together in my name, there am I in the midst of them." St Matthew 18:20 Not biblical. Jesus said he was the door. That would not put him inside of all the many churches and organizations with their different doctrines. Lucifer said he was controlling the mount (all) the congregations. (Churches) in Isaiah 14:13-14 "Hereafter I will not talk much with you: for the prince of this world cometh and hath nothing in me." St John 14:30

Jesus teaching on divorce

"For this cause shall a man leave father and mother, and shall cleave to his wife: and they twain shall be one flesh?" St Matthew 19:5 It reads God and Jesus are one but they are twain. "Wherefore they are no more twain, but one flesh. What therefore God hath joined together, let not man put asunder." 6 This is where it gets dicey. Which church? It reads about a person that died let the dead bury their dead. "But Jesus said unto him, Follow me; and let the dead (spiritually dead) bury their dead." St Matthew 8:22 It reads what God hath joined them together. According to this, those that are shacking up, did God join them together? I believe a couple must recognize the union came from God, and divorce or separation then, "would be out of the question."

"Master, which is the great commandment in the law?" St Matthew 22:36 "Jesus said unto him, Thou shalt love thy God with all thy heart, and with all thy soul, and with all thy mind." 37

"Think not that I am come to send peace on earth: I came not to send peace, but a sword." St Matthew 10:34 "For I am come to set a man at variance against his father, and the daughter against her mother, and the daughter-in- law against her mother-in-law." 35 "And a man's foes shall be they of his own household." 36 He that loveth father or mother more then me is not worthy of me: and he that loveth son or daughter more then me is not worthy of me." 37 "He that findeth his life shall lose it: and he that loseth his life for my sake shall find it."39 The question is what about the wife and children? When I was saved I had nothing going for me, and did

Jesus Have a wife and children? How important is it? It reads a man's foes shall be they of his own household. It reads to love God, and if a person finds a life they could lose it.

"And every one that hath forsaken houses, or brethren, or sisters, or father, or mother, or wife, or children, or lands, for my name's sake, shall receive a hundred-fold and shall inherit everlasting life." St Matthew 19:29 I'm not sure how the born again experience plays with this verse.

"But Jesus said, Suffer little children, and forbid them not, to come unto me: for of such is the kingdom of heaven." St Matthew 19:14 I went to the Alter in tears after two months of seeking God. "And he laid his hand on them, and departed thence." ??? 15 Jesus is allegorically trying to tell us that the Spirit will change our heart that a person needs.

The rich young ruler

"---but if thou will enter into life, keep the commandments." St Matthew 19:17 Most people that reads this lets it run off, like water on a ducks back. But this verse has everything to do with being born again and receiving the Holy Ghost physically for starters. It doesn't necessarily mean keeping the written commandments only. "And again I say unto you, It is easier for a camel to go through the eye of a needle, than for a rich man to enter into the kingdom of God." 24 What is the purpose of going to a divinity college to get a degree? Isn't it so you can preach in a big church with a big congregation? That means lots of money.: "---who then can be saved?" 25: "But Jesus beheld them (looked on their heart) and said unto them, with men this is impossible; but with God all things are possible." 26 "---Ye do err, not knowing the scriptures nor the power of God." St Matthew 22:29

(Back to Peter) "Then answered Peter and said unto him, Behold, we have forsaken all, and followed thee; what shall we have therefore?" St Matthew 19:27 "And every one that hath forsaken houses, or brethren, or sisters, or father, or mother, or wife, or children, or lands, for my name's sake, shall receive a hundredfold, and shall inherit everlasting life." 29 These verses are not biblical if you compare them with other verses. In St John born again and you must receive the Spirit to enter into the kingdom of God. St John 3:3-5 There is always the problem of the original sin of Adam, and in Ezekiel, it verifies that, it is written literally where Jesus spoke in parables. "A new heart also will I give you, and I will take away the stony (sinful) heart out of your flesh, and I will give you a heart of flesh. (Not spirit) Ezekiel 36:26-27

A mother asks greatness for her sons

She asked Jesus if her two sons could set on each side of Him in His kingdom? In St Matthew Jesus said it shall be given for whom it is prepared of my Father. Prepared, is a big word that is why some people go to college eight or so years to get prepared. If we go by the KJB of 1611 there is the matter of being chosen along with those that are drawn or couldn't we say selected. It reads many are called but few chosen. The guests are up to God, who He wants to invite, and not only invite but He is God, that will prepare a person to be perfect as He is perfect. "Be ye therefore perfect, even as your Father which is in heaven is perfect." St Matthew 5:48 If your name is written in the lamb's book of life, and called, can a person mess up his life to where they wouldn't be one of the chosen? Jesus said His body is a temple. Could a person disfigure their body to not be one of the chosen, I'll leave that up to you? Without the prayer of Jesus to His Father is it possible to be drawn to Him. St John 14:16 "And I will pray the Father, and he shall give you another (they have already been born again) Comforter, (Holy Ghost or Spirit) that (he) may abide with you forever." St John 14:16 "Even the Spirit of truth; whom the world cannot receive, because it seeth him not, neither knoweth him: but ye know him; for he dwelth with you, and shall be in you." 17 The Holy Ghost is referred to as a, him or he in some verses.

Back to the two sons, then those that are chosen, and drawn, they are able to drink of the cup, that I (Jesus) shall drink of, and be baptized with the baptism that I am baptized with? St Matthew 20:23 Above it reads the world cannot receive the Spirit. A person must receive the born again experience first. You see the power of God in St John 3:3 and learn of Jesus, it cleans the body, to get it ready to receive the Spirit. It is God's preparation so a person can receive the Holy Ghost or Comforter to be in you forever. In Ezekiel 36:26 It is first the new heart, the Comforter second, The Comforter is the Holy Ghost mentioned in St John 14:16 and

17 that will be with you for eternity. "And I will pray the Father, and he shall give you another Comforter, that he may abide with you forever."16

"And he saith unto them, ye shall drink indeed of my cup (receive the same things that I received) and be baptized with the baptism (Holy Ghost) that I am baptized with?" St Matthew 20:23 Jesus never needed to be born again (new heart) because he was born without sin. By this the original sin of Adam perhaps comes down only through the generations of the male. Jesus received the Holy Ghost in his mouth on the first breath that he took. That is why in St Matthew it reads straightway (immediately) He came out of the water. 3:16 God put a vision of a preacher in trouble, "and praying" to get me to open my mouth, I said out loud in a Ford car, "God help that BOY." On the word boy the Spirit, as a dove came through the windshield and went in my mouth, down my throat, when I was driving to work in a 1959 Ford Thunderbird.

The other thing that Jesus saw was an angel, it was after he came out of the wilderness tempted by the Devil, and his ordeal was over with. "Then the devil leaveth him, and, behold, angels came and ministered unto him." St Matthew 4:11 It only reads that He fasted 40 days and nights it doesn't say how long He was in the wilderness, I believe it was the Holy Ghost or Spirit at that time taught Jesus what to say and do sanctioned by His Father God. "For I have not spoken of myself; but the Father which sent me, he gave me a commandment, what I should say, and what I should speak." St John 12:49

In a Sunday school class at the climax, I looked up toward the ceiling and saw an angel pure white with no head, feet or hands. I blurted out, "The day of judgment is coming."

The triumphal entry into Jerusalem

It was prophesied in Isaiah "Behold the Lord hath proclaimed unto the end of the world, Say ye to the daughter of Zion, Behold thy salvation cometh; behold his reward is with him, and his work before him. Isaiah 62:11 "And they shall call them, The holy people, The redeemed of the Lord:---" 12 St Matthew 21:5 "Tell ye the daughter of Zion, Behold, thy King cometh unto thee, meek, and sitting upon an ass, and a colt the foal of an ass." ST Matthew 21:5 I believe it means the countries that are friendly to Israel the daughter of Zion. Was Jesus trying to tell people what God really thought of them sitting on an ass? "And it repented (grieved) the Lord that he had made man on the earth, and it grieved him at his heart." Genesis 6:6 This is definitely contrary to what people will tell you about God, that He loves everybody. it reads that the Father loves those that have been redeemed. "He that hath my commandments, and keepeth them he it is that loveth me: and he that loveth me shall be loved of my Father, and I will love him, and will manifest myself to him." St John 14:21 Manifest is a big word= apparent to the senses; reveal; be evident of; to appear to the senses. Does grace, faith, walk in righteousness, work it out etc. as Paul put it, fit this situation of manifest, to a person?

The cleansing of the temple

"And Jesus went into the temple of God, and cast out all them that sold and bought in the temple, and overthrew the tables of the moneychangers, and the seats of them that sold doves." St Matthew 21:12 "And said unto them, It is written, my house shall be called the house of prayer; but ye have made it a den of thieves." 13

Is the KJB of 1611 lying to us? "Gird yourselves, and lament, ye priests: howl, ye ministers of the Alter: come, lie all night in sackcloth, ye ministers of my God: for the meat offering and the drink offering is withholden from the house of your god." (God) Joel 1:13 Jesus used in St John 6:31-58 different terms of meat offering's and drink offerings, He used allegorically bread, flesh, blood, "For my flesh is meat indeed, and my blood is drink indeed."55 "He that eateth my flesh, and drinketh my blood, dwelleth in me, and I in him." 56 When my heart was removed it reads in Ezekiel that I would receive a heart of flesh, (meat offering) and when I received the Holy Ghost it went in my mouth, drinketh my blood, (drink offering) and both of these according to Joel has been removed from the house of your god. It reads that Lucifer would be in the mount (all) the congregation (churches). Isaiah 14:13 That is why it reads, "the house of your god."

"Hereafter I will not talk much with you: for the prince of this world cometh, and hath nothing in me." ST John 14:30 The prince of this world would be Satan.

God and Caesar

"Then went the Pharisees, and took counsel how they might entangle him in his talk." St Matthew 22:15 People have a notion on what they believe, it seems almost impossible to change a person's mind I have found that out on the social networks. Some of the people that I have been in contact with seem interested in truth I have offered to give them a book, and so far not one person has sent me an address. I identify with Noah, why there were only eight people on his boat. "But as the days of Noah were, so shall also the coming of the Son of man be." ST Matthew 24:37 (at the end time) "For as in the days of Noah were, before the flood, they were eating and drinking, marring and giving in marriage, (without God's sanctification) until the day that Noah entered into the ark."38

"But Jesus perceived their wickedness, and said, why tempt ye me, ye hypocrites?" St Matthew 22:18 It all makes sense when you consider either your father is the Devil or your Father is God. Can't you see how a divinity college graduate with thousands in their congregation, would listen to a carpenter from Wyoming? It reads that they wouldn't listen to the other carpenter's Son, why would they listen to me. "Ye are of your father the devil, and the lusts of your father ye will do. He was a murder from the beginning, and abode not in the truth, because there is no truth in him. When he speaketh a lie, he speaketh of his own: for he is a liar, and the father of it." St John 8:44 "And because I tell you the truth, ye believe me not."45 "Jesus answered and said unto them, Ye do err, not knowing the scriptures nor the power of God." St Matthew 22:29 What does the power of God have to do with Grace, Faith, Walk in righteousness, Charity, Love, Water baptism? Etc.

Peter said forsake all and enter into the kingdom of heaven. From The Act's –Jude are thousands of ways to be in the kingdom. Jesus said it is God's commandments or statutes, is the only way to the kingdom of God. Being born again and receiving the Spirit takes the power of God, and it comes from God in heaven. "A man can receive nothing, except it be given him from heaven," St John 3:27. I found out this verse is true.

Who teaches a person the statutes? The Holy Ghost or Spirit without it, there would be no kingdom of God or kingdom of heaven. "And I will put my spirit within you, and cause you to walk in my statutes, and ye shall keep my judgments, and do them." Ezekiel 36:27 "But the Comforter, which is the Holy Ghost, whom the Father will send in my name, he shall teach you all things, and bring all things to your remembrance, whatsoever I have said unto you." St John 14:26

When I was walking out the door of the church the night before receiving the Holy Ghost the next morning, the preacher asked me how I felt? I told him, 'at peace with myself.' "Peace I leave with you, my peace I give unto you: not as the world giveth, give I unto you. Let not your heart be troubled, neither let it be afraid." St John 14:27 Those that give you comfort now, it is only superficial at best. In a nursing home where my mother stayed, her worldly things after she died, were put outside under six inches of snow when I went to get them. It proves it is all about the money. I never got any authorization from a doctor, so I paid from the first day to the last day with about her last month on welfare.

The great commandment

"Master,which is the great commandment in the law?" St Matthew 22:36 "Jesus said unto him, thou shalt love the Lord thy God with all thy heart, and with all thy soul, and with all thy mind." The reference is Deut. 6:5 "And thou shalt love the Lord thy God with all thine heart, and with all thy soul, and with all thy -----might----." Deuteronomy 6:5 Can you see the difference? "And these words, which I command thee this day, shall be in thine heart." 6 Jeremiah 31:33 " But this shall be the covenant that I will make with the house of Israel; after those days, saith the Lord, I will put my law in their inward parts, and write it in their hearts; and will be their God, and they shall be my people." Jeremiah 31:33 "And I will give them one heart, and one way, that they may fear me forever, for the good of them, and of their children after them:"? 32:39 40 "---I will put my fear in their hearts, that they shall not depart from me." 40 Ezekiel 11:19 "And I will give them one heart, and I will put a new Spirit within you; (Holy Ghost) (again the cart is in front of the horse) and I will take the stony heart (sinful) out of their flesh: and will give them a heart of flesh:" Ezekiel 11:19 (Not spirit but flesh from God) This again is about the same as Ezekiel 36:26-27 In 25 there is no way that your body can have the filthiness removed before your heart is removed and replaced. "Create in me a clean heart, O God; and renew a right Spirit within me." Psalm 51:10 (After your body is clean in that order) "Cast away from you all your transgressions, whereby ye have transgressed; and make you a new heart and a new Spirit: for why will ye die, O house of Israel?" Ezekiel 18:31 When receiving the new heart in the transformation a person will die clinically, but you can't cast away your own transgressions on your own.

Master, which is the great commandment in the law? St Matthew 22:36 "And the second is like unto it, Thou shalt love thy neighbor as thyself." 39 "---Thou shalt love the Lord thy God with all thy heart, and with all thy soul, and with all thy mind." 37 In both these commandments, I'm not sure where Genesis fits in nor the love of the wife, "And it repented (grieved) the Lord that he had made man on the earth, and it grieved him at his heart." 6:6

Jesus denounces the scribes and the Pharisees

It seems devoted to what we have in the churches today, the 23 chapter of St Matthew, and it reads that your righteousness must exceed the righteousness of the scribes and Pharisees, "Ye shall in no case enter into the kingdom of heaven." St Matthew 5:20

The next chapter 24 they asked Jesus what shall be the sign of thy coming, and of the end of the world? St Matthew 24:3 "And Jesus answered and said unto them, Take heed that no man deceive you." 4 "For many shall come in my name, saying, I am Christ; (I don't believe they have to say I am Christ but those in charge of the church represent Christ, and in so doing say they are Christ) and shall deceive many." 5 Which church or religious organization has the doctrine that Jesus died for?

"For there shall arise false Christ's, and false prophets, and shall show great signs and wonders insomuch that, if it were possible, they shall deceive the very elect." St Matthew 24:24 A lot of preachers will tell you a story how the cancer disappeared, but the patient died. Etc. It reads if it were possible, they shall deceive the very elect. It is not possible to deceive the elect that is why I don't attend any church. When your salvation has been physical, and I received the Holy Ghost in the mouth, a person is not going to be deceived when the preacher never mentions those facts. That is how I could tell Paul was not of God.

No man knows the day

"---This generation shall not pass, till all these things be fulfilled." 34 "But of that day and hour knoweth no man, no, not the angels of heaven, but my Father only." St Matthew 24:36 "But as the days of Noah were, so shall also the coming of the Son of man be."37

Why worry be happy until the day that it is going to be too late. "And knew not until the flood came, and took them all away; so shall also the coming of the Son of man be."39 "Therefore be ye also ready: for in such an hour as ye think not the Son of man cometh." 44 I'm ready to live with God in His kingdom, it doesn't say a word about being sent to purgatory to get me ready to live with God in His kingdom, that I can find in my KJB Bible of 1611.

"---and they that were ready went in with him to the marriage: (couldn't we say marriage feast) and the door was shut." St Matthew 25:10 "But I say unto you, I will not drink henceforth of this fruit of the vine, until that day when I drink it new with you in my Father's kingdom." 26:29 "Afterward came also the other virgins, saying, Lord, Lord, open to us." St Matthew 25:11 "But he answered and said, Verily I say unto you, I know you not."12 When Noah was in the ark it reads in Genesis "And they went in, went in male and female of all flesh, as God had commanded him: and the Lord shut him in." 7:16 Where, was the love for mankind when God shut the door on Noah? And the door will be shut again when Jesus returns?

"And he shall set the sheep on his right hand, but the goats on the left." St Matthew 25:33 "Then shall the king say unto them on his right hand, Come, ye blessed of my Father, inherit the kingdom prepared for you from the foundation of the world:" 34 It is a question of what you are either you're a sheep or goat? The Goat's father is 'Satan,' the sheep's Father is God. "Ye are of your father the devil, ------When he speaketh a lie, he speaketh of his own: for he is a liar, and the father of it."St John 8:44

Judas Iscariot betrays Jesus

"Then one of the twelve, called Judas Iscariot went unto the chief priests." St Matthew 26:14 "And from that time he (she?) sought opportunity to betray him." 16 In most all the paintings of the Lord's supper, that I have seen, the person next to Jesus has no beard, and I believe it is Judas that could have been a cross dresser a girl?

"And he went a little farther, and fell on his face, and prayed, saying O my Father, if it be possible, let this cup pass from me nevertheless not as I will, but as thou wilt." 39 According to the preachers Jesus must have been talking to Himself. He was asking God His Father for permission to get out of the crucifixion, as let this cup pass from me. In St Matthew "---Ye shall drink indeed of my cup, and be baptized with the baptism that I am baptized with:" 20:23 I received the new heart but Jesus never needed that because He was born without sin, but He did need the new Spirit or Holy Ghost, which He received, when baptized by John. I received it in a 1959 Ford it came through the windshield. He saw an angel when He was through with being in the wilderness as I did two years after the born again experience. My reason for living is to explain the parables or allegorical teaching that Jesus spoke. It reads in Revelation, that I won't be hurt of the second death my first death, was when I received the new heart."Ye serpents, ye generation of vipers, how can ye escape the damnation of hell?" St Matthew 23:33 34 "Wherefore, behold, I send unto you prophets, and wise men, and scribes: and some of them ye shall kill and crucify: and some of them shall ye scourge in your synagogues, and persecute them from city to city:"34

This verse has troubled me for a long time. "Give not that which is holy unto the dogs, neither cast ye your pearls before swine, least they trample them under their feet, and turn again and rend (tear) you." St Matthew 7:6

Peter denies Jesus 26:69-75

In reading all about Peter, I can't find a verse that tells me in the Gospels, Peter 1-2 or 'The Acts', that he understood that a person had to be born again, and receive the Spirit to be saved or redeemed, to enter into the kingdom of God.

The crucifixion 27

"---If thou be the Son of God, come down from the cross." St Matthew 27:40 "He trusted in God; let him deliver him now, if he will have him: for he said I am the Son of God." 43 "The thieves also, which were crucified with him, cast the same in his teeth." 44 Luke (Is the only Gospel that has this about the two thieves that were crucified with Jesus) 42 "And he said unto Jesus, Lord, remember me when thou comest into thy kingdom." Luke 23:42 "And Jesus said unto him, Verily, I say unto thee, today shalt thou be with me in paradise." 43 In St Matthew the thieves were doing the same things mocking Jesus, and in Luke they were friends. Which way do we want to believe it? A woman told me one time that she wanted to go to heaven like the two thieves in Luke. Another problem is Jesus never went to paradise on that day, he had to spend time in the sepulcher. Etc.

"And the graves were opened; and many bodies of the saints which slept arose," St Matthew 27:52 "And came out of the graves after his resurrection, and went into the holy city, and appeared unto many." 53 There are no other references that this occurred so I find these verses troubling. Jesus said that He would go and make a place for the saints and what holy city are they referring to?

The resurrection

"And, behold, there was a great earthquake: for the angel of the Lord descended from heaven, and came and rolled back the stone from the door, and sat upon it." St Matthew 28:2 "His countenance was like lighting, and his raiment white as snow:" 3 The angel I saw it's raiment was white as snow. It reads that the angel sat on the stone. I believe, that the same Spirit that helped in creation of the heavens and earth, came after the door was removed, and put life back into the body of Jesus. The Spirit that saved me or gave me a new heart was a, "light" with the power of God behind it. The shroud of Turin they said a light had to put the image on the cloth, and if it is true, there is your light the same one that saved me. But again those involved with the Shroud don't want to hear about the light that I saw, because I connect the born again experience to it, and redemption.

Jesus commissions the disciples

"Go ye therefore, and teach all nations, baptizing them in the name of the Father, and of the Son, and of the Holy Ghost:" St Matthew 28:19 In several ways this verse is not biblical. It seems to give Peter's version of salvation some credence in The Acts "Then Peter said unto them, Repent, and be baptized every one of you in the name of Jesus Christ for the remission of sins, and ye shall receive the gift of the Holy Ghost." The Acts 2:38 There seems to be several problems, with this verse. What about being one of the chosen, or drawn in St John, or when John the Baptist said salvation comes from heaven, or when he said my way of baptism is not what you need, it is the baptism of the Holy Ghost or Spirit, that is what a person needs, 'that God will give you. Salvation is more than teach, and according to St Matthew it reads "He answered and said unto them, because it is given unto you to know the mysteries of the kingdom of heaven, but to them it is not given." St Matthew 13:11 This verse separates the masses, and they are either a goat or a sheep. "---he shall separate them one from another, as a shepherd divideth his sheep from the goats: St Mathew 25:32 "And he shall set the sheep on his right hand, but the goats on the left."33

The main thing about receiving the Spirit is your body must be clean first, before it will enter into your body, this includes the original sin of Adam must be removed from the heart. Ezekiel 36:26-25-27 These verses are not written in sequential order of occurrence, that happened to me. The Holy Ghost was received thirty days after receiving the new heart.

The Gospel according to St John
The pre-existent Word

"In the beginning was the Word, and the Word was with God, and the Word was God." St John 1:1 The problem lies with the, "Word was God." I have heard more than one preacher point to the problem, and say see; Jesus was God. There are many more verses that have God and Jesus separate, and God speaking telling of the fact that Jesus was His Son. A couple that gets married it reads the same way God and Jesus are as one. "To him that overcometh will I grant to sit with me in my throne, even as I also overcame, and am set down with my Father in his throne." Revelation 3:21 To overcome, is not excepting every doctrine of Tom, Dick, Harry, and Judy nor the doctrine of Islam, Buda, Hindu, Mormon, Baptist, or Catholic. During the two months I was seeking salvation I had a chance, 'more than once of what they call becoming a Christian,' but I felt like there is something wrong with their belief or doctrine. When I was a child, I had felt what I call the spirit of conviction, and was looking for that before I went to The Alter in 1968. (As told in this book)

The Word was from the beginning but it wasn't made flesh until the time was right, made in the form of Jesus the Son, the perfect sacrifice because of the righteousness of God. "And the Word was made flesh, and dwelt among us, (and we beheld his glory, the glory as of the only begotten of the Father,) full of grace and truth." St John 1:14 The reference is in Isaiah "And the glory of the Lord shall be revealed, and all flesh shall see it together: for the mouth of the Lord hath spoken it."Isaiah 40:5 The word in the Gospels of, 'grace' only occurs in three verses "And of his fullness have all we received, and grace for grace." 16 His fullness is being born again and receiving the Holy Ghost to enter into the kingdom of God. "For the law was given by Moses, but grace and truth came by Jesus Christ." 17 What it means is by God's grace He gave us Jesus for the sacrifice for sin because of the righteousness of God. The grace and faith spoken of by Paul has nothing to do with Salvation.

In St John in mentioned a light, what if it were true that a person will see a light when they are saved, I did. "In him was life; and the life was the light of men."4 "And the light shineth in darkness; and the darkness comprehended it not." 5 Those that are not saved will not understand the allegorical teaching of Jesus."---it is given unto you to know the mysteries of the kingdom of heaven, but to them it is not given." St Matthew 13:11

John the Baptist was, a witness, that Jesus came in the flesh, and that He received the Holy Ghost, when he baptized Him. Those around Him never understood that the Spirit went in His mouth, because of the speed that it occurred. The Spirit that gave me my new heart and the Holy Ghost was a light that I saw with my eyes and felt. Jesus said the Spirit was, "as a dove" or white in color descending from heaven. St Matthew 3:16 St "There was a man from God, whose name was John." St John 1:6 "The same came for a witness, to bear witness of the Light, (Jesus or Holy Ghost) that all men through him might believe." 7 "But as many as received him, to them gave he power to become the sons of God, (even to them that believe on his name:)" 12 it is not biblical I'm sorry. But a person must believe on one of the works that He did as in St John; "Believe me that I am in the Father, and the Father in me or else believe me for the very works' sake." St John 14:11 "Which were born, not of blood, (not inheritable) nor of the will of the flesh, (your desire) nor of the will of man, (preachers) but of God." St John 1:13

The Word was with God from the beginning but it wasn't made flesh 'Jesus' until the time was right. "And the Word was made flesh, and dwelt among us, (and we beheld his glory, as of the only begotten of the Father,) full of grace and truth." St John 1:14 It is by God's grace that He gave us Jesus for redemption of mankind because of the righteousness of God. Salvation has nothing to do with grace and faith, that Paul said it did. Salvation is physical that John the Baptist said it was."---A man can receive nothing, except it be given him from heaven." 3:27 "And they asked him (John the Baptist) what then? Art thou Elijah? And he saith, I am not. Art thou that prophet? And he answered, No". 21 (The preachers say that John was Elijah, but how could that be when he was to come at the end time as in Malachi 4:5. John was a witness of the Holy Ghost that descended from heaven, but it never abode on Him it went in his mouth, and down His throat. "And John bare record, saying, I saw the Spirit descending from heaven like a dove, and it abode upon him." St John 1:32 The preachers like that, because in The Acts it reads the Spirit set on each of them when it went in Jesus mouth.

(Receiving the Holy Ghost is the only way to the kingdom of God in the mouth or like a dove) "And I knew him not: but he that sent me to baptize with water, the same said unto me, Upon whom thou shalt see the Spirit descending, and remaining on him, (going in His mouth) the same is he which baptizeth with the Holy Ghost." St John 1:33 (There is no need to baptize a person in water) A vision was put on me to get my mouth open.

The first disciples

"---We have found him, of whom Moses in the law, and the prophets, did write, Jesus of Nazareth, the son of Joseph." St John 1:45 (Joseph had nothing to do with the birth of Jesus it was the Spirit of Genesis 1:2) In St Matthew (It reads the Holy Ghost, but it wasn't available for mankind until after Jesus went to His Father in heaven) St John16:7 Jesus received it in the mouth when He was baptized by John in St Matthew it never, 'lighting on him.' 3:16 ("But this spake he of the Spirit, which they that believe on him should receive: for the Holy Ghost was not yet given; because that Jesus was not yet glorified.) St John 7:39 "Nevertheless I tell you the truth; It is expedient for you that I go away: for if I go not away, the Comforter (Holy Ghost) will not come unto you; but if I depart, I will send him unto you." St John 16:7 "He that believeth on me, as the scripture hath said, out of his belly shall flow rivers of living water."7:38 It means "Believe me that I am in the Father, and the Father in me; or else believe me for the very works' sake." St John14:11 That is what triggers the Spirit in Genesis 1:2 to act to give a person a new heart.

St John Chapter 2
The miracle of Cana

It is about Jesus turning the water into wine at a marriage feast. This was what the Sunday school teacher was speaking on the morning I saw an angel at the end of the class. I blurted out, "the day of judgment is coming." "When the ruler of the feast had tasted the water that was made wine, and knew not whence it was: (but the servents which drew the water knew;)" 9 The question that I have, did the wine somehow come from the body of Jesus?

That evening I never went to the church service, and it was about midnight 1/12/1970. I was studding in the KJB of 1611, and went to the kitchen to get a drink of water in an audible voice it said, 'change the water into wine. I brought the glass of water back into the front room setting it on the coffee table, I lifted both arms, and said, 'my Father in heaven change the water into wine in Jesus name.' Nothing happened to the glass. I felt a sensation from the tips of my fingers to my toes. The only explanation of it is further in the book.

Jesus cleanses the temple

"And found in the temple those that sold oxen and sheep and doves, and the changers of money sitting:" St John 2:14 "And when he made a scourge of small cords, he drove them all out of the temple, and the sheep, and the oxen; and poured out the changers money, and overthrew the tables;" 15 Could we say that it is different today but with different products? "---make not my Father's house a house of merchandise." 16"---The zeal of thine house hath eaten me up." 17 A preacher with thousands in attendance how could they say I have been preaching this same message for 60 years and have been wrong. They might even have to get a job. It reads "But seek ye first the kingdom of God, and his righteousness:---." St Matthew 6:33 What if that meant be given a new heart and new Spirit physically as in Ezekiel 36:26—27.

The straight gate

"Enter ye in at the strait gate: (the one that I have provided for you) for wide is the gate, and broad is the way, that leadeth to destruction, and many there be which go in (there-at:)" St Matthew 7:13 The greatest stumbling block is taking the Bible or Word, literally when Jesus spoke either plainly, parables, or allegorically, and a lot of what He said was meant to be physical. The creation of the heavens, and the earth were physical, that is the main difference between Jesus and Paul with his faith, grace, work it out, walk in righteousness, etc. "Because strait is the gate, and narrow is the way, which leadeth unto life, and few there be that find it." 14 "Beware of false prophets, which come to you in sheep's clothing, but inwardly they are ravening wolves." 15 When Jesus was asked what will be the sign of the end? He said beware of false prophets. St Matthew 24:4-5

"Even so every good tree bringeth forth good fruit; but a corrupt tree bringeth forth evil fruit." St Matthew 7:17 The problem is telling the difference. His disciples asked Jesus, why speak thou unto them in parables? "He answered and said unto them, because it is given unto you to know the mysteries of the kingdom of heaven, but to them it is not given." St Matthew 13:11 It wasn't until after I was redeemed that I learned of the mysteries. My dad never had a clue, and he was an Assembly of God ordained minister for about five years.

St John 2:19 "---Destroy this temple, and in three days I will raise it up." St John 2:19 "Then said the Jews, Forty six years was this temple in building, and wilt thou rear it up in three days?" 20 He was referring to His body after the crucifixion. I was saved on a pay phone on the outside of a gas station. Is it true that God is not in the church building, that is what it reads in Joel 1:13 "----for the meat offering is withholden from the house of your God." (god) Joel 1:13 (Salvation, in allegorical form is in St John 6:31-58 and as plain as I could write it, it is in Ezekiel 36:26-27)

"Our fathers did eat manna in the desert; as it is written, He gave them bread from heaven to eat." St John 6:31 (This is only the second time I found 'He' with a capital in the Gospels. 32 "Then Jesus said unto them, Verily, verily I say unto you, Moses gave you not that bread from heaven; but my Father giveth you the true bread from heaven." 32 "For the bread of God is he which cometh down from heaven, and giveth life unto the world." 33 "Then said they unto him, Lord, evermore give us this bread." 34 "And Jesus said unto them, I am the bread of life: he that cometh to me shall never hunger; and (he that believeth on me) shall never thirst. (Not biblical) 35 "But I said unto you, that ye also have seen me, and believe not." (In the heart) 36 "All that the Father giveth me shall come to me, and him that cometh to me I will in no wise cast out." 37 " For I came down from heaven, (Word St John 1:14) not to do mine own will, but the will of him that sent me." 38

"No man can come to me, except the Father which hath sent me draw him: and I will raise him up at the last day." 44 "---Every man therefore that hath heard, and hath learned of the Father, (born again) cometh unto me." 45 (Afterward receive the Holy Ghost)

"Not that any man hath seen the Father, save (except) he which is of God, he hath seen the Father." 46 (The Spirit of Genesis in action at the time of being born again) "Verily, verily, I say unto you, He that believeth on me hath everlasting life." 47 (Not biblical) Somebody got lose, with the pencil.

"I am that bread of life." 48 49 "Your fathers did eat manna in the wilderness, and are dead. 49 "This is the bread which cometh down from heaven, that a man may eat thereof, and not die.50 (47 or 50 which verse do the preachers like?) 47 Is believe and 50 It cometh down from heaven. John the Baptist said, it is from heaven that I found out was true "John answered and said, a man can receive nothing, except it be given him from heaven." St John 3:27

"I am the living bread which came down from heaven: (Word) if any man eat of this bread, he shall (no doubt) live forever: which I will give for the life of the world." 51 (God told Adam he would die, and here we have life) 53 "Then Jesus said unto them, Verily, verily, I say unto you, Except ye eat the flesh of the Son of man, (born again) and drink his blood, (Holy Ghost) ye have no life in you." 53 "Whoso eateth my flesh and drinketh my blood, hath eternal life; and I will raise him up at the last day." 54 For my flesh is meat indeed, and my blood, is drink indeed." 55 I can understand why, "only believe" seems to be all there is to salvation.

"He that eateth my flesh, and drinketh my blood dwelleth in me, and I in him." 56 (it is matter or constituent of material and physical) 57 "As the living Father hath sent me, and I live by the Father: so he that eateth me, (receives the Holy Ghost in the mouth) even he shall (no doubt) live by me." 57 "This is that bread which came down from heaven: not as your fathers did eat manna, and are dead: he that eateth of this bread shall (no doubt) live forever." 58

"But he spake of the temple of his body." St John 2:21 If Jesus body is a temple what about mankind's body? That is why I say it is unwise to disfigure your body with tattoos etc.

St John Chapter 3
"Ye must be born again"

That statement means different things to different people, and in the world it is a major problem. "War is what Islam is about, until everyone is of that faith; it is the main vehicle for religious expansion. It is the Muslim duty to bring world peace via the sword." Muhammad demonstrated his success as a warrior, affirming himself as a prophet. Allah is everyone's god according to Islam. These are only a few false beliefs, but think of the other thousands of false doctrines from the other religions in the world, including even the King James Bible of 1611, and most of it comes from what Paul said. In Revelation it reads Satan deceived the whole world, and without Paul's writing half of the New Testament, it couldn't be done.

"Jesus answered and said unto him" (Nicodemus recognized that Jesus was a teacher that came from God the second verse.) "Verily, verily, I say unto thee, except a man be born again, he cannot see the kingdom of God." St John 3:3 Too 'see' means a person will see the power of God. It took the power of God (Spirit) to remove the heart I was born with ,and give me another from God. Ezekiel 36:26 "A new heart also will I give you---." Ezekiel 36:26 "---Ye do err, not knowing the scriptures, nor the power of God." St Matthew 22:29 "I have made the earth, the man and the beast that are upon the ground, by my great power and by my outstretched arm, (Spirit) and have given it unto whom it seemed meet (right) unto me." Jeremiah 27:5 "And God blessed them, (male and female) and God said unto them, Be fruitful, and multiply, and have dominion over the fish of the sea, and over the fowl of the air, and over every living thing that moveth upon the earth." Genesis 1:28

I believe Nicodemus established the fact that to be born again is physical.4

"Jesus answered, Verily, verily, I say unto thee, Except a man be born of water (born again 3rd verse, new heart) and of the Spirit (new Spirit or Holy Ghost) he cannot enter into the kingdom of God." St John 3:5 A New Heart, and a New Spirit (will I put within you.) Ezekiel 36:26-27

"That which is born of the flesh is flesh; (that has to do with the senses) and that which is born of the Spirit is Spirit." 6 (That a person will receive in the mouth) 7 "Marvel not that I said unto thee, ye must be born again." 7 "The wind bloweth where it listeth, and thou heareth the sound thereof, but canst not whence it cometh, and whither it goeth: so is every one that is born of the Spirit." 8 What Jesus is saying it comes on a person fast, and everyone must receive it to be redeemed or saved, so they can live eternally with God in His kingdom.' I have no idea where the heart I was born with went, but all I know is it went to the right of me, my body caving in or collapsing inward from the shoulders. Genesis 1:2

"---We (God and Jesus) speak that we do know, and testify that we have seen: and ye receive not our witness." 11 (Nicodemus did not understand nor comprehend)

"That whosoever believeth in him (In the heart St John 14:11) should not perish, but have eternal life." 15 It triggered the Spirit of Genesis 1:2 to act to give me a new heart.

"For God so loved the world, that he gave his only begotten Son, that whosoever believeth in him should not perish, but have everlasting life." 16 It is a play on 15 and shouldn't be in the Bible at all, it is not biblical. "It grieved God in His heart that He had made man on the earth. Genesis 6:6 At the time God gave the earth to mankind it just seemed right, but God regretted it later. Destroying everybody but Noah, and seven others, how much love did it take to do that? What about "No man can come to me, except the Father which hath sent me draw him:---" St John 6:44 What about; "---I speak not of you all: I know whom I have chosen:" St John 13:18 or "---for many be called, but few chosen." St Matthew 20:16

"For every one that doeth evil hateth the light, (truth) neither cometh to the light, lest his deeds should be reproved." St John 3:20 (examined or found out) The worst kind is those that go to church, and set on the front seat. The man that most preachers emulated joined the choir, to scope out the girls."How can ye believe, which receive honor one of another, and seek not the honor that cometh from God only." St John 5:44 "---A man can receive nothing, except it be given him from heaven," 3:27

"He (Jesus) must increase, but I (John) must decrease. 30 "He that cometh from above is above all: he that is of the earth is earthly, and speaketh of the earth: he that cometh from heaven is above all." 31 He is talking about the misinformed preachers, that don't know the allegorical meaning of the verses of Scripture, that go off on a tangent of their own the way Paul did.

"He that believeth on the Son hath (will be given) everlasting life: and he that believeth not the Son shall (no doubt) not see life; but the wrath of God abideth on him." St John 3:36 "----or else believe me for the very works' sake." St John 10:37-38 or 14"11 It triggered the Spirit to act, when I believed in my heart of Jesus healing a person.

The Samaritan women at the well

"---Whosoever drinketh of this water shall thirst again: St John 4:13 But whosoever drinketh of the water that I shall give him (shall be in him) a well of water springing up into everlasting life." 14 (Those that become saved) "Ye worship ye know not what: we know what we worship: for salvation is of the Jews." 22 Perhaps this is why the salvation plan is in Ezekiel, and not in parable form. It is true because I am an uncircumcised gentile that was saved as in Ezekiel 36:26 the same as the Jews will be some day. "But the hour cometh and now is when the true worshipers shall worship the Father in Spirit (Holy Ghost) and in truth (know the truth) for the Father seeketh such to worship him." 23 St John 6:31-58 above.

"God is a Spirit: and they that worship him must worship him in spirit and in truth" 24 If this is true than when I go to the kingdom of God it seems like my earthly body, will have to be changed into a spirit?

"But he said unto them, I have meat to eat that ye know not of." 32 (In the reference it reads, it means food, but it doesn't.) "---My meat is to do the will of him that sent me, and to finish his work." 34 Until the parables are explained the work of Jesus is not finished by Elijah. (Malachi 4:5) Verse 32 it means receiving the salvation plan physically of the new heart and Spirit in the mouth.

"For Jesus himself testified, (spoke) that a prophet hath no honor in his own country." 44 Can you visualize some of the mega church pastors with a divinity degree listening to a carpenter from Wyoming that graduated from a vocational school?

"---Verily, verily, I say unto you, the son can do nothing of himself, but what he seeth the Father do: for what things so ever he doeth, these also doeth the Son likewise." 5:19 The Jews said that He was equal, with God so let's kill Him. 18 Jesus could never be equal but a subordinate to God. "For I have not spoken of myself; but the Father which sent me, he gave me a commandment, what I should say, and what I should speak." St John 12:49

"For as the Father raiseth up the dead, (the spiritual dead from Adams sin) and quickeneth them; (the Spirit of Genesis makes them alive by giving them a new heart) even so the Son quickeneth (saves) whom he will." St John 5:21 It is the Son that prays to the Father for those that have received the new heart, that they can receive the Holy Ghost or new Spirit as well. "And I (Jesus) will pray the Father, and he shall (no doubt) give you another Comforter, that he may abide with you forever." St John 14:16

"Even the Spirit of truth: whom the world cannot receive, because it seeth him not, neither knoweth him: but ye know him; for he (Holy Ghost) dwelleth with you, and shall be in you." 17 When the son prays to the Father, He is judging that this person has received the new heart, and is eligible to receive the Holy Spirit.

24 "Verily, Verily, I say unto you, He that hearth my word, and believeth on him that sent me, hath everlasting life," (The trick in this verse is, 'believeth' we have to go to St John 10:38 or 14:11. It is in one of the works that Jesus did, I believed in my heart that perhaps I could

heal my mother it triggered the Spirit of Genesis to give me a new heart literally. "---it is given unto you to know the mysteries of the kingdom of heaven, but to them it is not given." St Matthew 13:11 Does this sound like all you have to do is believe, what is complicated about that? I couldn't tell you why God gave us the word as it reads or people contaminated the Word?. I found out Ezekiel is true, and it makes sense because in reads "Be ye therefore perfect, even as your Father which is in heaven is perfect." St Matthew 5:48 How can we be perfect with the sin of Adam in our heart? "---and shall not come into condemnation; but is passed from death unto life." St John 5:24 If I have passed from death unto life already why would I have to go to purgatory? Receiving the new heart and new Spirit, that makes me ready to go to God at this time. In St John it reads; you will, when this happens, after receiving the born again and new Spirit, enter into the kingdom of God. St John 3:5

"Verily, verily, I say unto you, The hour is coming, and now is, when the dead shall hear the voice of the Son of God: and they that hear shall live." 5:25 I heard the voice the night when it told me to change the water into wine, and the sensation went from my fingers to my toes. "But I receive not testimony from man: but these things I say, that ye might be saved." 5:34 The KJB of 1611 is the closest thing we have to the Words of truth, and man believes they can modify the truth? It reads few will find the way, how many were on the boat with Noah? Seven. It reads (And now is in 5:25) What that means is a person can be associated with God at this time or be in His kingdom, and yet still be living on the earth in bodily form, having been born again and have received the Holy Spirit. "Verily, verily, I say unto you, the hour is coming, and now is, when the dead shall hear the voice of the Son of God: and they that hear shall live." St John 5:25

It all happened to me physically, literally, that I felt with my senses. "And ye have not his word abiding in you:" (New heart-New Spirit or Holy Ghost) for whom he hath sent, him ye believe not." 38 It would be hard to find anybody on the earth that doesn't believe Jesus walked on the earth but just to Believe, has nothing to do with receiving His righteousness, and without that, a person can't be in His 'kingdom'.

"Search the scriptures; for in them ye think ye have eternal life: and they are they which testify of me." 39 "And ye will not come to me, that ye might have life." 40 At the end I knew I was a sinner that needed a savior, and after I left the church I couldn't believe I never felt something, but I was physically saved at a gas station. "How can ye believe, which receive honor one of another, and seek not the honor that cometh from God only." St John 5:44

"I receive not honor from men." 41 "But I know you, that ye have not the love of God in you." 42 Without the love of God in you, what do you have? "How can ye believe, which receive honor one of another, and seek not the honor that cometh from God only?" 44 "Do not think that I will accuse you to the Father; there is one that accuseth you, even Moses, in whom ye trust." 45 Moses name is only in the Bible, Paul's name is only in the Bible, Peter's name is only in the Bible. Because their names are in the Bible, they have nothing to do with becoming saved. Jesus or the Spirit, for this dispensation, is the only one that can save a person physically. Being religious from birth, is not going to help a person. Mentioning Moses, I believe He is referring to the law for the Old Testament dispensation before Jesus arrived.

"I am come in my Father's name, and ye receive me not: if another shall come in his own name, him ye will receive." (Paul) 5:43 "And because I tell you the truth, ye believe me not" 8:45 "---I (Lucifer) will exalt my throne above the stars of God: (Churches) I will sit also upon the mount (all) of the congregation (churches)" Isaiah 14:13 "Hereafter I will not talk much with you: for the prince of this world cometh, and hath nothing in me." St John 14:30 (Lucifer) If the Devil never had his word in the Bible could he deceive all the nations? I don't think so, and I don't read anything from The Acts – Jude except for this book.

Jesus feeds five thousand
The sixth Chapter of St John

In Branson, Missouri at Mickey Gillie's show, he said Jimmy Swaggart made more money than Jerry Lee Lewis and Mickey Gillie combined, they are both cousins of Jimmy. Who said there is no money in religion especially when a person stays away from the truth. It reads; if you speak the truth all men will hate you. "And ye shall be hated of all men for my name's sake: but he that endurth to the end shall be saved." St Matthew 10:22 It reads, they loved Paul and Paul loved them, it is not biblical.

"Jesus answered them and said, Verily, verily, I say unto you, Ye seek me, not because ye saw the miracles, but because ye did eat of the loves, and were filled." St John 6:26 27 "Labor not for the meat which perisheth, but for that meat which endureth unto everlasting life, which the Son of man shall give unto you: for him hath God the Father sealed." 27 The problem with the preachers most everything they say is in the Bible even the King James Bible of 1611, but it is not the truth, the sad part, most of what they say comes from what Paul wrote, or St John 3:16. Paul was the advocate for Satan. Isaiah 14:13-14.

"I am the Bread of Life" St John Chapter 6

In St John is the allegorical writing, that there are churches point to these verses, to give credence to the sacraments, see, "it mentions bread, and drink my blood. 6:31-58 What it all means is that salvation or being redeemed experiences, cometh from God only. "This is the bread that cometh down from heaven: that a man may eat thereof, and not die." 50 "Whoso eateth my flesh (bread, or receive the new heart) and drinketh my blood, (receive the Holy Ghost in the mouth) hath eternal life: and I will raise him up at the last day." 54

"Then Simon Peter answered him, Lord, to whom shall we go? Thou hast the words of eternal life." St John 6:68 Peter, the problem you have is the words, what some of them mean is what will happen to a person physically. In The Acts–Jude most of it is only words like have faith, grace, work it out, or walk in righteousness. Salvation is physical as the earth is physical and matter "And we believe and are sure that thou art that Christ, the Son of the living God." 69 Peter, there is more to salvation then just to believe that Jesus walked on the earth, even the Devil believed and talked to Jesus. In St Matthew 4:1-11

"Jesus answered them, Have not I chosen you twelve, and one of you is a devil? 70 He spake of Judas (Judy) Iscariot the son of Simon: for he, it was that should betray him, being one of the twelve." 71 No concrete proof just a hunch, that Judas was Judy. In the painting of the last supper, Judy looks like a girl with no beard.

"If any man will do his will, he shall know of the doctrine, (the doctrine is physical) whether it be of God, or whether I speak of myself." St John 7:17 "---Why speaketh thou unto them in parables?" St Matthew 13:10 "---Because it is given unto you to know the mysteries of the kingdom of heaven, but to them it is not given." 11 "---if it were possible, they shall deceive the very elect." St Matthew 24:24 This is why I don't go to any church. God removed the salvation Spirit from the churches, all they preach on is what Paul said or they make it up. Joel 1:13 and St John 5:43

You hear that a person cannot judge another person. "Judge not according to the appearance but judge righteous judgment." St John 7: "Thou hypocrite, first cast out the beam out of thine own eye; and then shalt thou see clearly to cast out the mote out of thy brother's eye." St Matthew 7:5 After a person receives redemption they are capable of judging righteously.

"Ye shall seek me, and shall not find me: and where I am, thither ye cannot come." 7:34 It is debatable with me if those in that day became righteous? That is, receiving the new heart and new Spirit, or Holy Ghost 38 "He that believeth on me, as the scripture hath said, (in St John according to 14:11) out of his belly shall flow rivers of living waters." 38 "But this spake he of the Spirit, which they that believe on him should receive: for the Holy Ghost was not yet given: because that Jesus was not yet glorified. 39 "Nevertheless I tell you the truth; It is expedient for you that I go away: for if I go not away, the Comforter will not come unto you; but if I depart, I will send him unto you." ST John 16:7

"Then spake Jesus again unto them, saying, I am the light of the world; he that followeth me shall not walk in darkness, but shall have the light of life." St John 8:12 The Spirit of Genesis 1:2 was a light that removed my heart and gave me another from God.

"The Pharisees therefore said unto him (Jesus) Thou bearest (give testimony) record of thyself; thy record (testimony) is not true." 13 (reliable) There is no difference today in the religious world, who would want to believe a carpenter from Wyoming without a divinity college degree? "For I say unto you, that except your righteousness shall exceed the righteousness of the scribes and Pharisees, ye shall in no case enter into the kingdom of heaven." St Matthew 5:20 "---Ye know that the princes of the Gentiles (Those that God has ordained) exercise dominion over them, (fat chance) and they that are great exercise authority upon them." St Matthew 20:25 (that is the way it is suppose to be) "But it shall not be so among you: (that is true) but whosoever will be great among you, let him be your minister:" 26 (servant) "And whosoever will be chief among you, let him be your servant:" 27 (I know of no one, preaching the Gospel that Jesus died for at this time) 98% is all about Paul, family, money, faith or grace, and hope, Jesus left the 99% and went after the 1 %. It reads few will find the way.

"Jesus answered and said unto them, though I bear record of myself, yet my record is true: for I know whence I came, (the Word) and whither I go; but ye cannot tell whence I came, and whither I go." St John 8:14 It is the same way with me I look about half normal, it all happened on the inside of me. "Ye judge after the flesh; I judge no man." 15 If there are 50,000 people in attendance, he must be a true, 'man of God' a real back slapper, with a divinity College degree, how could he be wrong? St John 8:44 They have not received His righteousness. St "But seek ye first the (kingdom of God,) and his righteousness---." St Matthew 6:38 "Except a man be born of water (born again 3rd verse) and the new Spirit he cannot enter into the (kingdom of God)" St John 3:5

"And he said unto them, Ye are from beneath; (made from the ground) I am from above: Ye are of this world; I am not of this world." St John 8:23 Joseph had nothing to do with the pregnancy of Mary, it was the Spirit in Genesis 1:2.

"And he that sent me is with me: the Father hath not left me alone; for I do nothing of myself; but as my Father hath taught me, I speak these things." 29 The Holy Ghost was with Jesus that He received, when baptized by John the Baptist in His mouth.

"If the Son therefore shall make you free, ye shall be free indeed." 36 You will not be dominated by the disobedience of Adam, and be free to live in the kingdom of God as have received His righteousness the only way to the kingdom.

"I speak that which I have seen with my Father: and ye do that which ye have seen with your father." 38 "Ye are of your father the devil, and the lusts of your father ye will do, He was a murderer from the beginning, and abode not in the truth, because there is no truth in him. When he speaketh a lie, he speaketh of his own: for he is a liar, and the father of it." 44

"And because I tell you the truth, ye believe me not." 45 If they never believed Jesus how can I expect anyone to believe me that salvation is physical?

"He that is of God heareth God's words: ye therefore hear them not, because ye are not of God." St John 8:47 In St Matthew Jesus recognized that it would be easier getting to the cross, because the Father's Words were in allegorical or parable form. St Matthew 11:25 Only those that become saved would understand His message. "He answered and said unto them, because it is given unto you to know the mysteries, of the kingdom of heaven, but to them it is not given." St Matthew 13:11 "---By hearing ye shall hear, and not understand; and seeing ye shall see, and shall not perceive:" 14 "But blessed are your eyes, for they see: and your ears, for they hear." 16

"For verily I say unto you, That many (false) prophets and (those that believe they are righteous men) have desired to see those things which ye see, and have not seen them; and to hear those things which ye hear, and have not heard them." St Matthew 13:17

"Verily, Verily, I say unto you, If a man keep my saying, he shall never see death." St John 8:51 Is it spiritual or physical death? In Revelation it reads a person will not be hurt of the second death, and don't you need to have a first death if not hurt of the second death? Clinically I believe, I died when my heart that I was born with was removed, and replaced. "---I will take away the stony (sinful) heart out of your flesh,---" Ezekiel 36:26

"My sheep hear my voice, and I know them, and they follow me." St John 10:27 The Word that Jesus spoke is the Word of truth, Paul, and his disciples only said, that what they say is true, it never came from God as the Word spoken by Jesus did. How could Paul get the Word right, when there was nothing at that time written down, nor did he ever meet Jesus'. Some of those around him questioned what he was saying, but he must have had a strong personality, and with the devils help, he overruled them. "I am come in my Father's name, and ye receive me not: (Jesus) if another shall come in his own name, him (Paul) ye will receive." (Believe) St John 5:43 If you don't believe me go to church.

"And I give unto them eternal life, (it is given to a person, physically) and they shall never perish, neither shall any man pluck them out of my hand." St John 10:28 "My Father, which gave them me, is greater than all; and no man is able to pluck them out of my Father's hand." 29 This is where the Baptist get once saved always saved, now read about my salvation or redemption, and is there anything about St John 3:16? It is usually written somewhere on the outside announcement board of their churches.

"I and my Father are one." 30 Now you have found another one of my headaches. This is true in what their goals are of redemption for mankind, because of the righteousness of God. It reads the same for a married couple that they are one, but I have always counted two.

"If I do not the works of my Father, believe me not." St John 10:37 Jesus did the works of His Father. "But if I do, though ye believe not me, believe the works: (I believed that perhaps I could heal my mother, it triggered the Spirit of Genesis 1:2 to act and it gave me my new heart) that ye may know, and believe, that the Father is in me, and I in him." 38 14: "Believe me that I am in the Father, and the Father in me, or else believe me for the very works' sake." St John 14:11 I was saved at a pay telephone on an outside wall of a gas station at 9pm 12/1/1968. In Spain they have been working on a church for about two hundred years.

42 "And many believed on him there." St John 10 42 The other headache is when people read that all you have to do is believe, they assume that they are saved. Then most all the preachers preach that is all there is to salvation, just asked Jesus to come into your heart? They never mention that your entire body must be clean before the Spirit or Holy Ghost will come into your body after being born again. The reason that is never mentioned, it never happened to them.

"I am the Resurrection and the Life"

If Jesus is the Resurrection and the Life, why preach Paul?

"Jesus said unto her, I am the resurrection, and the life; he that believeth in me, (there is a lot of difference between In and on) though he were dead, (spiritually separated from God) yet shall he live:" St John 11:25 (in communion with God) St John "And whosoever liveth and believeth in me shall never die. Believest thou this?" 11:26 If, it is a clinical death he is speaking about, are we that close to Jesus second coming? It also is written in Revelation that a person won't be hurt of the second death. My first death was when I received my new heart. "Jesus said unto her, Said I not unto thee, that if thou wouldest believe, thou shouldest see the glory of God?" 40 The Acts –Jude there are many different ways for salvation that speak, of seeing the glory of God? When you see and feel the glory of God it leaves no doubt of the existence of God. "But if I with the finger of God cast out devils, (your sin) no doubt the kingdom of God is come upon you." Luke 11:20

Mary's brother had died and she told Jesus if He had been there he wouldn't have died. When Jesus saw him He wept. "Jesus wept." St John 11 35 Why? I believe Jesus knew that he was not saved. People don't have a clue but it is not about this life, but the next life that is going to count. That is why I don't really seek after the things of this world. God has given me more than enough, and saved my life more than once, so like the song says, 'this world is not my home I'm just passing through.' "He that loveth his life shall lose it; and he that hateth his life in this world shall keep it unto life eternal." St John 12:25

"He that rejecteth me, and receiveth (physically receive) not my words, hath one that judgeth him: the word that I have spoken, the same shall judge him in the last day." St John 12:48 Paul and his disciples said go by what we say; now there is a choice to be made. I'm not sure how a person can see the movie recently about the crucifixion of Jesus and preach from The Acts –Jude? "For I have not spoken of myself: but the Father which sent me, he gave me a commandment, what I should say, and what I should speak." 49 "And I know that his commandment is life everlasting: whatsoever I speak therefore, even as the Father said unto me, so I speak." 50 How anybody can say that God is Jesus, God is God, and God is the Spirit or Holy Ghost I have never been able to figure that out. It even confounds the Islam faith also, but they dropped the Holy Ghost and included Mary as a part of the trinity. Why anyone would pray to Mary I don't have a clue? As the Muslims say how does 1+1+1=1. What if it is the one creator of 1+1+1=4 in the God Head. The' Spirit in Genesis 1:2, Jesus, Holy Ghost and God the creator is four or quadruple.

Jesus washes his disciples' feet
Chapter 13

"Jesus saith to him, (Peter) He that is washed needeth not save (only) to wash his feet, but is clean every whit (bit or way) and ye are clean, (on the outside) but not all." St John 13:10 Peter needed to be born again. I believe Jesus is speaking about Peter's heart. "A new heart also will I give you" Ezekiel 36:26 which to my knowledge none of the disciples received? The Bible is difficult to understand, that is why the preachers grab on to a few verses like faith, grace, hope, believe, and the money.

Jesus the way to the Father
Chapter 14

On this planet earth, is there anything more important than to live with God in His kingdom when a person dies? "Jesus saith unto him, I am the way, the truth, and the life: no man cometh unto the Father but by me." St John 14:6 Did God need help by the preaching of Paul, and his disciples? Paul never met Jesus nor at that time there wasn't anything written down that he could study? How could Paul's half of the Bible be the same as the Gospels?

Salvation, in a physical sense is found in a verse St John when a person believes in their heart of one of the works that Jesus did. St John 14:11 Superficially believing, as in St John 3:16 it has nothing to do with salvation, one of the most quoted scriptures in the Bible, and memorized by children. When I believed in my heart that I could heal my mother it was one of the works that Jesus did, and that is what triggered the Spirit to act. It removed my heart that I was born with and gave me another from God. Ezekiel 36:26 The new Spirit or Holy Ghost, is another matter that came thirty days later, and that verse is found in 26 & 27 but 25 comes after the new heart but before the new Spirit. "Then will I sprinkle clean water upon you, (born again) And ye shall be clean: from all your filthiness, and from all your idols, will I cleanse you." 25 After receiving my new heart, God put a fast on me for three days and nights, the beginning of the cleaning up process.

"If ye love me, keep my commandments." St John 14:15 (It includes receiving the new heart and when keeping the commandments Jesus said, He would pray to the Father to give you the new Spirit) 'Holy Ghost to be with a person forever.

"And I will pray (asked) the Father, and he shall give you another Comforter, (after the new heart) Spirit or Holy Ghost, that (he) may abide with you forever;" 16

Scriptures, about receiving the Holy Ghost are from St John 14:17 through 26Then In 21 It reads; that the Father loves those that have been redeemed, OR 'are the preachers right,' does God love everybody? Like at the time of Noah's flood, or Sodom when they couldn't find 10 righteous people.

"Hereafter I will not talk much with you: for the prince of this world cometh, and hath nothing in me." St John 14:30 Do you think God is in charge of all the religions of the world? That God has created all the different doctrines and bibles in the world? Common sense should be enough to warn or give notice to the religious community that there is something wrong. Is money all that valuable to make a person blind to the truth? I will give Timothy a little credit, is he speaking to the bar tender when he said, "the love of money is the root of all evil" or to the religious community? In the mega-churches are they talking through their wallet? It doesn't appear to me, they certainly aren't using their head, and the sad part is, everything they say is found in the Bible with most of it what Paul or his disciples said. Doesn't it say Jesus is the way the truth and the life or is Paul the way the truth and the life as he said?

"Ye are my friends, if ye do whatsoever I command you." St John 15:14 Paul and his disciples will tell you their way is the only way. "Ye have not chosen me, but I have chosen you, and ordained you,----." 16 My dad was proud that he was an ordained minister in the Assembly of God Church, that couldn't remember going to school. He only preached about four years. His salvation plan was that a person had to, "pray through," and I never found out when you got through, what happened. The last time that we went to church or Sunday school, I believe the teacher told him that Billy Graham said all you had to do was believe, and that is what got the fireworks started, our last day of church.

The hatred of the world

"If the world, hate you, ye know that it hated me before it hated you." St John 15:18 Billy was at least once voted in as, 'the most admired man in the United States.' Do you see anything wrong with that? "If ye were of the world, the world would love his own: because ye are not of the world, but I have chosen you out of the world, therefore the world hateth you." 19 It reads Paul loved them, and they loved Paul, do you see anything wrong with that?

"If I had not come and spoken unto them, they had not had sin: but now they have no clock (covering) for their sin." 22 "He that hateth me, hateth my Father also." 23 "But when the Comforter is come, whom I will send unto you from the Father, even the Spirit of truth, which proceedeth from the Father, he (Holy Ghost or Spirit) shall testify of me:" 26 What part of this verse do you think it means speaking in tongues? " And ye also shall bear witness, because ye have been with me from the beginning." 27 Before the earth was made God had those He called, but few chosen, which is the sad part. "So the last shall be first, and the first last: for many be called, but few chosen." St Matthew 20:16 ""For many are called, but few are chosen." St Matthew 22:14

Jesus speaks of his leaving and the coming Comforter

"Nevertheless I tell you the truth; It is expedient for you that I go away: for if I go not away, the Comforter (Holy Ghost or Holy Spirit) will not come unto you; but if I depart, I will send (him)unto you." St John 16:7 At 12/30/1968 at 6:30am I received it in my mouth. St Matthew It reads, it lighting upon him, "as a dove" but it never, it went in His mouth as it did mine. St Matthew 3:16 Verses15:26 and 16:7 above repeats almost the same thing, so how could it be truthful in Luke the first chapter, of the presents of the Holy Ghost?

"I have yet many things to say unto you, but ye cannot bear (grasp) them now." St John 16:12 He answered and said unto them, because it is given unto you to know the mysteries of the kingdom of heaven, but to them it is not given." St Matthew 13:11 (Saved or unsaved ?) "---thou hast hid these things from the wise and prudent, and has revealed them unto babes." St Matthew 11:25

Sorrow to turn into joy

Most preachers will tell you,' if you are not joyful,' that is how I can tell, you are not saved. The Bible tells us that those in the world are joyful, but those that have been redeemed will be joyful at the end time. How can a person be joyful when they know the truth? Are all the doctrines from God? Are all the religious organizations from God? Are all the bibles from God? Defacing your body is that safe to do, when Jesus said His body is a temple? Speaking in tongues as being of the (Holy Ghost) is that from God? When it is, 'as a dove' that goes in the mouth, the way Jesus received it. The truth is sad, not joyful when a person knows the mystery. "Verily, verily, I say unto you, that ye shall weep and lament, but the world shall rejoice: and ye shall be sorrowful, but your sorrow shall be turned into joy." St John 16:20 Sunday night a preacher said if you don't have Joy you don't have grace.

Does God love everybody? For the Father himself loveth you, because ye have loved me, and have believed that I came out from God." St John 16;27 "---and he that loveth me shall be loved of my Father, and I will love him, and will manifest myself to him." St John 14:21 Ezekiel 36:26-27

"And the glory (Holy Ghost) which thou gavest me I have given them: that they may be one, even as we are one:" St John 17:22 One in goals, and the glory is when Jesus received the Holy Ghost in St Matthew because it is the only way to the kingdom of God. St Matthew 3:16 "Be ye therefore perfect, even as your Father which is in heaven is perfect." St Matthew 5:48

The betrayal and arrest of Jesus

I couldn't say it better then the movie, "The Passion of Christ." It shows humanity, that they say God loves at its worst, but I'm not to say how much of it was made up.

The crucifixion

The preachers say a lot of what happened during the crucifixion. Most of what they say I believe they get it from The Acts-Jude or make it up, that He went to hell, took on our diseases, our unhappiness, etc.. I believe Jesus was the perfect sacrifice, to achieve, the righteousness of God. He fulfilled the sacrifices of Leviticus for this dispensation eliminating all of the rules that governed that dispensation of the Old Testament.

Jesus appears to Mary Magdalene
And His disciples

"And seeth two angels in white sitting, the one at the head, and the other at the feet, where the body of Jesus had lain." St John 20:12 When Jesus finished His time in the wilderness after receiving the Holy Ghost this happened. "Then the devil leaveth him, and, behold, (that's what I saw, and the angels were clothed in white) angels came and ministered unto him." St Matthew 4:11 (Made the demons flee) I'm the only mortal that saw an angel in a Sunday school class that I know of, and blurted out, "the day of judgment is coming, "Behold, I will send you Elijah the prophet before the coming of the great and dreadful day of the Lord." Malachi 4:5 Now all I have to do is find someone to believe me, it is strange God made the earth and heavenly bodies, but they can't believe my redemption, a nonfiction story.

"And many other signs truly did Jesus in the presence of his disciples, which are not written in this book:" 30 "But these are written, that ye might believe that Jesus is the Christ, (Paul and his disciples used the word Christ as being God) the Son of God: and that believing ye might have life through his name." 31 I found out that Ezekiel is true, but not in sequence of occurrences, it is the mystery of God, but Jesus spoke allegorically, or in parables, or plain language. 36:26-25-27

On T V they had what is called 'game changers' last night. That is people that the experts believe had something to do with the course of humanity. The most famous of all was Jesus which of course was not one of the game changers. The problem with him is the parables that He spoke, and the understanding of those parables. Those that came after Him that were redeemed understand the parables or as Jesus spoke allegorically or even literally at times. Those that are redeemed could be 'game changers' but if no one believes them they're not going to change anything. All the different religions on the earth are going to remain the same.

"ye are of your father the devil, and the lusts of your father ye will do. He was a murder from the beginning, and abode not in the truth, because there is no truth in him. When he speaketh a lie, he speaketh of his own: for he is a liar, and the father of it." St John 8:44 How could I expect any help from the Devils children? If they never believed Jesus how can I expect any help from any of the religious communities? "And because I tell you the truth, ye believe me not." 8:45 In other words they never believed the parables, and the simple truth is they never understood them. It was designed this way by God the Father so that Jesus would get to the cross, and the Word that He spoke would be written down for mankind, that those redeemed, would understand the parables.

"At that time Jesus answered and said, I think thee, O Father, Lord of heaven and earth, because thou hast hid these things from the wise and prudent, and hast reveled them unto babes." St Matthew 11:25 (Those redeemed, or saved)

If there are no 'game changers' religiously, then it will be as it was in the days of Noah and the Bible will be true again. "Verily I say unto you, This generation shall not pass, till all these things be fulfilled." St Matthew 24:34" Heaven and earth shall pass away, but my words shall not pass away." 35 "But of that day and hour knoweth no man, no, not the angels of heaven, but my Father only." 36 "But as the days of Noah were, so shall also the coming of the Son of man be."37

"But he that is greatest among you shall be your servant." St Matthew 23:11 That is easier said than done. Who would believe a carpenter, from Wyoming, that graduated from a vocational school? Shall' is it will happen, and should' it might not happen which one will happen? Can you see those in some of these Meg-a Churches, the pastor sitting on the back seat? I can't.

Chapter 11

Is God Love?

"And God saw that the wickedness of man was great on the earth, and that every imagination of the thoughts of his heart was only evil continually." Genesis 6:5

"And it repented (grieved) the Lord that he had made man on the earth, and it grieved him at his heart." 6:6

"But those things which proceed out of the mouth come forth from the heart: and they defile the man." St Matthew 15:18 "For out of the heart proceed evil thoughts, murders, adulteries, fornications, thefts, false witness, blasphemies:" 19

There were only eight people on Noah's boat, and it only reads that Noah was a just man and perfect in his generations, and Noah walked with God. The others on the boat were they perfect in God's eyes, or to replenish the earth?

"And the Lord God commanded the man, saying, Of every tree of the garden thou mayest freely eat." Genesis 2:16 17 "But of the tree of the knowledge of good and evil, thou shalt not eat of it: for in the day that thou eatest thereof thou shalt surely die." 17 Evidently the original sin only comes down through the generations, from the male, because how could Jesus be free from sin because Mary was His mother, conceived by the Spirit of Genesis 1:2. The Holy Ghost mentioned in St Matthew is not biblical, as the conceiver of Mary, because the Holy Ghost wasn't to be until after Jesus went back to His Father. St Matthew 1:18 It was the Spirit in Genesis 1:2 that was the conceiver of Mary. St John 16:7

Eve did eat of the knowledge of good and evil, and gave also unto her husband with her, and he did eat. It doesn't matter what the tree consisted of God told them not to eat of it. Than we read of the curse on the earth. Genesis 3:14-21

In Sodom and Gomorrah they couldn't find ten people that were righteous, and God destroyed those two cities because their sin was deplorable to God, 'it is His party.'

To get God's people the Israelites out of Egypt, we have all the plagues up to the death of the first born in the land of Egypt. How much love did that take? The first born at the time of the birth of Jesus were killed, trying to kill the Son of God. "---and slew all the children that were in Bethlehem, and in all the coasts thereof, from two years old and under, according to the time which he had diligently inquired of the wise men." St Matthew 2:16

In Leviticus we have the sacrifices for sin usually animals.

We have in the Old Testament wars that usually pertained to the Israelites, which God always favored. In Joshua chapter 10 "The defeat of the Amorites the Lord cast down great stones from heaven upon them unto A-ze'kah, and they died:" There were more which died with hailstones than the children of Israel slew with the sword. Joshua needed more time to defeat the Amorites he spoke to the Lord for permission to stop the Sun? Joshua 10:12 "Sun stand thou still upon Gibeon: and thou, Moon, in the valley af Ajalon" 13 "And the sun stood still, and the moon stayed, until the people had avenged themselves upon their enemies." Why make the sun still when the heavy hitters say it is not the sun, but the earth that is moving? What if the earth is still and the Sun is circling the earth. I have read that in Russia that is what is believed, and two books "A Geocentricity Primer" and "The Genocentric Bible 6" by Gerardus D. Bouw, Ph,D. He believes the earth is still in one place, with the Sun going around it.

Is God still love?

The Old Testament is bloody with other wars that you never hear preached about, but what about mankind from the crusades to the present?

The crusades marked the brutality and ruthlessness of both sides, and Christians believed the slaughter showed God's approval.

What if you look out the window, what do you see?

"For many are called but few chosen." St Matthew 22:14 It is beyond me why I haven't heard any preacher worn people to not get a tattoo. I don't think that is a good idea. Jesus said His body is a temple. "---Is not the life more than meat, and the body than raiment?" St Matthew 6:25 " ---Destroy this temple, and in three days I will raise it up" St John 2:19 "But he spake of the temple of his body." 21 In the concordance it reads A house or dwelling (could it be a person's body allegorically?). When I was in the Navy only a few sailors had a tattoo but now it seems almost everyone you meet has one. The preachers would lose most of their congregation if they said anything.

St Matthew 20:16 "So the last shall be first, and the first last: for many be called, but few chosen." St Matthew 20:16" For many are called, but few are chosen" 22:14 "Because strait is the gate: and narrow is the way, which leadeth unto life, and few there be that find it." St Matthew 7:14

"And there shall in no wise enter into it anything that defileth, neither whatsoever worketh abomination, or maketh a lie: but they which are written in the lamb's book of life." Revelation 21:27 "No man can come to me, except the Father which hath sent me draw him: and I will raise him up at the last day." St John 6:44 (Worketh abomination= doing things that God doesn't approve of. Wouldn't a tattoo be one of those things? Remember, the Father in heaven must draw a person to Him, and after a person is saved their name is written in the lamb's book of life.

My friend on the ship called me Mutton's that was ironic because God has always mentioned lamb's one way or the other.

Who maketh a lie? 22:15 "For without are dogs, and sorcerers, and whoremongers, and murderers, and idolaters, and whosoever loveth and maketh a lie." Revelation 22:15 Wouldn't that be those in the religious world that start from scratch, the many different religious denomination. "But seek ye first the kingdom of God, and his righteousness: and all these things shall be added unto you." St Matthew 6:33

Does it say anything about getting your aunt, 'thinking she is doing God a service' to pay your way through a divinity school. What kind of righteousness is that? What about being born again first, that is what the verse mean's. Without God's righteousness a person then would be making a lie for himself. To put it bluntly they are not saved. I stayed drunk most of the time, until I was thirty one years old, who did Jesus say he came to save, wasn't it the sinner?

"For I say unto you, that except your righteousness shall exceed the righteousness of the scribes and Pharisees, ye shall in no case enter into the kingdom of heaven." St Matthew 5:20 The reason for this is salvation is physical receiving a new heart and Spirit as told in this book for this dispensation.

If you can't see anything on the earth that literally turns your stomach, it is an exceptionable day. "And God saw that the wickedness of man was great in the earth, and that every imagination of the thoughts of his heart was only evil continually." Genesis 6:5 Is it any different today? On T V last night it said Russia has five times the murder rate, then the United States.

The crusades according to the Moslems have never ended, the endeavor of wanting every human being dead, if they are not of their faith or religion. Accordingly this will never stop until they convert everybody. You can pay rent and live.

Sense the crusades until about 1900 I consider life was relatively mild' because this country had a lot of different denominations but were tolerant of each other. I believe that has changed recently, in the fact that Islam wants you dead.

Sense 1900 according to the religious community the love for man, has really shown its ugly head.

Millions of Jews were put in the oven, Stalin killed a lot of his own countrymen. In Cambodia after the Viet Nam war death was everywhere. Millions were killed during World War 1, World War 11, Korean War, Viet Nam, and the first war with Iraq. A magistrate in Kuwait told Husain that they were going to make prostitutes out of all their women. According to a journalist George Piro talking to Husain before he was hung, said, that is why Iraq attacked Kuwait in the first place. What the answer girl said in the news paper it was over oil, and that is what is in the archives in Washington D.C. Husain then set his own oil wells on fire if he won the war. Does that make any sense to you?

Than we had the building blown up in Oklahoma City, and on to the Trade Center in New York where 3000 people lost their lives. It brought on a skirmish with Afghanistan but the good targets to bomb were in Iraq, and Husain said he would like to kill the presidents dad that had a lot to do with moving on to Iraq. Millions lost their lives in Iraq, and the soldiers of the United States.

We have had the slaughter in Africa, and it seems like at the moment the whole Middle East is ablaze with no end in sight with the Isis movement.

Yes, God certainly loves the world as it says in St John "For God so loved the world" St John 3:16 or did God get it right in "And it repented (grieved) the Lord that he had made man on the earth, and it grieved him at his heart." Genesis 6:6 On the computer a man said there were 38,000 different denominations in the world, somebody must be wrong.

Which churches doctrine do you think is right?

It reads, "There will be a generation" that will witness all things. I was born in 1937 in the middle of World War 11 we surly have seen the decadence of men, with his inventions, sense then. It reads that men will (think) they are gods in Genesis, or they will become gods.

Recently it has been noted that 1968 was the turning point for a lot of things, and that was the year that I had my redemption 12/1/1968 at 9pm, and received the Holy Ghost 30 thirty days after the born again experience of receiving the new heart.

One Sunday at the end of a Sunday school class I saw an Angel toward the ceiling and I blurted out, 'the day of judgment is coming.' That night I never went to church but was studying the Bible. At about midnight 12/30/1968 there was a voice that said change the water into wine in a glass of water, the second chapter of St John. Asking God to do that, nothing happened in the glass, there was a sensation that came over me from my fingers to my toes. Having found nothing in the New Testament scriptures to validate it, there is only one explanation. In Genesis 3:22 "And the Lord God said, Behold, the man is become as one of us, to know good and evil: and now, lest he put forth his hand, and take also of the TREE OF LIFE, EAT, AND LIVE FOR EVER:" Was I given the tree of life? It reads in Revelation "He that hath an ear, let him hear what the Spirit saith unto the churches; He that overcometh (from the false doctrine) shall not be hurt of the second death." Revelation 2:11 A person needs a first death to have a second death? That happened when my heart I was born with, was removed, and replaced. In the seventh verse it reads "---To him that overcometh will I give to eat of the (tree of life) which is in the midst of the paradise of God." Revelation 2:7 Now the tree of life is not in the forest but in the paradise of God, as it reads in Genesis.

"Blessed and holy is he that hath part in the first resurrection: (the first death was when I received the new heart) on such the second death hath no power, but they shall (no doubt) be priests of God and of Christ, and shall reign with him a thousand years." Revelation 20:6 Ezekiel 36:26

What has always been confusing is in Revelation "And death and hell were cast into the lake of fire. This is the second death." Revelation 20:14 "But the fearful, and unbelieving, and the abominable, and murderers, and whoremongers, and sorcerers, and Idolaters, and all liars, shall have their part in the lake which burneth with fire and brimstone, which is the second death." Revelation 20:8 The second death hath no power, 'if your saved." In other words they will reign with Him a thousand years verse 20:6.

"For God doth know that in the day ye eat thereof, than your eyes shall be opened, and ye shall be as gods, knowing good and evil." Genesis 3:5 There were two trees in the Garden of Eden, the tree of the knowledge of good and evil, and the tree of life, to live forever. "So he drove out the man; and he placed at the east of the garden of Eden cherubim, and a flaming sword which turned every way, to keep the way of the tree of life."Genesis 3:24 It must have been this tree of life that I was given, and it is debatable if I will ever die? I'm 80 years old and I would be concerned, at when the end time is going to be. My biblical name is Elijah of Malachi "Behold, I will send you Elijah the prophet before the coming of the great and dreadful day of the Lord:" Malachi 4:5

Chapter 12

Revelation

: "For I testify unto every man that heareth the words of the prophecy of this book, If any man shall add unto these things, God shall add unto him the plagues that are written in this book:" Revelation 22:18 19 "And if any man shall take away from the words of the book of this prophecy, God shall take away his part out of the book of life, and out of the holy city, and from the things which are written in this book." 19

It is my opinion, that God is only having John give the warning to Revelation, and not the whole Bible. What other book of the Bible is almost all prophecy like Revelation?

Chapter 13

Satan

What are some of the attributes of Satan? It doesn't say exactly why he was removed from the kingdom of heaven or God, but he was. It gave us a little hint when he said that he wanted to exalt my throne above the stars of God. Satan said that he will sit also upon the mount (all) of the congregation (churches and religious organizations) Satan also said that he would be like God. To be like God than he needed an advocate like Jesus was to God, He chose Paul to be his advocate. In all of this God could see in his heart the evil that was there. Jesus said that people will follow the person that comes after me. Didn't Paul come after Jesus? He was never heard of before that. When Stephen was stoned to death, It never took a rocket scientist to see that they couldn't stone everybody on the earth, so why not contaminate the Word of God as it is today. Everybody waves there bible around, and speak of how wonderful and infallible it is cover to cover. Isaiah 14:13-14 St John 5:43 "How can ye believe, which receive honor one of another, and seek not the honor (salvation or truth) that cometh from God only?" St John 5:44 What about Isaiah 14:13-14 and St John 5:43

In The Acts chapter 6 and 7 I see very little that is not true coming from Stephen, and it reads he was full of the Holy Ghost. Because in the second chapter of The Acts it reads of a different Holy Ghost than what the author received, and experienced, then he questions chapter 6-7.

When Satan lied to Eve it is another attribute of Satan. It is also an attribute of mankind. It reads that after a person is lucky enough to be born, a person starts speaking lies. "The wicked are estranged from the womb: they go astray as soon as they be born, speaking lies." Psalm 58:3

"I speak that which I have seen with my Father: and ye do that which ye have seen with your father." St John 8:38 "At that time Jesus was talking to the children of Abraham who needed a savior." "I know that ye are Abraham's seed: but ye seek to kill me, because my word hath no place in you." 8:37 "But now ye seek to kill me, a man that hath told you the truth, which I have heard of God: this did not Abraham." 40

"Ye are of your father the devil, and the lusts of your father ye will do. He was a murderer from the beginning, and abode not in the truth, because there is no truth in him. When he speaketh a lie, he speaketh of his own: for he is a liar, and the father of it." St John 8:,44 "And because I tell you the truth, ye believe me not." 45 "He that is of God hearth God's words, ye therefore hear them not, because ye are not of God." 47

"Verily, verily I say unto you, if, a man keep my saying, he shall never see death." St John 8:51 Could that verse be true? In just a few days I will be eighty years old. According to St John, I was born again and received the Holy Ghost in my mouth the same as Jesus on His first breath, when He came out of the water baptism. I saw an angel as Jesus did at the end of His time in the wilderness in St Matthew. The angel I saw was in a Sunday school class in San Pedro, California. I blurted out, "the day of judgment is coming" the same thing happened to me as in Ezekiel. It reads also that a person won't be hurt of the second death in Revelation. If you won't be hurt of the second death, doesn't a person need a first death? I was clinically dead when the heart that I was born with was removed and replaced by one from God. I believe God gave me the 'tree of life' because there is no other explanation that I have found in the King James Bible of 1611. God asked me to change the water into wine verbally as in St John and nothing happened in the glass, but in my body. In Genesis it reads if you eat of the 'tree of life' you will live forever, as I have stated in this book. The question is am I going to die a physical death?

"Verily I say unto you, All these things shall come upon this generation." St Matthew 23:36 It is mentioned, the generation of Jesus Christ. "Verily I say unto you, this generation shall not pass, till all these things be fulfilled." 24:34 Heaven and earth shall pass away, but not my words shall not pass away. (shall and should)

"Ye do the deeds of your father, Then said they to him, We be not born of fornication; we have one Father, even God." St John 8:41"Jesus said unto them, If God were your Father, ye would love me: for I proceed forth and come from God; neither came I of myself, but he sent me." 42 "He that hath my commandments, and keepeth them, he it is that loveth me: and he that loveth me shall be loved of my Father: and I will love him, and will manifest myself to him." St John 14:21 (The second time Jesus manifested himself to me was giving me the Holy Ghost, it is a must have, to be saved) That is why it is unwise to blasphemy it. "Wherefore I say unto you, All manner of sin and blasphemy shall be forgiven unto men but the blasphemy against the Holy Ghost shall not be forgiven unto men." St Matthew 12:31 "And whosoever speaketh a word against the Son of man, it shall be forgiven him: but whosoever speaketh against the Holy Ghost, it shall not be forgiven him, neither in this world, neither in the world to come." 32

"Ye are of your Father the devil, and the lusts of your father ye will do. He was a murderer from the beginning, and abode not in the truth, because there is no truth in him. When he speaketh a lie, he speaketh of his own: for he is a liar, and the father of it." St John 8:44 "And because I tell you the truth, ye believe me not." 45 "He that is of God heareth God's words: ye therefore hear them not, because ye are not of God." 47

"Verily, verily, I say unto you, If a man keep my saying, he shall never see death." 51 (It reads in Revelation, that a person will not be hurt of the second death) When my heart was removed, and replaced I had my first death.

"For out of the heart proceed evil thoughts, murders, adulteries, fornications, thefts, false witness, blasphemies:" St Matthew 15:19 "These are the things which defile a man: but to eat with unwashed hands defileth not a man." 20 When Eve took the forbidden fruit, and gave it to Adam I believe their bodies were physically changed, that is the reason a person receives the new heart and a new Spirit.

(King James Bible of 1611) "When they fast I will not hear, their cry; and when they offer burnt offering, and an oblation, I will not accept them: but I will consume them by the sword, and by the famine, and by the pestilence." Jeremiah 14:12 "Then said I Ah, Lord God! Behold the prophets say unto them, ye shall not see the sword, neither shall ye have famine; but I will give you assured peace in this place:" 13 (The redeemed)

Oblation is an interesting word it means an offering of a sacrifice or the thing offered, it reads, 'I will not accept them.' It seems to be, most all religions of the world has oblation as offerings to God for appeasement to satisfy the demands of their denomination. The dictionary as an example mentions the Eucharist, and I have said it is unnecessary but what about other oblations? Baptism in water, it never happened to me by man, and the Catholics Mormons and Moslem have a lot of this sort of thing from jihad to special temples.

"Then the Lord said unto me, the prophets prophesy (preach) lies in my name: I sent them not, neither have I commanded them, neither spake unto them: they prophesy unto you a false vision and divination, and a thing of nought, and the deceit of their heart." Jeremiah 14:14

Paul was on his own without God, and the preachers' slap each other's back without knowledge of the truth. "I am come in my Father's name, and ye receive me not: (Jesus) if another shall come in his own name, him ye will receive." (Believe, Paul) St John 5:43 "How can ye believe, which receive honor one of another, and seek not the honor that cometh from God only?" 44

Mark put it this way, "And he said, that which cometh out of the man, that defileth the man." (out of the mouth) St Mark 7:20 "For from within, out of the heart of man, proceed evil thoughts, adulteries, fornications, murders, 21 "Thefts, covetousness, (greed) wickedness, deceit, (the act of deceiving, or lying, to lie; a dishonest action or trick. the quality of being deceitful.) lasciviousness, (expressing lust or tending to excite lust) an evil eye, blasphemy, pride, foolishness:" 22 Women don't give it a second thought, expressing lust in men, with their nakedness, as being an abomination to God.

"All these evil things come from within, and defile the man."23 Most preachers they love to speak Paul's words, without knowing his words never came from God.

"He that is of God hearth God's words: ye therefore hear them not, because ye are not of God." St John 8:47

"Beware of false prophets which come to you in sheep's clothing, but inwardly they are ravening wolves." St Matthew 7:15

"Hereafter I will not talk much with you: for the prince of this world cometh, and hath nothing in me." St John 14:30 When Lucifer was removed from heaven in Isaiah, it reads that he (Lucifer) would sit upon the mount (all) of the congregation, (Churches and religious organizations.) "For thou hast said in thine heart, I will ascend into heaven, I will exalt my throne above the stars of God: (churches) I will sit also upon the mount (all) of the congregation, (churches) in the sides of the north: (North America) Isaiah 14:13 "I will ascend above the heights of the clouds; I will be like the most High." 14 (God) To do this Lucifer needed an advocate, and Paul fit that bill. "I am come in my Father's name, and ye receive me not: (Jesus) if another shall come in his own name, him (Paul) ye will receive." St John 5:43 (Believe is superficial according to the standards, but unknown to the populace God made, "belief in your heart" a catalyst for the Spirit to act for your redemption.) Receive = To take in one's possession, to encounter; experience; take the effect or force of. (I said Ezekiel 36:26-25-27 happened to me physically, it explains it in St John chapter 3:3-5 but allegorically.)

"Therefore said some of the Pharisees, This man is not of God, because he keepeth not the Sabbath day, others said, how can a man that is a sinner do such miracles? And there was a division among them." St John 9:16 Where have I heard the phrase, 'divide and conquer?' That seems to be exactly what Lucifer does, with all the various denominations, and religious organizations. I believe that is a military term, and common sense tells me it would probably work militarily or religiously for Satan.

Islam has the same disparities of being divided as does the religions of North America.

The war in Iraq, 2014 is between the Sunnis and Shiites, and the United States name came up. When Mohammad died he never left a person to be in charge which has been the difficulty between them. I read in a book that the Sunni believe the Shiite is worse than the Jew.

Good and corrupt fruit

"Either make the tree good, and (his) fruit good; or else make the tree corrupt, and his fruit corrupt: for the tree is know by his fruit." St Matthew 12:33 34 "O generation of vipers, how can ye being evil, speak good things? For out of the abundance of the heart the mouth speaketh." 34 "A good man out of the good treasure of the heart bringeth forth good things: and an evil man out of the evil treasure bringeth forth evil things." 35 "For by thy words thou shalt be justified, and by thy words thou shalt be condemned." 37 According to this it is the words from your mouth will either justify or condemn a person. Is it safe to preach from The Acts- Jude or Qur'an when it never came from God? Sin is no problem that is what Jesus died for, but words from the mouth of a person, not sanctioned by God, there are no forgiveness only Judgment.

Common sense should reveal to mankind that what has happened is Allah never showed his face, until Muhammad declared him, sanctified by his wives. They call it sound doctrine?

When Jesus was in the wilderness Satan tried to get Him to worship him but Jesus said it is written, "Thou shalt worship the Lord thy God, and him only shalt thou serve.---" St Matthew 4:10

If that is true what are the chances for people to enter the kingdom of God going by the Words that God hasn't sanctioned? Paul was on his own as it reads in St John 5:43.

"And I saw an angel come down from heaven, having the key of the bottomless pit and a great chain in his hand." Revelation 20:1. "And he laid hold on the dragon, that old serpent, which is the Devil, and Satan, and bound him a thousand years." 2 "And cast him into the bottomless pit, and shut him up, and set a seal upon him, THAT HE SHOULD DECEIVE THE NATIONS NO MORE, till the thousand years should be fulfilled: and after that he must be loosed a little season." 3 (a short time) We might be in the period of Satan's short release, but that could last a thousand years?

We have had over two thousand years sense Jesus went to His Father in heaven. It would be nice if the Holy Ghost inside of me, would explain this phenomenon. When it occurred or did it occur, the beginning and end of the thousand years. If it occurred already, are we in the period that Satan was let loose for a season? It would be nice if a person knew the reason that he was let loose? Sense 1900 a lot has occurred, but wars seem to have been in existence continuously from the time of man, but it seems to be getting worse every day all over the world.

There is every kind of religion that a person could think up. Jesus said His body was a temple, so whose body is it, your body might not be your body to deface? That might be why it is written that many are called but few chosen. The wars, and diseases, are getting more vicious every day. Some of the diseases are incurable. I understand global warming is upsetting nature that will eventually, effect if it hasn't already, mankind. Because of over population, etc. goods and services have become more expensive. Greed has become a nightmare and wasteful governments with their taxes, sale taxes, property taxes, lotteries, income taxes, gasoline taxes, etc. while money seems to be getting worthless in value.

Some of the disciples asked Jesus, tell us when shall be the sign of the end time? "Take heed lest any man deceive you: St Matthew 24:4 "For many shall come in my name, saying, I am Christ, and shall deceive many." St Mark 13:6 (I believe he is saying that many religious doctrines will appear that will deceive many.) I don't attend any Church, it should give some indication where we are at today. Paul and his disciples were the greatest deceivers?

"For nation shall rise against nation, and kingdom against kingdom: and there shall be earthquakes in diverse places, and there shall be famines and troubles: these are the beginning of sorrows." St Mark 13:8

I know Paul said the gospel must first be preached, but in St Mark it reads "And the gospel must first be published among all nations." St Mark 13:10 I have never heard a preacher say published they always say preached, and in St Matthew that is not what it reads "Take heed that no man deceive you." St Matthew 24:4 Every Tom, Dick, Harry, Mary, Judy, and Samantha, with a computer, has mostly fiction religious books in the public domain. So many that it is almost impossible to get any truth out. The Galilean religious book store's owner told me one time, fiction was all the Christians will buy, and if you don't leave I'm calling the police.

"And in the synagogue there was a man, which had a spirit of an unclean devil, (demon) and cried out with a loud voice." St Luke 4:32 How many other people have a spirit that is unclean? Wouldn't this encompass the human race, because of Adam's sin? That is what salvation is, it gives a person a new Spirit which is called the Holy Ghost, in the new Gospel message of Jesus. If a person is not saved, common sense tells me that they are unclean as far as being righteous. Without becoming righteous according to St Matthew it reads , seek ye first His righteousness. 6:33 St,

It also reads, unless you are born again, and receive the Holy Spirit, they can't live with God in his kingdom. St John 3:3-5

"Woe unto you, scribes and Pharisees, hypocrites!, For ye are like unto whited sepulchers, which indeed appear beautiful but are within full of dead men's bones, and of all uncleaeanness." St Matthew 23:27 " Woe unto you, scribes and Pharisees, hypocrites! For ye , make clean the outside of the cup and of the platter, (Your body) but within they are full of extortion and excess." St Matthew 23:25 Extortion is getting money by the misuse of authority. (Preacher's) The sad part is they don't know they are feeding their congregation false doctrine. Every church pastor will tell you that, "their way or the hi-way." As a carpenter from Wyoming do you think any of them would listen to me? Some of them would tell me they have a Divinity degree, top of the class. Jesus would say –you do. In St Matthew it is all about the religious leadership, and there fallacies the 23rd chapter.

Mohammad said: know that paradise is under the shades of the sword. " ---he that killeth with the sword must be killed with the sword---." Revelation 13:10

The sad part: it reads that Islam wants total dominance of the earth. You say it can't happen, but in Revelation there is a verse that reads like it does happen.

"And all that dwell upon the earth shall worship him, (Anti-Christ and or the false prophet Paul) whose names are not written in the book of life of the Lamb slain from the foundation of the world." Revelation 13:8 "And the devil that deceived them was cast into the lake of fire and brimstone, where the beast and the false prophet are, and shall be tormented day and night forever and ever. Revelation 20:10 The preachers will tell you that the false prophet will come in the future, and they say Elijah was John the Baptist that has already came.

"And it was given unto him to make war with the saints, and to (overcome) them: and power was given him over all kindreds, and tongues, and nations." Revelation 13:7 I believe this is about the anti-Christ ,'it can happen' the total dominance, of the earth by an evil force. "And all that dwell upon the earth shall worship him, whose names are not written in the book of life of the Lamb slain from the foundation of the world." 8

Chapter 14

God

God was the creator of the heavens and the earth. From the ground He made man, from man he took a rib out, and made a help mate called women. "I (God) have made the earth, the man and the beast that are upon the ground, by my great power and by my outstretched arm, and have given it unto whom it seemed meet (right) unto me." Jeremiah 27:5 It grieved God in His heart that He made man on the earth. Genesis 6:6 "Hast thou not known? Hast thou not heard, that the everlasting God, the Lord, the Creator of the ends of the earth, fainteth not, neither is weary? There is no searching of his understanding." Isaiah 40:28 People on the social net works try, and use their intellect, in understanding God.

It reads that to help him with His creation, He had the Spirit, help Him. Genesis 1:2 Along with this Spirit according to St John the Word was with God, but the time had not come for it to be made flesh. The Word would eventually be made flesh, and would be given the name of Jesus. Mary was conceived by the same Spirit when the time came about six thousand years later In St Matthew 1:18. It reads Mary was found with child of the Holy Ghost but it was a mistake, the Holy Ghost is a special Spirit for those that become saved or born again. Jesus received the Holy Ghost in the mouth, and it never became active again until Jesus went to His Father in heaven. "Nevertheless I tell you the truth: It is expedient for you that I go away: for if I go not away, the Comforter (Holy Ghost) will not come unto you; but if I depart I will send him unto you." St John 16:7 In the first chapter of Luke the Holy Ghost is mentioned several times but the author doesn't believe it happened the way as it is written.

In Leviticus the King James Bible of 1611 the sacrifices are mentioned or atonement for sin because of the righteousness of God. The Sacrifices had nothing to do with Love, it was all about righteousness. Just as Jesus never had anything to do with love it is all about sin must be eliminated, for a person to live with God in His kingdom. Jesus said it this way, "unless a person is born again (receive a new heart, and given the new Spirit called the Holy Ghost) he cannot enter into the kingdom of God." Jesus spoke in parables or allegorically so the stumbling block for mankind is the meaning of being born again and receiving the Spirit. I addressed this more fully in the chapter on Jesus.

When I was in the Navy I went with a woman that went to some kind of church. At the time I was not interested in going to church with her. At times I had my child with me, but divorced, I was married about three years, during my first enlistment in the Navy. She gave him a children's bible with all the pictures of gore in it, from the many wars that are recorded in the Bible. I threw it in the trash.

The God we serve was not hesitant in war, especially when it came to the apple of His eye the Jewish people. Some battles are recorded that there were thousands slaughtered. I can see that it should give Muhammad credibility when he slaughtered, what he called his enemies. I believe it shows that God is realistic, in dealing with reality or as they say He wasn't a wall flower or what we call a do-gooder. .

Would it be safe to use God as an example in regard to killing people? I don't think so, one of the Ten Commandments is, a person shall not kill, never mind what God does. In the end time death is going to be more natural than living, sanctioned by God. In Noah's flood there were only eight people on the boat. But, those that have been found guilty of a horrible crime for humanities sake putting them to death might be a deterrent. Remember, God was not hesitant when He felt like something must be done for humanities sake.

The difference in killing of people it was God himself in the Old Testament that was the instigator or supervisor, of most battles, and in the Qur'an it was Muhammad, himself, as the Moslem's put it, killed by the sword. The opposite in stature of Muhammad, was Jesus, and He never killed anybody but made people well.

A person must look at who is equal with one another? Wasn't Allah and God suppose to be equal but wasn't, with one a figurehead or imagination of Muhammad. Wasn't Muhammad and Jesus, each one the advocate of 'their' supreme being or 'their' god, but only one can be right? It doesn't seem to be in the cards that there are two Gods. Not even the Moslems believe there are two Gods.

In the book, "Unveiling Islam" Satan is mentioned very little, and I assume it is the same in the Qur'an. In this book I devoted a chapter on basically Satan's attributes, that will be the difference between heaven or hell, 'for all the people of the world,' and or their doctrines that they represent.

It is beyond me why the Bible and the religions of the world are in such a mess. The beginning of wisdom would be a person that agreed with that statement. I couldn't begin to express the names of all the denominations or religious organizations that are in the world. All I know is, I don't attend any church nor am I a member of any religious organization. That should tell a person something, that St John 3:16 is false doctrine along with The Acts 2:38. There are people in church that would die for those two verses. Those so called Christians, that are being killed all over the world which verses do they believe in? Sorry to say, salvation is physical that a person won't be told in any church doctrine, so are they being killed in vain. The sadness of the world would overcome me, but I believe God has made a way that I can tolerate it until Jesus comes back.

"No man putteth a piece of new cloth unto an old garment, for that which is put in to fill it up taketh from the garment, and the rent (tear) is made worse. Neither do men put new wine into old bottles: else the bottles break, and the wine runneth out, and the bottles perish: but they put new wine into new bottles, and both are preserved." St Matthew 9:16-17 My 'wine' is a metaphor, when I was given the new heart and new Spirit, so I could tolerate the discrepancies in the different religions, and both the (Holy Ghost & my-self) are preserved. It reads the Comforter will be in you forever.

Then came to him the disciples of John, saying, Why do we and the Pharisees fast often, but thy disciples fast not? And Jesus said unto them,

Can the children of the bride chamber mourn, as long as the bridegroom is with them? But the days will come, when the bridegroom shall be taken from them, and then shall they fast." St Matthew 9: 14-15 When I received the new heart I fasted three days and nights, also when receiving the Holy Ghost I fasted three days and nights, it wasn't my idea.

That is why I received a new heart physically and a new spirit in the mouth so that I could tolerate the information given to me by the new Spirit or Holy Ghost, or grasp the meaning of the parables or allegorical writing of the KJB of 1611. Which church has the two concepts as a part of their doctrine?

The three pages of Joel

My Dad who was an Assembly of God preacher until I was nine years old, I heard him say more than once when I was a child, 'read-em and weep.' I knew he was referring to the Bible, but people believe St John 3:16, why worry, be happy.

"The word of the Lord that came to Joel the son of Pe-thu'el." Joel 1:1 "Hear this ye old men, and give ear, all ye inhabitants of the land---." 2 (I believe when the word Lord is used it means God and the Spirit of Genesis, it has nothing to do with the other Spirit the Holy Ghost)

"The meat offering and the drink offering is cut off from the house of the Lord; (Churches) the priests, the Lord's ministers, mourn." 9 (They say send revival, or God show yourself.) The meat and drink metaphor is another way that God talks about being born again and receiving the Holy Ghost. Meat new Heart, and drink the Holy Ghost or Spirit St John 6:31-58

"Be ye ashamed, O ye husbandmen; (keepers of the flock) howl, O ye vinedressers, (those that make the church service look good) for the wheat and for the barley; (those inside the church) because the harvest of the field is perished." 11 (There isn't anyone at this time being saved in any church or religious organizations)

"Gird yourselves, and lament, ye priests: howl, ye ministers, of the alter: (most old fashion alters have been thrown in the trash, why have an alter, when all you have to do is raise your hand, "if you want it.") come, lie all night in sackcloth, (leave your $1000 suit and alligator shows at home) ye ministers of my God: for the meat offering and the drink offering is with holden from the house of your God." (g) Joel 1:13 (That is why I was saved after I left an alter of a protestant church, at a gas station, and received the Holy Ghost driving to work in a 1959 Ford)

"Sanctify ye a fast, call a solemn assembly, gather the elders and, all the inhabitants of the land unto the house of the Lord your God, and cry unto the Lord," 14 "Alas for the day! For the day of the Lord is at hand, and as a destruction from the Almighty shall it come."15 (It is His call and His alone, there is no doubt it will come.)

"Is not the meat (salvation) cut off before our eyes, yea, (also) joy and gladness from the house of our God?" 16 (There are those that see and know the mystery) "But blessed are your eyes, for they see: and your ears, for they hear." St Matthew 13:16 There are those that preach that if you don't have joy there is something wrong with you. " Verily, verily, I say unto you, that ye shall weep and lament, but the world shall rejoice: and ye shall be sorrowful, but your sorrow shall be turned into joy." St John 16:20 "No lion shall be there, nor any ravenous beast shall go up there on, it shall not be found there; but the redeemed (saved) shall walk there:" Isaiah 35:9 "And the ransomed of the Lord shall return, and come to Zion (God's kingdom or possibly the city of Jerusalem?) "With songs and everlasting joy upon their heads: they shall obtain joy and gladness, and sorrow and sighing shall flee away." 10

"The seed is rotten under their clods (what the churches are planting, their doctrine) the garners (churches) are laid desolate, the barns are broken down; for the corn is withered." Joel 1: 17 (the truth is not in the churches, and it has been going on generation after generation) When I was a child sitting in my dad's church I had felt at times a convictive Spirit (yes tearful), and that was what I was seeking over two months when I decided to find out,' if religion was real' at thirty one years old.

"And they brought young children to him, that he should touch them: and his disciples rebuked those that brought them." St Mark 10:13 "But when Jesus saw it, he was much displeased, and said unto them, Suffer (let) the little children to come unto me, and forbid them not: for of such is the kingdom of God." 14 "Verily I say unto you, who so ever shall not receive the kingdom of God as a little child, he shall not enter therein." 15 "And said, (Jesus) Verily I say unto you, except ye be converted, (saved, transformed, changed, redeemed, according to Ezekiel 36:26) and become as little children, ye shall not enter into the kingdom of heaven." St Matthew 18:3 "A new heart also (chosen and drawn by the Spirit) will I give you, and a new Spirit (Holy Ghost) will I put within you: (it will go in your mouth), and I will take away the stony heart (born with) out of your flesh, and I will give you a heart of flesh." (From God) Ezekiel 36:26 "John answered and said, A man can receive nothing, except it be given him from heaven." St John 3:27

"How do the beasts groan! The herds of cattle are perplexed, because they have no pasture; (truth) yea, the flocks of sheep (those in the religious organizations) are made desolate." Joel 1:18 (The sad part is, they don't know that, until it is going to be too late)

"O Lord, to thee will I cry: for the fire (word that has been preached) hath devoured the pastures (substance, or truth)) of the wilderness, and the flame hath burned all the trees of the field." 19 In church I have heard the song sung, (just like a tree planted by the water I will not be moved.) Jesus couldn't move the Sadducees or Pharisees either. The sad part, salvation wasn't for them but my generation of 1937? Jesus had His generation and Noah had his generation. There is a lot to be said for the end time generation. "Verily I say unto you, All these things shall come upon this generation." St Matthew 23:36

(It is about the end time calamity of the environment that is going to take place) "The beasts of the field cry also unto thee: for the rivers of water are dried up, and the fire hath devoured the pastures of the wilderness". (The food supply) Joel 1:20

In Revelation the seven churches there wasn't one of them that had the true doctrine, that Jesus died for.

The message to the church of Ephesus

"Nevertheless I have somewhat against thee, because thou hast left thy first love." Revelation 2:4 I found out when I was thirty one that being born again and receiving the Holy Ghost or Spirit is physical as in St John 3:3-5. The tree of life is separate from these two experiences.

"He that hath an ear, let him hear what the Spirit saith unto the churches; to him that overcometh (from false doctrine) will I give to eat of the tree of life, which is in the midst of the paradise of God." Revelation 2:7 (explained above) I believe I received the 'Tree of Life,' and according to Genesis a person will live forever. "And the Lord God said, Behold, the man is become as one of us, to know good and evil: and now, lest he put forth his hand, and take also of the 'tree of life,' and eat, and live forever: Genesis 3:22

The message to the church of Smyrna

Because I was given a new heart, and thirty days later received a new Spirit, it says "fear none of these things which thou shalt suffer: behold the devil shall cast some of you in prison, that ye may be tried; and ye shall have tribulation ten days: be thou faithful into death, and I will give thee a crown of life." Revelation 2;10 "---He that overcometh shall not be hurt of the second death." 11 Overcometh of what? (False doctrine) And a person needs to have a first death, to not be hurt of the second death. When I received the new heart it was my first death.

The message to the church at Pergamos

"I know thy works ---even where Satan's seat is: and thou holdest fast my name," Revelation 2:13 It could be the, 'Church of Christ.' "But I have a few things against thee, " 14 "---To him that overcometh will I give to eat of the hidden manna, and will give him a white stone, and in the stone a new name written, which no man knoweth saving (except) he that receiveth it." Revelation 2:17 (It is referring to the Holy Ghost it is a white Spirit or stone as it reads in St Matthew (like a dove a white blob) It never, Lighting on him" as it reads, St Matthew 3:16 It went in His mouth, on His first breath, when He came out of the water. That is why it reads straightway or immediately He came out of the water.

"He that hath an ear, let him hear what the Spirit (Holy Ghost) saith unto the churches; to him that overcometh will I give to eat of the hidden man'-na, and will give him a white stone, and in the stone a new name (Elijah) written, which no man knoweth saving (except) he that receiveth it." Revelation 2:17 "Our fathers did eat man'na in the desert; as it is written, He gave them bread from heaven to eat." St John 6:31 (to sustain life physically) "Then Jesus said unto them, Verily, verily, I say unto you, Moses gave you not that bread from heaven; but my Father giveth you the true bread from heaven." 32 "For the bread of God is he (Holy Ghost) which cometh down from heaven, and giveth life unto the world." 33 Most preachers would tell you it means Jesus, and not the Holy Ghost.

The message to the church at Thyatira

"I know thy works and charity, and service, and faith, and thy patience and thy works; and the last to be more than the first." Revelation 2:19 (Charity) "Notwithstanding, I have a few things against thee." 20 "And I will give him the morning star," 28 "---as I received of my Father." 27 Jesus received the Holy Ghost when he was baptized by John in the mouth, wouldn't this be the morning star? It is a white blob as the color of a star. "And he said unto them, ye shall drink indeed of my cup, and be baptized with the baptism that I am baptized with:" St Matthew 20:23 It explains why it reads 'as I received of my 'Father.'

The message to the church at Sardis

"----I know thy works, that thou hast a name that thou livest, and art dead." Revelation 3:1 "Be watchful, and strengthen the things which remain, that are ready to die: for I have not found thy works perfect before God." 2 "He that overcometh, the same shall be clothed in white raiment; and I will not blot out his name out of the book of life, but I will confess his name before my Father, and before his angels." 5 When I was given the new heart the Spirit that did the work was a light here it reads white raiment.

(Clothed in white raiment) When I was born again and received the new heart, there was a white light that entered my body with the power of God behind it. "If you love me, keep my commandments." St John 14:15 "And I will pray the Father, and he shall give you (another) Comforter, that he may abide with you forever;" 16 "Even the Spirit of truth: whom the world cannot receive, because it seeth him not, (the first comforter of white raiment is the new heart or born again) neither knoweth, him but ye know him; for he dwelleth with you, and shall be in you." 17 (The second Comforter is the Holy Ghost St John 3:5) "Verily, verily, I say unto thee,

(Nicodemus) Except a man be born again, he cannot (see) the kingdom of God." St John 3:3 (the power that God has to remove a person's heart, and give them a new heart;) "---Except a man be born of water (5rd verse, or born again 3rd verse) and of the Spirit, (Holy Ghost) cannot enter into the kingdom of God." St John 3:3-5 **(Born again and The Holy Ghost) Ezekiel 36:26--27** I'm not sure why God wrote water in verse 25 or St John 3:5 except to confuse people. Ezekiel 36:25 (It should read Born again)

The message to the church at Philadelphia

"Him that overcometh will I make a pillar in the temple of my God, and he shall go no more out: and I will write upon him the name of my God, ---which is new Jerusalem, which cometh down out of heaven from my God: and I will write upon him my new name." Revelation 3:12

"Behold, the days come, saith the Lord, that I will make a new covenant with the house of Israel, and with the house of Judah:" Jeremiah 31:31 "Not according to the covenant that I made with their fathers in the day that I took them by the hand to bring them out of the land of Egypt; which my covenant they brake, although I was a husband unto them, saith the Lord:" 32 "But this shall be the covenant that I will make with the house of Israel; (After those days,) saith the Lord, I will put my law in their inward parts, and write it in their hearts; and will be their God, and they shall be my people." 33 (this covenant cannot be broken as the other one was in Egypt) "A new heart also will I give you, and I will take away the stony heart (sinful heart) out of your flesh, and I will give you a heart of flesh." (from God) Ezekiel 36:26 ***and a new Spirit will I put within you."** 26 "And I will put my Spirit (within) you, and cause you to walk in my statutes, and ye shall keep my judgments, and do them." 27

"Thus saith the Lord, which giveth the sun for a light by day, and the ordinances of the moon and the stars for a light by night, which divideth the sea when the waves thereof roar; the Lord of hosts is his name:" Jeremiah 31:35

The message to the church at Laodicea

"I know thy works, that thou art neither cold nor hot---. " Revelation 3:15 "So then because thou art lukewarm, and neither cold nor hot, I will spew thee out of my mouth." 16 "Behold, I stand at the door, and knock: if any man hear my voice, and open the door, I will come in to him, and will sup with him, and he with me." 20 "To him that overcometh will I grant to sit with me in my throne, even as I also overcame, and set down with my Father in his throne." 21 "He that hath an ear, let him hear, what the Spirit saith unto the churches." 22 "But blessed are your eyes, for they see: and your ears for they hear." St Matthew 13:16 "For verily I say unto you, that many prophets (false) and righteous (believe their righteous) men have desired to see those things which ye see, and have not seen them; and to hear those things which ye hear, and have not heard them." 17

"He that hath an ear, let him hear what the Spirit saith unto the churches; To him that overcometh will I give to eat of the hidden manna, and will give him a white stone, and in the stone a new name written, which no man knoweth saving (except) he that receiveth it." (Elijah) Revelation 2:17 (the problem is no one wants to know what the truth is outside of what they already believe or through the preachers on the radio or the Trinity broadcasting Network.) I call them the back slappers, and Jesus said "How can ye believe, which receive honor one of another, and seek not the honor that cometh from God only?" St John 5:44 "let him hear what the Spirit saith unto the churches; to him that overcometh will I give to eat of the hidden man'-na," Revelation 2:17 (the Spirit of Genesis is uttering these words, and I know of no other verse like it. The manna came from God because it came from heaven to sustain their very life on this earth.) "For the (true) bread of God (manna) is he (Jesus or Holy Ghost) which cometh down from heaven, and giveth life (made it possible to get saved) unto the world." St John 6:33 I said made it possible because a person must receive the Holy Ghost in the mouth to truly be saved." And Jesus said unto them, I am the bread of life: he that cometh to me shall never hunger; and he that believeth on me shall never thirst." St John 6:35 Does your common sense tell you that God is speaking about, 'just believe' AS IN St John 3:16. It reads the bread or manna is hidden in Revelation 2:17

What about being born again and receiving the Spirit, (Holy Ghost) and unless this happens a person cannot enter into the kingdom of God. St John 3:5 Believeth is true, but it is only the condition or catalyst that triggers the Spirit of Genesis to operate. Born again is having the Spirit remove your heart that you were born with, and give you a new heart, without the original sin of Adam plus your accumulative sin. This must happen before the Holy Ghost or other Spirit will enter your clean body. When I was born again not only did I quit sin but it was the beginning of a three day and night fast, to get the body clean for the Holy Ghost to enter it.

"---To him that overcometh (from the false doctrine) will I give to eat of the hidden manna; and will give him a white stone, and in the stone a new name written, which no man knoweth except he that receiveth it." Revelation 2:17 " (What is that?) When Jesus was baptized by John it reads immediately He came out of the water, and on his first breath of air that He took in the mouth (because His nose was full of water) the white stone (parable) entered Jesus mouth which was the Holy Ghost. It reads it was, "like a dove" and it, "lighting on Him" but it didn't, it went in His mouth. St Matthew 3:16 Thirty days later I received the hidden manna, after my body was clean, the white stone or Holy Ghost in my mouth, after a vision was put on me to get my mouth open. On the word BOY it went in my mouth and down my throat. Even the Spirit of truth; (white stone) whom the world cannot receive, because it seeth him not,---" St John14:17 Except a man be born again, he cannot (see) the kingdom (power) of God" St John 3:3 "---neither knoweth him: but ye know him (Spirit, Holy Ghost or white stone) for he dwelleth with you, and shall (no doubt) be in you. St John 14:17 "And in the stone a new name written, which no man knowrth saving (except) he that receiveth it." Revelation 2:17 My new name is Elijah. "Behold, I will send you Elijah the prophet before the coming of the great and dreadful day of the Lord:" Malachi 4:5 "And he shall turn the heart of the fathers to the children, and the heart of the children to their fathers," (It doesn't matter that people believe that all feeling comes from the head or mind, God says it comes from the heart) "---lest I come and smite the earth with a curse." Malachi 4:6 This curse is going to be the curse mentioned in St Matthew 24 and Mark the 13th chapters for the end time. God knows that Elijah isn't going to be able to overhaul the established religions of the world. If people wouldn't believe Jesus what are my chances, a carpenter from Wyoming? "And because I (Jesus) tell you the truth, ye believe me not." St John 8:45

The preachers they like what the King James Bible says, that John the Baptist was Elijah. If a true, 'Man of God' came like Elijah will, his message would be different, than what would the preachers preach? What would they do with the mortgage? What would they tell their congregation? How would they make a living, if they have spent it all? Would she leave him for the garbage man? Would the apple cart be turned over as they say?

Jesus said (but hard to believe) that John the Baptist was Elijah, and the disciples said John the Baptist was Elijah, that is hard to overcome. "---Elijah truly shall first come," St Matthew 17:11 "---Elijah is come already, 12 "Then the disciples understood that he spake unto them of John the Baptist." St Matthew 17:13 "And they asked him, (John the Baptist) what then? Art thou Elijah? And he saith, 'I am not' Art thou that prophet? And he answered NO." St John 1:21

"But I say unto you, That Elijah is come already, and they knew him not, but have done unto him whatsoever they listed. (Pleased) Likewise shall also the Son of man (Jesus) suffer of them." St Matthew 17:12 (John lost his life by two persons that hated him or wanted his head.) The daughter of Herodias was promised to be given whatsoever she would ask. She asked for John the Baptist's head in a charger. (bowl) "Then the disciples understood that he (Jesus) spake unto them of John the Baptist." St Matthew 17:13 (Did they get it right?) I don't think so.

"And his disciples asked him, saying, Why then say the (scribes) that Elijah must first come?" St Matthew 17:10 "And Jesus answered and said unto them, Elijah truly shall first come, and restore all things." 11(To explain the allegorical spoken Word and parables) "Behold, I will send you Elijah the prophet before the coming of the great and dreadful day of the Lord:" Malachi 4:5

"For all the prophets and the law prophesied until John." St Matthew 11:13 "And if ye will receive it, this is Elijah, which was for to come." 14 How could Elijah be John the Baptist when he was to come at the end time as Malachi says? Elijah then lived at the time of Jesus and never portrayed the true salvation plan, I believe God had John the Baptist killed.

"And this is the record of John, when the Jews sent priests and Levites from Jerusalem to ask him, who art thou?" St John 1:19 "And he confessed, and denied not; but confessed, I am not the Christ." 20 "And they asked him, What then? Art thou Elijah? And he saith, I am not. Art thou that prophet? And he answered NO." 21 (I wonder what part of No, don't they understand?) The Elijah of the Old Testament is not the same Elijah or Elias for the New Testament and this dispensation. The Elijah that appeared was the other Elijah. "And, behold there appeared unto them Moses and Elijah talking with him." St Matthew 17:3 If you can believe this happened? Peter had a tendency to not be right, he wanted to build another monstrous church building, remember I was saved at a gas station. "Then answered Peter, and said unto Jesus, Lord it is good for us to be here: if thou wilt, let us make three tabernacles; one for thee, and one for Moses, and one for Elijah." 4

"And I saw another angel ascending from the east, having the seal of the living God: and he cried with a loud voice to the four angels, to whom it was given to hurt the earth and the sea," Revelation 7:2 "Saying hurt not the earth, neither the sea, nor the trees, till we have sealed the servants of our God in their foreheads." 3

(In their foreheads) When I received the Holy Ghost driving to work, when I went inside the factory, the workers faces were distorted or gross looking. I looked up a Baptist friend I thought his face would be normal, but it wasn't. "For Jerusalem is ruined, and Judah is fallen: because their tongue and their doings are against the Lord, to provoke the eyes of his glory." Isaiah 3:8

"The show of their countenance (face) doth witness against them; and they declare their sin as Sodom, they hide it not. Woe unto their soul for they have rewarded evil unto themselves." Isaiah 3:9 "Say ye to the righteous, (true righteous) that it shall be well with him: for they shall eat the fruit of their doings." 10 (Good) " Woe unto the wicked! It shall be ill with him: for the reward of his hands shall be given him." 11(Not good)

At the 'day of judgment,' the faces of those not saved, will look distorted or gross looking. I lost this phenomenon in a few days.

There are at least one or more preacher that says the two witnesses in Revelation, one of them is Elijah, and I see no reason to believe that, because they are both Jews in the great city. Revelation 11: The great city must be Jerusalem, and it's not the Jews that are spreading false doctrine all over the earth, If we want to put a name to the country it would be the United States. Common sense tells me Elijah would come from that area, or be a true gentile. I was never circumcised because a mid-wife delivered me.

Chapter 15

Allah

It seems strange to me that Allah never showed his face until Muhammad said he was the messenger of Allah, with approval of his wives.

A King James Bible of 1611 that I got at the Salvation Army had all the major bibles written for 1,611 + years and not one mention of Allah.

What about the millions of years during the dinosaur period, did Allah have anything to do with that? If you, as a person could do anything that you wanted to do, and had the power to do it, some of the dinosaurs weighed tons, it had an article about it in the news paper today. It seems reasonable to me, that God made the dinosaurs just because He could and did.

The God of the Bible can look on a person's heart, and know their thoughts. People's countenance or face is grossly distorted also, if they are not saved.

1. Muhammad had seizures, during which he sweat vigorously during revelations, and according to his wife Aishah, bells rang in his ears. He became upset, and his face changed, Umar ibnul Khattab tells that Muhammad shivered, his mouth foamed, and he roared like a camel.
2. Revelation came in dreams.
3. Inspiration came in visions.

4. Sometimes he saw an angel in the form of a young, tall man.
5. At other times he saw actual angels. (I saw an angel one time but only the extremely white robe with no hands, feet or head)
6. During one evening (known as the Mi'raj) he received his revelation as he crossed the "seven heavens" to receive the revelation.
7. Allah spoke to him from behind a veil.

Muhammad told his wife Khadija that he feared he was possessed by Demons and wondered whether others might consider him possessed.

The scriptures were given by Allah to Moses and Jesus, as prophets of Allah: according to the Islam faith.

Muslims see the Quran not as contradicting the Old and New Testaments, but rather as fulfilling them.

Man has had free will, and there has been 500 to 1000 men and organizations working on what they considered the true gospel after 1611. Sense 1900 there has been more than that, with every kind of bible imaginable. That is why this author believes this is truly the end of time.

The Author seems to think that when convenient Muhammad took parts of others belief systems, for his own revelations as the messenger of Allah.

Chapter 16

Clash of cultures

**Moslem discrepancies of the other religion
What if, "What they say, some of it is true?"**

How can one person get the whole world to change their religion? Jesus did that, and I'm working on it.

What if most of Moslem discrepancies are true, and I will give you the verses in the King James Bible of 1611 to verify what they believe about us is true.

We find in Isaiah "How art thou fallen from heaven, O Lucifer, son of the mourning, how art thou cut down to the ground, which didst weaken the nations." Isaiah 14:12-13-14 In Revelation It is about Satan being bound a thousand years, but what I want to concentrate on is "that he (Satan) should deceive the nations no more." Revelation 20:3 "–for thy merchants (is it churches?) were the great men of the earth; for by thy sorceries, were all nations deceived." 18:23 "And the great dragon was cast out, that old serpent, called the Devil, and Satan, which DECEIVETH the whole world: he was cast out into the earth, and his angels were cast out with him." Revelation 12:9

What does it mean (thy merchants were the great men of the earth) It is next to impossible to get any truth to the people of the earth. Unless writing about St John 3:16 that is as far as the Christian people want to go. What if the merchants are the media, publishing, and the leader's of religions. It would be OK if they were preaching the true Gospel. Common sense should tell them that there is something wrong.

"But Jesus perceived their wickedness, and said, Why tempt ye me, ye hypocrites?." St Matthew 22;18 "And Jesus knowing their thoughts said, wherefore think ye evil in your hearts?" St Matthew 9:4

"For thou hast said in thine heart, I (Satan) will ascend into heaven, I will exalt my throne above the stars of God: (churches) I will sit also upon the mount (all) of the congregation(s) (Churches)---."Isaiah 14:13 "I (Satan) will ascend above the heights of the clouds, I will be like the most High." 14 God used Jesus as His advocate' doesn't Satan need an advocate in the likeness of Jesus to be like Him? "I am come in my Father's name, and ye receive me not: (Jesus) If another shall come in his own name, him ye will receive." (Believe, Paul) St John 5:43

Paul and his companions never altered the message of Jesus or the Gospels, they never did know what the message was in the first place. The Moslem scholars said they cheapened salvation.

What if salvation is physical, that is something you don't hear of in either religion. I believe neither religion would want to know the truth. That would make St John 3:16 obsolete, and seventy two virgins nonexistent, and warfare for the cause of Allah or Jihad, those men have died in vain. Upon the Moslem's man's death, there is no Paradise or seventy virgin women waiting with open arms. There is no purgatory as suggested in two major religions. The reason I say that is, after I was saved (physically) I entered the kingdom of God without leaving the earth. It reads that a person must become perfect as God in heaven is perfect. With the sin of Adam in the heart, and a person's accumulative sin, it must be removed before a person can become perfect. This must be done physically on this earth, as it happened to me.

Jesus was no help He said that, "Except a man be born again, he cannot SEE the kingdom of God." What you SEE (feel) is the power of God, and that translates into, "there is truly a God." "Jesus answered and said unto them, Ye do err, not knowing the scriptures nor the power of God." St Matthew 22:29 What do you mean you felt something? After my mother sent me a King James Bible of 1611 my Dad gave me a Cruden's Complete Concordance of that Bible. The best verses that I found in the Bible are recorded in Ezekiel. Other books in the Old Testament have similar quotations. As I said above it happened to me physically, and as it reads, a person will see and feel the power of God. "A new heart also (a person is first chosen and drawn) will I give you, and I will take away the stony heart (sinful heart) out of your flesh, and I will give you a heart of flesh." Ezekiel 36:26

After I had left a protestant church's Alter, I went to a telephone on the outside of a gas station to tell my mother. She said pray for your dad and me. I believed in my heart that perhaps I could heal her. At that instant when I believed it triggered the Spirit of Genesis to act and it removed my heart that I was born with. A long stream of light began replacing the heart that had been removed. This happened 12/1/1968 at 9pm. "Believe me, that I am in the Father and the Father in me: (Holy Ghost) OR ELSE believe me for the very works' sake." St John 14:11 Also St John 10:37-38. Tonight on T V was the huge Catholic Church in Barcelona Spain that they have been working on for about one hundred forty years, and still at it, on sixty minutes. It reminded me of the shack, of a cut rate gas station that I was saved at. Your common sense should tell a person that the building has no connection on a person's salvation when it is physical.

What does redemption do for a person? Not only did I quit drinking, swearing, smoking, but fasted three days and nights. It started the cleaning process of my body to get it ready to receive the Holy Ghost or Spirit. Then will I sprinkle clean water upon YOU, (born again) (Why water is expressed in this manner, I don't know.) and ye shall be clean: from all your filthiness, and from all your idols, will I cleanse you." Ezekiel 36:25 Water baptism has nothing to do with being born again. "---my Father giveth you the true bread from heaven." St John 6:32 "For the bread of God is (he) which cometh down from heaven, and giveth life unto the world." 33 "And Jesus said unto them, I am the bread of life: he that cometh to me shall never hunger; and he that believeth on me shall never thirst." 35 (This believeth is a condition or catalyst to trigger the Spirit to act) "AND ye shall be clean: from all your filthiness, and from all your idols, will I (Spirit) cleanse you." Ezekiel 36:25

"and a New Spirit (Holy Ghost) will I put (within) you:" Ezekiel 36:26 "And I will put my Spirit (within) you, and cause you to walk in my statutes, and ye shall keep my judgments, and do them." 27 After I received the Holy Ghost, God put a fast on me again for three days and nights.

Jesus never needed the born again experience but He did need to receive the Holy Ghost or Holy Spirit. Evidently the original sin of Adam can only come down through the generations of the male, and His Father made the Spirit of Genesis 1:2, It wasn't the Holy Ghost as in St Matthew 1:18

Jesus received the Holy Ghost on His first breath, when He came out of the water, when He was baptized by John the Baptist. It never, "lighting on him, "as it reads in St Matthew 3:16 it was the, "Like a dove" a blob. God put a vision on me to get my mouth open, and that is when the Holy Ghost went in my mouth down my throat. In the vision a preacher was in trouble, from one of the churches I attended, and I said," God help that BOY: On the word boy it went in my mouth.

After Jesus received the Holy Ghost it reads He went in the wilderness and fasted forty days and nights. He was afterward ahungered. What that is telling us is, He was in the wilderness for some time coping with the Devil and learning what God wanted Him to do and say. The Holy Ghost is the teacher of the Word of God both to Jesus, and us, after the born again experience and receiving the Spirit. "For I have not spoken of myself, but the Father which sent me, he gave me a commandment, what I should say, and what I should speak." St John 12:49 My ordeal lasted two years with the Devil trying to get me to worship him, learning the statutes and commandments from the Holy Ghost. "If ye love me, keep my commandments." (born again) St John 14:15 "And I will pray the Father, and he shall give you ANOTHER Comforter, that (he) may abide with you forever." 16 'Another comforter' means that a person received a Comforter before, but it was the (New Heart or born again). Usually Comforter means receiving the Holy Ghost. "Even the Spirit of Truth; whom the world cannot receive, because it seeth him not, neither knoweth Him:" 17 It means the first Comforter, they haven't been born again and received the new heart. "---But ye know him; for he dwelleth with you, and shall be in you." 17 "At that day ye shall know that I am in my Father, and ye in me, and I in you." St John14:20 12/30/1968 at 6:30 am I received the Holy Ghost, and it went in my mouth, down my throat.

Does God love everybody? "He that hath my commandments and keepeth them, he it is that loveth me: and he that loveth me shall be loved of my Father.

and I will love him, and will manifest myself to him." St John 14:21 (The only person that the Father in heaven loves, are those that have been born again) (Give them the Holy Ghost after their body is clean) The preachers say that God loves everybody, but according to the Bible if you are not of God, your father is Satan. "But the Comforter which is the Holy Ghost, whom the Father will send in my name, he shall teach you all things, and bring all things to your remembrance, whatsoever I have said unto you." 26

"Hereafter I will not talk much with you: for the prince of this world cometh, and hath nothing in me." St John 14:30 (Satan and his advocate Paul)

At the end of Jesus time in the wilderness it reads; "Then the devil leaveth him, and, behold, angels came and ministered unto him." St Matthew 4:11 Two years after I received the Holy Ghost my time in the wilderness was over. In a Sunday school class in San Pedro, California in a protestant church, a woman was teaching the scriptures of Jesus turning the water into wine in St John 2: 1-12. At the end of the class I looked up toward the ceiling and saw an angel, extremely white with no head, feet, or hands, sort of like a graduation uniform. When it disappeared I blurted out "THE DAY OF JUDGMENT IS COMING."

That night I never went to church, but was studding the Bible, and at midnight I was going to the kitchen to get a glass of water. I heard an audible voice say, 'change the water into wine.' Filling the glass I set it on the coffee table, and lifted up both arms and asked God to change the water into wine in Jesus name. Nothing happened in the glass. I felt a sensation from my hands to my feet. What this is for I couldn't tell you, there is nothing about it in the Bible, but the wine might have came from Jesus body at the marriage in Cana. It reads in St John "When the ruler of the feast had tasted the water that was made wine, and knew not whence it was: (but the servants which drew the water knew; ---")." St John 2:9 It could be the tree of life mentioned in Revelation "He that hath an ear, let him hear what the Spirit saith unto the churches: To him that overcometh (from the false doctrine in the churches) will I give to eat of the tree of life, which is in the midst of the paradise of God." Revelation 2:7 "And the Lord God said, the man is become as one of us, to know good and evil: and now, lest he put forth his hand, and take also of the tree of life, and eat, and live forever." Genesis 3:22

Complaint's That Moslems Have.

Christians cannot defend the Bible, nor Jesus as the Son of God. No, they believe He was God, which I differ on that or the Trinity. I believe God was the creator of the other three as helpers, the Spirit found in Genesis 1:2, Jesus, and the Holy Ghost are for those that are born again. Paul wrote one third of the New Testament, it is a fraud that changed the course of history through his ambition and lies. Paul never had anything to do with the four Gospels with possibly, the exception of Luke or at the end of each Gospel, some verses are questionable?

Jesus represented the sacrifices in Leviticus because God cannot live with unrighteousness and love has nothing to do with being righteous. When a person is saved as (above) they become righteous to live with God in His kingdom.

Moslems say, "Jesus the Son of Mary" to give Him an earthly connotation instead of divine, but He never had an earthly father He was conceived by the Spirit of Genesis, so that made him divine, and truly the Son of God. Pure in righteousness, fit to be the offering for sin for righteousness sake. It is through Him that a person is saved. The Trinity in Islam is the definite example of the unreasonableness of Christian faith. How can 1+1+1=1? It doesn't make sense the Moslems say. That is true, and I have been expressing that fact for years with very little if any results. The Word was with God from the beginning but it wasn't made flesh until the time was right, and then Mary was conceived by the Spirit of Genesis. "And the Word was made flesh, and dwelt among us, (and we beheld his glory, the glory as of the only begotten of the Father,) full of grace and truth." St John 1:14 When two people get married, the Bible says they are one. The same as Jesus and His Father, "they should have the same goals." Another thing, why is it that you can use both Jesus and God's name in vain, but do not blasphemy the Holy Ghost? It is because the Holy Ghost is separate, and part of the salvation plan.

I agree above that Paul was a false prophet.

The Moslems are correct even the Gospels have flaws in them to be corrected or eliminated entirely. God has never been able to protect His Word. There are two or more preachers on the Radio that are dead, not even death, can stop the false doctrine, from being preached. People are making money on recordings, I have contacted a few running these programs with no results.

Flaws of the King James Bible of 1611

(A verse should not be in the Bible) "For God so loved the world," (what about a verse in Genesis?) "And it repented 'grieved' the Lord that he had made man on the earth, and it grieved him at his heart." Genesis 6:6 God killed all but eight that were on Noah's boat, and they couldn't find ten righteous people in Sodom and Gomorrah. About all a person hears is how much God loves them. 'He gave his only begotten Son,' that is true but it wasn't because of love, it was a way for people to become righteous to live with God in His kingdom. 'That whosoever believeth in him should not perish,' that is true but believing is a condition, for the Spirit to act and give you a new heart. When you believed did you receive a new heart, was the heart you were born with removed? 'But have everlasting life,' that is true but a person needs to receive the Holy Ghost after receiving the new heart, and with me that happened thirty days afterward. It is my belief that God would have used the word eternal if He wrote it. St John 3:16

St Luke chapter one is a nightmare. The Holy Ghost was not to be until after Jesus went to His Father in heaven, except that Jesus received it when he was about 30 years old in St Matthew 3:16 on His first breath, it went in His mouth down His throat. It never, "lighting on him as it reads."

It takes time between receiving the new heart and the Holy Ghost. Your body must be clean before the Holy Ghost will enter it, it took me thirty days. I question "Then opened He (Jesus) their understanding, that they might understand the scriptures." Luke 24:45

"And that repentance and remission of sins should be preached in his name among all nations, beginning at Jerusalem." Luke 24:47 The salvation of John the Baptist was not the salvation plan and salvation is an individual physical thing, it can happen anyplace. Somebody is trying to give what Peter said in The Acts credence. If it never worked for John the Baptist, why should it work for Peter? There are congregations that would die for what Peter said. "---Men and brethren, what shall we do?" The Acts 2:37 "Then Peter said unto them, Repent, and be baptized every one of you In the name of Jesus Christ for the remission of sins, and ye shall receive the gift of the Holy Ghost." 38 In Jerusalem is where the Holy Ghost (speaking in tongues were suppose to have occurred), which has nothing to do with the Holy Ghost. "And he (Jesus) saith unto them, ye shall drink indeed (there is no doubt about it) of my cup, and be baptized with the baptism that I am baptized with:" St Matthew 20:23

"He that believeth and is baptized shall be saved; but he that believeth not shall be damned." St Mark 16:16 Here again, man is projected into the equation. Water baptism is not necessary nor the sacraments, smoke, or rosary. Jesus said Mary were no better than the pilgrims are. "For whosoever shall do the will of my Father which is in heaven, the same is my brother, and sister, and mother." St Matthew 12:50"----who then can be saved?" St Matthew 19:25 "But Jesus beheld them, (looked on their heart) and said unto them, with men this is impossible; but with God all things are possible." 26 "John answered and said, A man can receive nothing, except it be given him from heaven." St John 3:27

"And these signs shall follow them that believe; In my name shall they cast out devils; they shall speak with new tongues;" St Mark 16:17 There has never been a documented case where somebody was healed by being prayed for, and tongues has nothing to do with the Holy Ghost that Jesus spoke of. "They shall take up serpents; and if they drink any deadly thing, it shall not hurt them; they shall lay hands on the sick, and they shall recover." 18 What if they were not saved in the first place, did they get suckered in by St John 3:16?

"Go ye therefore, and teach all nations baptizing them in the name of the Father, and of the Son, and of the Holy Ghost:" St Matthew 28:19 If as you say the Trinity is one; why baptize in all three? Again man has projected himself into the equation. 20 "Teaching them to observe (Salvation is physical) all things whatsoever I have commanded you: and lo, I am with you always, even unto the end of the world. A'men." 20 I'm not sure when they started believing Jesus? "And because I tell you the truth, ye believe me not." St John 8:45

It is true that Christians often read only material by writers that only share their beliefs In what they call Sunday school, only, literature that comes from the individual head quarters is used, they don't want to rock the boat so to speak, at least in the church that I attended.

The Qur'an is uncorrupted by man so they say. (Given from a man, that couldn't read nor write, give me a break) How can the word of God be corrupted by man? By people that put verses in, and thought they were correct but they never came from God. All of The Acts through Jude is from man. You are not fooling God any. "Hereafter I will not talk much with you: for the prince of this world cometh, and have nothing in me." St John 14:30

"I speak that which I have seen with my Father: and ye do that which ye have seen with your father." St John 8:38

Perhaps people need to be inspired to open their own Bibles, and read what Scripture actually says. When finished with this book, instead of relying upon preachers to spoon feed bits of proof, try to read the Bible yourself. (So what is the problem?) "And the disciples came, and said unto him, Why speakest thou unto them in parables? St Matthew 13:10 "He answered and said unto them because it is given unto you to know the mysteries of the kingdom of heaven, but to them (Unsaved) it is not given." 11 "But blessed are your eyes, for they see: and your ears, for they hear." 16 God does have people, on the earth that understands His Word, walking on the earth today. The problem is there is so much false doctrine that the truth is impossible to be believed. Jesus said they never believed Him either. St John 8:45

Chapter 17

Biblical

Biblical in the dictionary is, 'in keeping with, or according to the other verses.' I have a King James Bible of 1611, with a Cruden's Complete Concordance of that Bible.

In my social net working a couple of people said they were going to go by what happened to the thief on the cross. In "Then were there two thieves crucified with him, one on the right hand, and another on the left." St Matthew 27:38 It is recorded in Matthew, Mark, and St John but only that two thieves were crucified with Him.

In Luke whom I have said can get a person in trouble; "And he said unto Jesus, Lord, remember me when thou comest into thy kingdom" Luke 23:42 "And Jesus said unto him, Verily, I say unto thee, Today shall thou be with me in paradise." 43 According to this verse the thief got to paradise before Jesus did, because it was several days afterward that Jesus left. In accordance with the Bible a person must be born again and receive the Spirit or Holy Ghost first, before they can enter into the kingdom of God. In St John Born again, and receiving the Holy Ghost, there were a thirty day period, between the experiences. That is what is recorded in Ezekiel in as plain language as I could write it. Ezekiel 36:26-27

These two people mentioned above, believe, that they want to follow the thief, when it is only recorded in the one Gospel. Evidently they will just leave the earth, and go to God's kingdom, that's easy enough.

Who was The-oph'-i-lus? "It seemed good to me also, having had perfect understanding of all things from the very first, to write unto thee in order, most excellent The-oph'-i-lus." Luke 1:3

(John the Baptist before he was born) "For he shall be great in the sight of the Lord, and shall drink neither wine nor strong drink; and he shall be filled with the Holy Ghost, even from his mother's womb." Luke 1:15 The only time the Holy Ghost came to be was when Jesus received it when He was baptized in water by John in St Matthew 3:16. To save paper all the times in the first chapter of Luke, the Holy Ghost mentioned was not biblical. The Holy Ghost wasn't to be until after Jesus went to His Father in heaven. "Nevertheless I tell you the truth; it is expedient for you that I go away: for if I go not away, the Comforter will not come unto you; but if I depart, I will send him unto you." St John 16:7 (John the Baptist) "I indeed baptize you with water unto repentance: but he (Jesus) that cometh after me is mightier than I, whose shoes I am not worthy to bear: he shall baptize you with the Holy Ghost, and with fire." St Matthew 3:11 (New Word) "Ye shall drink indeed of my cup, and be baptized with the baptism that I am baptized with:" St Matthew 20:23

John the Baptist Father, said his son was to give knowledge of salvation unto his people by the remission of their sins. (False doctrine) The salvation message of John had nothing to do with the true salvation plan of God. Luke 1:77 I believe that is why he was killed.

"And the angel came in unto her, (Mary) and said, Hail, thou, that art highly favored, the Lord is with thee: blessed art thou among women." Luke 1:28 In my KJB of 1611 the concordance sends me to Judges "And the Angel of the Lord, appeared unto (him,) and said unto (him,) The Lord is with thee, thou mighty (man?) of valor." Judges 6:12 (False doctrine) Unless you are born again and receive the Spirit a person cannot enter into the kingdom of God.

"While he yet talked to the people, behold, his mother and his brethren (brother) stood without, desiring to speak with him." S Matthew 12:46 "And he stretched forth his hand toward his disciples, and said, behold my mother and my brethren!" 49 "For whosoever shall do the will of my Father which is in heaven, the same is my brother, and sister, and mother." St Matthew 12:50 It reads here that Mary is a pilgrim no better or worse off than the rest of us. Again this is only recorded in Luke's gospel, that Mary is blessed. What about the rosary and the beads? You figure that out.

The Trinity of the Father, Son, and Holy Ghost, It seems like they left Mary out. The book, "Unveiling Islam" says the trinity is Father, Son, and Mary, according to Islam. The Holy Ghost doesn't like that, because a person must receive it, to become saved. But to my knowledge, there is the first Spirit mentioned in Genesis 1:2, so the trinity is quadruple with God the creator of the other three with the Son, Holy Ghost, and Spirit mentioned in Genesis subject to God. So the trinity is quadruple if that makes any sense to you.

"---It is written, that man shall not live by bread alone, but by every word of God." Luke 4:4 That would cover Paul, Peter, James John 1,2, and 3, Peter 1and 2 Etc., and all those that wrote different bibles or worked on the gospel message sense Jesus left, and the preachers call the Bible infallible? It means incapable of error; never wrong; reliable, an infallible person or thing. "Man shall not live by bread alone, but by every word that proceedeth out of the mouth of God." (Jesus) St Matthew 4:4 One verse never came out of the mouth of Jesus. Fifteen did, it is allegorically written, part of the mystery or hidden truth. St John 3:16-15

The problem is, according to scripture only those that become saved can understand the parables or allegorical verses. "And the disciples came, and said unto him, Why speakest thou unto them in parables?" St Matthew 13:10 "He answered and said unto them, because it is given unto you to know the mysteries of the kingdom of heaven, but to them it is not given." 11 "But blessed are your eyes, for they see: and your ears for they hear." 16 "But I say unto you, That it shall be more tolerable for the land of Sodom in the day of judgment than for thee," St Matthew 11:24 (God made it easy for Jesus, because people never knew what He was speaking about: It is much more difficult, when a person knows what the parables mean) "At that time Jesus answered and said, I thank thee, O Father, Lord of heaven and earth, because thou hast (hid) these things from the wise and prudent, (learned) and hast revealed them unto babes." 25 Jesus recognized that those He was talking to never understood what He was saying. "Even so, Father; for it seemed good in thy sight." 26 The reason for this is Jesus had to die on the cross for our sins, if He spoke plainly He might have never got to the cross. For instance what if it is true? (The generation will not pass until all is fulfilled, and which generation is it that Jesus is referring too?) "Verily I say unto you, all these things shall come upon this generation." St Matthew 23:36 What if Jesus said the end time is not for you, it is for the generation that is going to be born in 1937, the year I was born, they might have went back home?

"I (John the Baptist) indeed baptize you with water unto repentance: but he that cometh after me is mightier than I, whose shoes I am not worthy to bear: he (Jesus) shall baptize you with the Holy Ghost, and with fire:" St Matthew 3:11 (a new message) What is complicated with this verse? It must have not been plain enough because Peter had the answer for salvation. "Then Peter said unto them, Repent, and be baptized every one of you in the name of Jesus Christ for the remission of sins, and ye shall receive the gift of the Holy Ghost." The Acts 2:38 It never worked for John the Baptist, why should it work for Peter? The problem is a person's body must be clean before the Holy Ghost will enter it, as explained in earlier Chapters. Jesus is the one that prays to the Father, giving the qualified person the right to receive the Holy Ghost. "And I will pray the Father, and he shall (no doubt) give you another Comforter, that he may abide with you forever." St John 14:16

Preachers read that Jesus fasted forty days and forty nights, so the time He was in the wilderness was forty days according to them. Why did my ordeal last two years, and I fasted three days and nights when I received the Holy Ghost also when being born again.

"And Jesus when he was baptized, went up straightway out of the water: (on His first breath) and lo, the heavens were opened unto him, and he saw the Spirit of God descending like a dove, (blob) and lighting upon him." St Matthew 3:16 (It never lighting on Him but the Spirit (Holy Ghost) entered His mouth and went down His throat.) "Even the Spirit of truth; whom the world cannot receive, because it seeth him not, (Jesus saw the Spirit that looked like a dove, blob) neither knoweth him: (Spirit or Holy Ghost) but ye know him; for (He) dwelleth with you, AND SHALL BE IN YOU." St John 14:17 It went in my mouth after a vision was put on me.

There is one verse I like, in Luke. "But if I with the finger of God (power of God) cast out devils, (born again and receiving the Spirit) no doubt the kingdom of God is come upon you." Luke 11:20 Born again 12/1/1968 at 9: pm and received the Holy Ghost 12/30/1968 at 6;30 am.

At the end of every Gospel are verses that are not Biblical in comparison with the rest of the Bible.

"Go ye therefore, and "teach" all nations, baptizing them in the name of the Father, and of the Son, and of the Holy Ghost." St Matthew 28:19 (I found out salvation or being born again, is physical that comes from God, and John the Baptist said it comes from heaven.), St John 3:27 Jesus never did nothing in water, assuming water is what is meant here in Matthew. It never worked for John the Baptist. I believe they are just trying to tie the Gospels in, with what Peter said in The Acts 2:38

"He that believeth, and is baptized shall be saved: but he that believeth not shall be damned." St Mark 16:16 (believeth) God made it a condition for the Spirit (not the Holy Ghost) to act, or it is a catalyst when a person believes in his heart as of St John 10; 37-38 and 14:11. It is the trigger of action by the Spirit to give a person a new heart. (The only thing water will do for you is get yourself wet) "Shall be saved ?" (not on your life) "but he that believeth not shall be damned." 16 That is true, but they haven't believed in their heart on one of the works that Jesus did. (14:11 above) "And these signs shall follow them that believe; In my name shall they cast out devils; (there has never been a documented case of a person being healed by being prayed for) they shall speak with new tongues;" 17 (tongues has nothing to do with the Spirit or Holy Ghost) "They shell take up serpents; (do you believe anyone should harass, any of God's creatures?) "And if they drink any deadly thing, it shall not hurt them: they shall lay hands on the sick, and they shall recover." 18 It reminds me of when Jesus was in the wilderness He told Satan "thou shalt not tempt the Lord thy God." St Matthew 4:7

"And when he had said this, he (Jesus) breathed on them, and said unto them, receive ye the Holy Ghost:" St John 20:22 (Never mind your body must be clean before a person can receive the Holy Ghost) "Whosesoever sins ye remit, they are remitted unto them; and whosesoever sins ye retain, they are retained." 23? (No wonder there is a confessional to get rid of sins but it is not Biblical.) According to St John "Jesus answered, Verily, verily, I say unto thee, Except a man be born of water (born again 3rd verse) and of the Spirit (Holy Ghost) he cannot enter into the kingdom of God." St John 3:5

"And he was there in the wilderness forty days, (my ordeal lasted two years, and I believe Jesus was in the wilderness more than forty days) tempted of Satan; and was with the wild beasts; and the angels ministered unto him." St Mark 1:13 Jesus had just received the Holy Ghost the teacher of God, and Mark says that the angels ministered unto Him ? At the end of His time in the wilderness it was a sign that Satan wouldn't bother Him anymore when He saw the angels.

"Then the devil leaveth him, and behold, (surprise from God) angels came and ministered unto him. St Matthew 4:11 "And when he had fasted forty days and forty nights, he was afterward ahungered." 2 It doesn't say how long Jesus was in the wilderness.

Is Satan down at the local bar having a few beers? When Jesus was in the wilderness Satan tried to get Jesus to worship him by promising Him, He could set in the holy city, (Jerusalem?) and setting him on a pinnacle of the temple, He also showed him the kingdoms of the world, and the glory of them. All these things will I give thee, if thou wilt fall down and worship me."

"How art thou fallen from heaven, O Lucifer, son of the morning! How art thou cut down to the ground, which didst weaken the nations." Isaiah 14:12

In the thirteenth verse it might have been in Lucifer's heart before he was removed from the kingdom of God, and it might have been the reason that Lucifer was removed.

"For thou hast said in thine heart, I will ascend into heaven, I will exalt my throne above the stars of God: (churches) I will sit also upon the mount (all) of the congregation, (churches) in the sides of the north: (America?) 13 "I will ascend above the heights of the clouds; I will be like the most High." 14 (God) All of this might have occurred before the 13th verse, and it was the reason that Lucifer was removed from the kingdom of God because it mentions that he weaken the nations, which are on the earth?

If Lucifer was going to be like God wouldn't he need an advocate such as Jesus was to God? Wouldn't that be Paul? "I am come in my Father's name, and ye receive me not: (Jesus) if another shall come in his own name, him ye will receive. (Believe, Paul) St John 5:43

Chapter 18

Noah

"But as the days of Noah were, so shall also the coming of the Son of man be." St Matthew 24: 37 "But as in the days that were before the flood they were eating and drinking, marring and giving in marriage, until the day that Noah entered into the ark," 38 "And knew not until the flood came, and took them all away; so shall also the coming of the Son of man be." 39 "Then shall two be in the field; the one shall be taken, and the other left. 40 "Two women shall be grinding at the mill; the one shall be taken, and the other left." 41"Watch therefore: for ye know not what hour your Lord doth come." 42"Therefore be ye also ready: for in such an hour as ye think not the Son of man cometh." 44

Luke, who I said before can get a person in trouble with two men in one bed, but he could have been more realistic. "I tell you, in that night there shall be two men in one bed; the one shall be taken, and the other shall be left." Luke 17:34 If one of them is truly saved that could be possible. I'm at a place, where I'm not going to try and judge this one.

In these verses it appears that 50% is used, but Jesus left the 99 and went after the 1, so I don't think a person can know what the percentage is that will live in God's kingdom when Jesus returns. It reads few will find the way in St Matthew "Enter ye in at the strait gate: (narrow) for wide is the gate, and broad is the way, that leadeth to destruction, and many there be which go in there-at:" St Matthew 7:13 "Because strait is the gate, and narrow is the way, which leadeth unto (life), and few there be that find it." 14 (When Adam disobeyed God he said that he would die, but here it reads a few people will find (life or the kingdom of God).

"Watch therefore, for ye know neither the day nor the hour wherein the Son of man cometh." St Matthew 25:13

You can't say that Luke discriminates, "I tell you, in that night there shall be two men in one bed; the one shall be taken, and the other shall be left." Luke 17:34 Is it possible? I would say it was possible (if) a person has received the new heart and new Spirit, and the other hasn't. Perhaps God isn't concerned with what a person does in the bedroom. In other words; one of the men has received salvation and the other hasn't. "Not that which goeth into the mouth defileth a man; but that which cometh out of the mouth, this defileth a man." St Matthew 15:11 "But those things which proceed out of the mouth come forth from the heart; and they defile the man. 18 "For out of the heart proceed evil thoughts,---": 19 (Those that have not been saved) "Ye are of your father the devil, and the lusts of your father ye will do. He was a murderer from the beginning, and abode not in the truth, because there is no truth in him. When he speaketh a lie, he speaketh of his own: for he is a liar, and the father of it." St John 8:44 "I am come in my Father's name, and ye receive me not: (Jesus) if another shall come in his own name, him (Paul) ye will receive." (Believe) St John 5:43

"Watch ye therefore, and pray always, that ye may be accounted worthy to escape all these things that shall come to pass, and to stand before the Son of man." Luke 21:36 I don't believe that a person saved, will stand before Jesus. If a person has received salvation and been transformed I see no reason to be judged as it seems to read. "And except those days should be shortened, there should no flesh be saved: but for the elect's sake (saved) those days (shall) be shortened." St Matthew 24:22

"For where so ever the carcase is, (false preachers) there will the eagles (congregation) be gathered together." St Matthew 24:28 "How can ye believe, which receive honor one of another, and seek not the honor that cometh from God only?" St John 5:44 The first thing that Jesus said when they asked him in St Matthew "---What shall be the sign of thy coming, and of the end of the world?" St Matthew 24:3 "---Take heed that no man deceive you." St Matthew 24:4 The 24th chapter of Matthew is mostly about false doctrine, and the end time so carcase must mean what I said above. (false preachers)

It is almost an impossibility to get any truth through the media, publishing, and in the churches. The preacher will tell you I'm a divinity college graduate in a big church, with thousands in (my) congregation, we all believe in St John 3:16. All our missionaries believe in St John 3:16. All my colleagues, along with my Mother believe in St John 3:16.

Is TBN spreading the true Gospel all over the world as they say? Or are all of them back slappers (agreeable to one another)? Jesus said in St John "How can ye believe, (get saved) which receive honor one of another, and seek not the honor that cometh from God only?" St John 5:44 (Seek His righteousness first," the kingdom of God)" In Ezekiel I know this book, and verses are in the Old Testament but the allegorical verses are in St John they are no help. "He answered and said unto them, because it (salvation) is given unto you to know the mysteries of the kingdom of heaven, but to them (unsaved) it is not given." St Matthew 13:11

How bad was it before Noah? It is hard to know for sure. The only thing I believe we can go by is what is happening today.

(Eating and drinking) In the fifties we said there is a gas station on every corner. Today there seems to be an eating establishment on every corner. In 1971 in Casper, Wyoming you could count on one hand the family restaurants. Today it is hard to choose which one to go too. The Bull Pen across from the Beacon Bar was one of the most active family restaurants in town, but now there is a place to eat on every corner.

The Bible reads; who God has put together let not man put asunder or separate, between a man and women as husband and wife. It reads these two are one. That is one of my reasons the way it is worded, that Jesus and God are two, but the Bible says they are one. They are one with the same goals, the salvation of man.

One of the things that a pastor does is marriages and funerals, but what does it say about the dead? "And another of his disciples said unto him, Lord, suffer me first to go and bury my father." St Matthew 8:21 "But Jesus said unto him, follow me and let the dead bury their dead." 22 I believe he is referring to this end time, of so many false preachers that haven't received their 'redemption' or His righteousness first. "But seek ye first the kingdom of God, and his righteousness; and all these things shall be added unto you." St Matthew 6:33

Instead of a gas station on every corner, and between the restaurants, we find a church with a different doctrine.

There are two programs on television with the men and women naked, and the, "pill for women" they needed that, because most men just want to get it done and over with. I'm not supposed to condone fornication but reality is reality. It is hard to say what it was like before Noah, but it probably wasn't much different then today. It were the sinful nature of man, was why Jesus had to die on the cross for redemption sake, and because of the righteousness of God.

One day it happened In the book of Genesis "And God saw that the wickedness of man was great in the earth, and that every imagination of the thoughts of his (heart) was only evil continually." Genesis 6:5 "And it repented the Lord that he had made man on the earth, and it grieved him at his heart." 6 "And the Lord said, I will destroy man whom I have created from the face of the earth; both man, and beast, and the creeping thing, and the fowls of the air; for it repenteth (grieved) me that I have made them." 7 "But Noah found grace, in the eyes of the Lord." 8

"These are the generation of Noah: Noah was a just man and perfect in his generation, and Noah walked with God." Genesis 6:9 "Be ye therefore perfect, even as your Father which is in heaven is perfect." St Matthew 5:48 Noah must have followed the rituals in Leviticus or whatever he had to do in his day, to be perfect. I'm perfect because the sinful heart was removed and I received a new heart from the Lord. Thirty days later I received in my mouth the new Spirit or Holy Ghost.

If Noah was perfect, did the other seven on the boat were they perfect, or just to replenish the earth? (Food for thought)

The great supper with God in His kingdom at the end time, I'm not sure if Noah will be there or not, or any of the other prophets in the Old Testament. The Preachers don't seem to have any trouble lumping it all together but I do, because the salvation plan for this dispensation is different. The preacher in charge, that is His domain, for speculation, I don't speculate. Jesus said the law ended with John the Baptist, a person would think it ended when Jesus began his ministry. "For all the prophets and the law prophesied until John." St Matthew 11:13

As far as the sacraments go Jesus said, He would not drink henceforth (from now on) of this fruit of the vine, until that day (the end time) when I drink it new; (it will be different) with you in my Father's kingdom." (in heaven) St Matthew 26:29 If you think Jesus is down in the punchboll your sadly mistaken, and He isn't in the cracker barrel either. While we are at it, is there a purgatory that a person will get out of, until they get straightened out.? The Moslems believe the same thing, but a good murderer (like the Devil) will miss purgatory. In St John it reads the devil was a murderer from the beginning, and will be cast into the lake of fire. Why doesn't it read that the Devil, beast, and false prophet are sent to purgatory? It reads they were cast into the lake of fire and brimstone Revelation 20:10

How bad is the earth going to be or get at the end time? In Noah's day it reads one day God saw that the wickedness of man were great in the earth, and He decided to destroy man, which He did, except Noah, and the seven with him.

The Roman Empire was destroyed from within, the greatest empire in the history of the world. The only difference is, the earth is in the crosshairs of God, which will be so much worse according to St Matthew. "For many shall come in my name, saying, I am Christ; (or a true man of god?) and shall deceive many." St Matthew 24:5 "And ye shall hear of wars and rumors of wars: see that ye be not troubled: for all these things must come to pass, but the end is not yet.6 "For nation shall rise against nation, and kingdom against kingdom: and there shall be famines, and pestilences, and earth quakes, in divers (various) places." 7 "All these are the beginning of sorrows." 8 "And many false prophets, shall rise, and shall deceive many." 11 "For then shall be great tribulation, such as was not since the beginning of the world to this time, no, nor ever shall be." 21 "And except those days should be shortened, there should no flesh be saved: but for the elect's sake those days shall be shortened." 22

"Immediately after the tribulation of those days, shall the sun be darkened, and the moon shall not give her light, and the stars shall fall from heaven, and the powers of the heavens shall be shaken;" St Matthew 24:29 30 "And then shall appear the sign of the Son of man in heaven: and then shall all the tribes of the earth mourn, and they shall see the Son of man coming in the clouds of heaven with power and great glory." 30

"And he shall send his angels with a great sound of a trumpet, and they shall gather together his elect from the four winds, from one end of heaven to the other." 31 "Verily I say unto you, this generation shall not pass, till all these things be fulfilled. 34 "Heaven and earth shall pass away, but my words shall not pass away." 35 Not only the Word, but what I say it shall happen at the end time.

In the Casper Star Tribune of December 22/ 2015 there was an article of opinion written by George F. Will, "Ballooning welfare state in America" If you can see any hope, I can't.

"America's national character will have to be changed if progressives are going to implement their agenda. So changing social norms is the progressive agenda.

To understand how far this has advanced and how difficult it will be to reverse the dependency, consider the Nicholas Eberstadt deploys in "National Affairs Quarterly:"

"America's welfare state transfers more than 14 percent of GDP to recipients, with more than a third of Americas taking "need-based" payments. In our wealthy society, the government officially treats an unprecedented portion of the population as" needy."

Transfers of benefits to individuals through social welfare programs have increased from less than one federal dollar in four (24 percent) in 1963 to almost three out of five (59 percent) in 2013. In that half-century, entitlement payments were, Eberstadt says, America's "fastest growing source of personal income," growing twice as fast as all other real per capita personal income. It is probable that this year, a majority of Americans will seek and receive payments.

This is not primarily because of Social Security and Medicare transfers to an aging population. Rather, the growth is overwhelmingly in means-tested entitlements. More than twice as many households receive "anti-poverty benefits than receive Social Security or Medicare. Between 1983 and 2012, the population increased by 67 million. Food stamp recipients increased from 19 million to 51 million-more than the combined populations of 24 states.

What has changed? Not the portion of the estimated population below the poverty line (15.2 percent in 1983; 15 percent in 2012). Rather, poverty programs have became un-tethered from the official designation of poverty: In 2012, more than half the recipients were not classified as poor but accepted being treated as needy.

Expanding dependency requires erasing Americans traditional distinction between the deserving and the undeserving poor. This distinction was rooted in this nation's exceptional sense that poverty is not the unalterable accident of birth, and is related to traditions of generosity arising from immigrant and settler experiences.

Eberstadt's essay, "American Exceptionalism and the Entitlement State," argues that this state is extinguishing the former. America "arrived late to the 20th century's entitlement party." He notes that the structure of U,S government spending "has been completely overturned within living memory," resulting in the "remolding of daily life for ordinary Americans under the shadow of the entitlement state."

Causation works both ways between the rapid increase in family disintegration (from 1904 to 2012, the percentage of children born to unmarried women increased from 7 to 41) and the fact that, Eberstadt says, for many women, children and even working-age men, "the entitlement state is now the breadwinner of the household." In the last 50 years, the fraction of civilian men ages 25 to 34 who were neither working nor looking for work approximately quadrupled.

Eberstadt believes that the entitlement state poses "character challenges" because it powerfully promotes certain habits, including habits of mind. These include corruption. Since 1970, Americans have become healthier, work has become less physically stressful, the workplace has become safer, and yet there has an almost six fold increase in claims from Social Security Disability Insurance. Such claims (including fraudulent ones) are gateways to a plethora of other payments..

As a growing portion of the population succumbs to the entitlement state's ever-expanding menu of temptations, the costs, Eberstadt concludes, include a transformation of the nation's "political culture, sensibilities, and tradition," the weakening of America's distinctive "conceptions of self-advancement," and perhaps a "rending of the national fabric."

As a result, "America today does not look exceptional at all." Unquote
Walter E Williams is a professor of Economics at George Mason University. He wrote in the Star Tribune in Casper, Wyoming on 3/21/2018 an article "It has not always been like this" a modified version of the article.

"It turns out that according to 2016 FBI statistics, rifles accounted for 368 of the 17,250 homicides in the U. S. that year. Gun ownership is not our problem. Our problem is a widespread decline in moral values that has nothing to do with guns. That decline includes disrespect for oneself, little accountability for anti-social behavior and a scuttling of religious teachings that reinforced moral values. If people would come back who passed away before 1960 were to return, they would not believe the kind of personal behavior all too common today. They wouldn't believe that some school districts, such as Philadelphia employ more than 400 school police officers.

There are other forms of behavior that would have been deemed grossly immoral yes-teryear There are companies, such as National Debt Relief, CuraDebt and Lending Tree, which advertise that they will help you to avoid paying all the money you owe. There are companies that counsel senior citizens on how to shelter their assets from nursing home care costs. In my book, that's immoral, but it is so common that most of us give it no thought.

There is one moral failing that is devastating to the future of our nation. That failing, which has wide acceptance by the American people, is the idea that Congress has the authority to forcibly use one American to serve the purpose of another American. That is nothing less than legalized theft and accounts for roughly three-quarters of federal spending. For the Christians among us, we should consider that when God gave Moses the commandment "Thou shalt not steal." He probably didn't mean thou shalt not steal unless you get a majority vote in the U. S. Congress. Unquote.

My Mother contacted polio when she was three years old, and worked like a dog until about fifty five years old. It ruined her left leg, and she never drove a car in which she could have. Her first major work was on the two farms in Missouri and Oklahoma with three children and no electricity in Missouri. My brother did most of the heavy farm work he was twelve years old. Dad would read his Bible under a shade tree, getting ready for the church services. He was an ordained minister in the Assembly of God Church, after he quit his deferred railroad job twice, during World War 11, he was called to preach only for about four years.

After selling the farm Dad became a union carpenter, and the family, without Paul, 'he went in the Air force,' we traveled all over the mid-west living in a 29 foot trailer.

Mom's first Job was a commercial laundry in two towns, and she studied typing and short hand but couldn't do that, so she became the janitor. In Rapid City, South Dakota she got a job at a motel, first, than a dish washer in a small cafe. The cook never came to work so she became a cook, with a raise of $10.00 a week before taxes. After she got a divorce she had to pay Dad for half of the value of the house that he had built on $25.00, $35.00 a week. She never got any alimony, because she filed for the divorce, the judge said Dad never had to give her any money, so he sent me $5.00 every Christmas. Over the years she worked at about four restaurants until she got rheumatoid arthritis, and with only one leg she finally had to start drawing Social Security Disability at the age of about fifty five years old.

Not long ago a relative about twenty one that didn't like to work, got on one of the Entitlement Programs, and others that look capable are on welfare. This year the government reduced my Social Security check by $87.00, somebody has to pay for those that don't like to work. Because of my Mother, I have very little sympathy for them. A lady on TV had a joint bank account with her mother that was on Social Security, and after her mother died she neglected to inform S. S. It was years before she was caught. There are a lot of people 112+years old on S.S.

In the article above, "the government officially treats an unprecedented portion of the population as "needy." Last year the IRS billed me for $7.10 cents 3 cents' interest, and 7 cents' penalty, they said the accountant made a mistake. In the last "State of the Union address" I never heard one word about the 20 trillion + that we are in debt? I hope my $7.10 helped out, I would hate to think it was in vain when I sent it in. When you get 105 years old a person is unable to re-invest money, so you get stuck with all the capital gain taxes. This year I gave them $16,000 after selling a house, I hope that helped out.

The bread winner now is the entitlement programs, but at one time, it was the man of the family.

"In the last fifty years, the fraction of civilian men ages 25 to 34 who were neither working nor looking for work." They just make babies as the population attest to. Pope Francis said, "you don't have to act like rabbits."

The sad part of all this is who needs God, if everybody is on entitlements of one kind or another?

"But as the days of Noah were, so shall also the coming of the Son of man be." St Matthew 24:37 "But of that day and hour knoweth no man, no not the angels of heaven, but my Father only." 36

In Noah's day it reads in Genesis "And God saw that the wickedness of man was great in the earth, and that every imagination of the thoughts of his heart was only evil continually." Genesis 6:5 "And it repented the Lord that he had made man on the earth, and it grieved him at his heart." 6 "And the Lord said, I will destroy man whom I have created from the face of the earth; both man, and beast, and the creeping thing, and the fowls of the air; for it repenteth (grieved) me that I have made them." 7

So one day God came down and saw the wickedness of man. It wouldn't be any different today, one of the things mentioned is people will be eating. It is almost unimaginable the number of eating establishments in existence now.

I noticed that Paul and his disciples, seemed to know all about the condition of man in the last days, with no mention of the things of the earth and heavens. That should wake the preachers up but they are dead, to the things of God.

Sense I have been born, in 1937, I believe there has been a war going on someplace on the earth, but it seems to be getting worse every day. Mankind has had plagues etc. but those seem to be getting worse every day. The penitentiaries are full and running over most of the time. Who are the peacemakers of the King James Bible of 1611? It reads "Blessed are the peacemakers: for they shall be called the children of God." St Matthew 5:9 In Islam they believe peace will come when everybody becomes a Moslem, or dead, at least pay rent to live. If they would only read their own book, instead of fleeing, they can charge them rent to live. With some, that would be better than cutting their head off. Nobody reads the Bible either, that is one thing that we have in common. A reverend on T V said last night, that the peacemakers are soldiers. Have you ever heard that a soldier is the other half of the verse? "For they shall be, called the children of God." St Matthew 5:9 They are human beings that need salvation, just like the rest of mankind, and there seems to be something wrong with calling them, "boots on the ground" but, I'm just a carpenter from Wyoming.

Becoming children of God, think of all the things that would be different. There would be no drinking, so domestic violence would end by 99%. Driving while drunk would end the destruction both in lives and property. It would be the end of physical damage, smoking or black lungs, and all it cost insurance companies. They would lower our insurance bill by a dollar. It would cut back on people wondering, 'who, is my daddy?' It would cut the bleeps out on T V with nobody swearing, people would have to learn how to talk all over again. People would put on clothes not only for their benefit but for the lust in others, and it would help save perhaps a child being molested. In judgment day that is what judgment is all about. Will you be judged on how you have lived your life? I believe so.

Children of God they take everything in moderation, they don't spend all their time in any one sport, devoting all their time to it. They get more pleasure from reading the Bible, and if they are a true child of God they will understand the parables and allegorical writing which makes the Bible more interesting.

They will take care of their bodies realizing that there body is not their body but it is God's body. Defacing it, would close down a lot of businesses, and there body wouldn't look like a wall you might find in New York City. A child of God is obligated to God, to keep their body as healthy as possible, for His benefit.

Doing anything that would harm your body a child of God wouldn't do, like rodeo, rock climbing, skiing, and or snowboarding down hellish slopes would not be in the cards. The tax payers would miss out taking care of them until they died, with their paralyzed bodies.

War would be no more, with the billions of dollars spent on shells etc. and, no one would have a chest full of medals in recognition of dead soldiers.

With greed, 'he catalyst for living' I'm not sure how it is going to end, property taxes, sales taxes, license plate fees, drivers license fees, fishing license fees, use fees, lottery, hunting fees, gasoline tax, telephone taxes and fees, capital gain tax, when a person gets old they can't re-invest in income property, their body won't let them, so the government has your number, they can wait. New curb and gutter fee, electricity fees, natural gas choices; park fees, gun permit fees, bank fees, income tax, rules of the road, fines etc.. .

At the tower of Babel In Genesis it reads nothing will be restrained from them, which they have imagined to do. Does mankind bring about his own demise by his imagination? In the cartoon of Dick Tracy about seventy two years ago he was talking on a phone on his wrist as a fantasy, and recently a cell phone has achieved that in reality.

The movies are into subject matter that is pure fantasy, out of this world so to speak, and most of it is. It looks to me like the depth of hell with Satan setting in the driver's seat. The hard rock bands resembles hell in drag with the noise and lingo, but thankfully I can't hear all that well. If you can't pat your foot, the noise is grating on your soul. I believe the Lawrence Welk Band, is the last of the pure musical sounds, a classic. Very seldom do you find a dancer that is the leader of a band, real dancing, not jumping up and down. Some women are in Dallas and their boy friend is in Huston.

I went in a bar in Illinois with a band playing. It was so loud I had to get within an inch of the bartenders ear to get a glass of orange juice, of course there wasn't anyone on the dance floor. The leader had such a foul mouth, I never heard anyone speak like that sense leaving the United States Navy. Of course there was football on one T V, hockey on the other the third T V, baseball. I tried to figure out where the fun was, I left. In my day there was a Jukebox with the kind of music as on the Lawrence Welk show that we danced too, in the bar, sometimes at noon with a girl that loved me.

The music today, either country or religious, I can't tolerate either one, at least 90% of it.

Chapter 19

Inconvenient Truth

Who is correct, of all the religious in the world? Pope Francis was in the United States this year in 2015, and at the same time about a thousand people were killed in Saudi Arabia trying to throw rocks at the devil, they were crushed to death. Thousands of people gathered in the different major cities to greet the Pope, and he wasn't bashful at all asking different people to pray for him. The only spiritual word that I heard him say was, "religion." Both Islam and the Catholic religion, after death, they have what they call "purgatory."

There are three verses with the same wording in St Mark, it is writing about hell, the fire that never shall be quenched.

"Where their worm (soul) dieth not, and the fire is not quenched." St Mark 9:44-45-46 In Luke the rich man was telling Lazarus "For I have five brethren, (brothers) that he may testify unto them, lest they also come into this place of torment." Luke16:28 "---send Lazarus, that he may dip the tip of his finger in water, and cool my tongue; for I am tormented in this flame." 24

"And the devil that deceived them was cast into the lake of fire and brimstone, where the beast (anti-christ) and the false prophet are. (Paul) and shall be tormented day and night forever and ever." Revelation 20:10

Reading about my physical redemption, why would I need purgatory? A person can be in the kingdom of God, and still be on the earth. "---Verily,

...ee, Except a man be born again, he cannot see (power) of God." "Except a man be born of water (born again) and ...rit, (Holy Ghost) he cannot enter into the kingdom of God." St ... 3:3-5 Water doesn't mean water baptism nor does it mean, 'Washing of the Word' whatever that means? A person can be in the Kingdom of God, and never leave the earth.

"For I say unto you, that except your righteousness shall exceed the righteousness of the scribes and Pharisees, ye shall in no case enter into the kingdom of heaven." St Matthew 5:20 They probably went to church every Sunday sitting in the a-men corner, agreeing with everything that is being said. Their parents were probably Pharisees. I understand 80% of people wouldn't even give it a thought, that their parents were wrong. They probably paid there tithes' of 10% or more, and prayed over every meal. They probably received their last rights, when necessary, did the beads, candles, smoke, signing, and confession. They were probably baptized in water when they were a baby. They probably, "witnessed" every chance that they got, and told them all you have to do is, "believe" to enter into the kingdom of God like in St John. Then they become missionaries, and told those in Japan, that all you have to do is, "believe."

"Not everyone that saith unto me, Lord, Lord, shall enter into the kingdom of heaven; but he that doeth the will of my Father which is in heaven." St Matthew 7:21 "Many will say to me in that day, Lord, Lord, have we not prophesied (preached) in thy name? And in thy name have cast out devils? And in thy name done many wonderful works?" 22 "And then will I profess unto them, I never knew you: depart from me, ye that work iniquity." 23

"But seek ye first the kingdom of God, and his righteousness: and all these things shall be added unto you." St Matthew 6:33 When a person receives, 'His righteousness' is when you find out what God wants you to do. His righteousness is in Ezekiel as given the new heart and about thirty days later the new Spirit which is the Holy Ghost, the teacher that went in your mouth and down your throat. "---But you know him, for he dwelleth with you, and shall be in you." St John 14:17

The problem with the preachers are, I have never heard one of them say you have to receive the Holy Ghost in your mouth the same as Jesus when baptized by John. They say when the sinner's prayer is spoken, that is when the Spirit, from then on, resides with you, which is as far from the truth as you can get. The sad part is not receiving the Spirit in the mouth a person will not enter into the kingdom of God. That is why to blasphemy the Holy Ghost is not what you should do. "Wherefore I say unto you, all manner of sin and blasphemy shall be forgiven unto men: but the blasphemy against the Holy Ghost shall not be forgiven unto men." St Matthew 12:31 "And whosoever speaketh a word against the Son of man, it shall be forgiven him: but whosoever speaketh against the Holy Ghost, it shall not be forgiven him, neither in this world, neither in the world to come." 32 As they say on the street, the Holy Ghost is the only game in town.

"---Ye shall drink indeed of my cup, (receive the same thing that I received) and be baptized with the baptism that I am baptized with:" (Spirit or Holy Ghost) St Matthew 20:23)

Explaining this on the social media they seem to have trouble with believing that the "like a dove," In St Matthew was the Holy Ghost. Why not, it had to be reduced to get into the inside of Jesus in the mouth, and then it expands. We are talking about God here. St Matthew 3:16

How close are we to the second coming of Jesus? When receiving the new heart by the clinical standards they would probably say without a heart the person would be dead. The first thing that went out of me was the heart that I was born with. My shoulders sank inward, and my lungs might have been removed also but the KJB of 1611 only says that the Spirit of God will give you a new heart. It reads; "and I will take away the stony heart (sinful) out of your flesh, and I will give you a heart of flesh." Ezekiel 36:26 (A new heart from God) In this transition I must have died. It happened 12/1 1968 at about 9pm on a pay phone at a gas station in Long Beach, California. When my mother asked me to pray for your dad and me, I, "believed in my heart" that perhaps I could heal her. It triggered the Spirit of Genesis to act, and it did the work. That is what it means by believing, that we read so much about. This was my first death, and the Bible reads that you won't be hurt of the second death in Revelation 2:1. I'm eighty years old, is it saying that I'm not going to die, the second death and perhaps only time will tell.

"Blessed and holy is he that hath part in the first resurrection: on such the second death hath no power, but they shall be priests of God and of

Christ, and they shall reign with him a thousand years." Revelation 20:6 Resurrection means rising from the dead, or coming back to life. Isn't that what happened to me above, I needed the new heart to come back to life. "And death and hell were cast into the lake of fire, this is the second death." 14 So you can take this two ways, either I'm not going to die, or I won't be cast into the lake of fire?

"For God so loved the world, that he gave his only begotten Son, that whosoever believeth in him should not perish, but have everlasting life." St John 3:16 Isn't this verse a play on the 15th verse? "That whosoever believeth in him should not perish, but have eternal life." I believe another miss-informed person thought verse 16 sounded better, and put it in the Bible. I explained believe above as a catalyst for the Spirit to act, only. You have to believe in your very soul or heart one of the works that Jesus did. This is found in "Believe me that I am in the Father, and the Father in me: or else believe me for the very works' sake." St John 14:11 and 10:37-38

Does God love the world? It reads; that it grieved God in His heart that He made man on the earth. Genesis 6:6 God gave his only Son, yes, God never died on the cross it was His Son. It reads, "Whosoever" what about being one of the chosen and drawn? "No man can come to me, except the Father which hath sent me draw him:---." St John 6:44 "And except those days should be shortened, there should no flesh be saved: but for the elect's sake those days shall be shortened." St Matthew 24:22 "---Take heed that no man deceive you." 4 What about Paul it reads a man will come after I leave, what about Mohammad, or Buda they came after Jesus lived and left?

Not everybody that is called will be chosen or drawn. The Father must draw a person, It doesn't matter if your name is, "written in the book" that is the beginning, not the end result.

Jesus said that His body is a Temple, what about your body. Your body is not your body to deface, or swear allegiance to a ruler, government, country or another person. As a child of God you have nothing to do with this world, or anybody on the earth.

(When you become a child of God that is what the new heart is about) "Then will I sprinkle clean water upon you, (born again) ye shall be clean: from all your filthiness, and from all your idols, will I cleanse you." Ezekiel 36:25 The Holy Ghost, Spirit, Comforter, or Spirit of Truth will not reside in an unclean body. It was thirty days afterward that I received it in the mouth going to work in a 1959 Ford Thunderbird in Los Angeles, 12/30/1968 at 6:30am that is when I became a true child of God. Afterward I received the "tree of life" that I explained earlier.

In St Matthew it is about the sacraments and Jesus said "But I say unto you, I will not drink henceforth of the fruit of the vine, until that day when I drink it new with you in my Father's kingdom." St Matthew 26:29 It doesn't sound like to me, Jesus is participating in the sacraments, on this earth in any way at this time.

What about water baptism? John the Baptist said I baptize you with water, but Jesus baptism in the Holy Ghost is what is needful. "I indeed baptize you with water unto repentance: but he that cometh after me is mightier than I, whose shoes I am not worthy to bear: he shall baptize you with the Holy Ghost, and with fire:" St Matthew 3:11It is a Spirit not associated with the other Spirit or Holy Ghost that gave me the new heart. There are churches of different denominations that have literally made a denomination out of baptism in water which has nothing to do with the salvation experience. ""Woe unto you, scribes and Pharisees, hypocrites!, For ye make clean the outside of the cup and the platter, but within they are full of extortion and excess." St Matthew 23:25

A word that everybody loves is, "Love." It has nothing to do with God being righteous so what good is love? "It grieved God in His heart that He made man." Genesis 6:6 He loved them so much that He killed all but eight during the flood in Noah's day. He loved people so much that in Sodom and Gomorrah, ten righteous people couldn't be found so God destroyed both of those cities. He loved people so much after Adam and Eve disobeyed Him, he put a curse on the earth. He loved people so much we have Paul writing half of the New Testament of false doctrine. It reads that He knew Paul would come after Him to do that, in St John 5:43. God saw in the heart of Lucifer that he would be over the mount (all) of the congregation (churches) Isaiah 14:13-14 The New Testament reads of words; like chosen, elect, drawn, and using words like this, salvation is not for everybody.

Believe is a word that is quite prevalent, but it is not absolute in itself it is based on a condition that very few understand, it is the catalyst for the Spirit first mentioned in genesis that you might say is the right hand of

God. When a person believes in the heart, on one of the works that Jesus did it triggers the Spirit to act. St John 10:37-38 and 14:11

I found salvation with verification of what happened to me in the King James Bible of 1611, so what would be the reason for me to read now days in 2018 every bible or Qur'an that Tom, Dick, Harry, Judas, Muhammad, and Mary has in the market place. I was physically transformed, the word's in the Bible, has nothing to do with me, but verification of my redemption gave me a piece of mind when I found Ezekiel 36:26-25-27.

What about evolution? There are a few signs of changes, for instance I believe our ancestors were shorter, but does that prove evolution, and I read a bees tongue is shorter recently. In both instances the species are basically the same. In a magazine I saw pictures of close to a hundred different insects, and it amazed me the delicate workmanship that went into their creation.

Reincarnation; I lived in Missouri, you are going to have to show me. Originally mankind has a curse, because of Adam and Eve disobeying God. That would prevent a person from becoming a cow.

On T V the religious channel the different preachers seem to have selected a few catch words like faith, grace, God, and money, I have never heard them say Jesus that through Him, physically, is the only way to the kingdom of God. On the radio is family, money, sports, etc., and dead preachers still conveying their false doctrine. The only spiritual word that I heard the Pope say was, "religion" when he was in the United States in 2015. The King James Bible of 1611 has verses with meaning, allegorically or in parable form, and even literally. The big problem with preachers is Jesus said, what will condemn a person is what comes out of their mouth. "For by thy words thou shalt be justified, and by thy words thou shalt be condemned." St Matthew 12:37 "O generation of vipers, (preachers) how can ye being evil, speak good things? For out of the abundance of the heart the mouth speaketh." 34 A person must receive God's righteousness, of being born again and receiving the Holy Ghost as in Ezekiel. It is why on television they slap each other's back because they don't know any better. With them they are all men of god. In Joel it reads your god, and then it reads if you are not of the true God your Father is the Devil. "How can ye believe, which receive honor one of another, and seek not the honor that cometh from God only?" St John 5:44

One of the biggest miss-informed-preachers in the U S today I sent a letter to his dad of the truth, who was a preacher, shortly afterward he had a heart attack, and died. I have often thought perhaps it was my letter that caused that, we will never know. How can a person tell their congregation they have been wrong for sixty years?

Who is it Allah or God? In the book it reads that the Islam religion is based on sound doctrine. The first time that Allah was ever mentioned was Muhammad declared him, "his messenger" and in the chapter on Satan the Qur'an justifies all of the traits of Lucifer, which the Qur'an seldom if ever mentions Lucifer. It reads that they didn't know why, Jesus never slew a few of his transgressors, Muhammad was a warrior, and Islam's leader. If Jesus would have broken a law, or commandment sin, etc.; then He couldn't be the perfect sacrifice for our sin. One of the Ten Commandments is thou shall not kill.

A word that is used in religious circles is enlightenment, but the Word of God is the only truth. I believe it was Buda that said he was enlightened but if it doesn't come from the Bible or the Word of God, it is a false enlightenment. Believing in such then will never lead a person to the kingdom of God.

The Moslems of the Islam faith of the Qur'an has said for a long time, that the United States is the, "Great Satan." What if they are right? They recognized that Paul gave a watered down version of Christianity, and they thought Jesus should have been a warrior like Muhammad. It is worse than a watered down version, Paul was never saved, to give a correct version, and they know that is about all that is preached, 'what Paul said.'

According to my research the only verse in the KJB of 1611that has anything to do with tongues in the gospels, as a phenomenon, is found in St Mark, "And these signs shall follow them that believe; (there is more to believe, then to just believe) In my name shall they cast out devils; (there is no record of any devils leaving anybody except myself) "they shall speak with new tongues." St Mark 16:17 From The Acts through Jude last night, a preacher proved that speaking in tongues were in the Bible, and he impressed his mother, 'when he was a child.' According to The Acts tongues, is a manifestation of the Spirit or Holy Ghost, but it has nothing to do with the Holy Ghost. If it did it would be recorded in St Matthew, during the time John, baptized Jesus in water, on His first breath. The Holy Ghost descended from heaven, "like or as a dove," and it went in Jesus mouth down His throat. How do I know this? That is the way it happened to me but without the baptism in water, God put a vision on me to get my mouth open. It reads in St Matthew "---Ye shall drink indeed of my cup, and be baptized with the baptism that I am baptized with:" St Matthew 20:23

In an article in the Casper Star-Tribune by Susan Stamper Brown December 26, 2015 Christmas day, "Do you see what I see." Professor Peter Stoner lays out the statistical odds that one man, Jesus, could fulfill every Old Testament Messianic prophecy. Quote

"Foretold the Messiah would be born in Bethlehem. Micah 5:2 Predicted the Bethlehem-born Messiah would have a "forerunner" sent to prepare the way." (John the Baptist) Malachi 3:1

Predicted this ruler who had a forerunner was born in Bethlehem, but entered Jerusalem as a king riding on a Ass. Zechariah 9:9 (as recorded in St Matthew 21:5) said this ruler would be betrayed for 30 pieces of silver. 12 Predicted that remorse would inspire the betrayer to return the silver and the priests would use it to purchase a field from a potter, rather than return the blood money to the temple treasury.13; predicted an innocent man who was betrayed, oppressed, and afflicted yet would remain silent during his trial." Isaiah 53: 7 also 1-12 Unquote

The entire chapter fifty three of Isaiah; is devoted to Jesus. "No beauty, that we should desire him." 2 "He is despised and rejected of men." 3 "The Lord hath laid on him, the iniquity of us all."6 For he was cut off out of the land of the living:" 8 "neither was any deceit in his mouth."9 "Yet it pleased the Lord to bruise him; he hath put him to grief: when thou shalt make his soul an offering for sin, he shall see his seed, (those that become saved) he shall prolong his days, (die at the right time, using parables) and the pleasure of the Lord shall prosper in his hand." 10 Isaiah 53: 1-12

Predicted the death of this innocent man by crucifixion, an execution method not yet invented. Psalm 22:16 Unquote

To the author's knowledge there is only one verse that has Paul, who wrote half of the New Testament, and Satan as being a factor after Jesus left except in Isaiah, we find Lucifer just after he was removed from heaven. "---I will exalt my throne above the stars of God: I will sit also upon the mount (all) of the congregation, (churches)---." Isaiah 14:13-14 "Hereafter

I will not talk much with you: for the prince (Satan) of this world cometh, and hath nothing in me." St John 14:30 "I am come in my Father's name, and ye receive me not: (Jesus) if another shall come, in his own name, him ye will receive. (Believe, Paul) St John 5:43

In my quest for redemption according to this book, if I were lying than I would say that Islam, Hinduism, Christianity as it is presented, Shinto, Buddhism, Taoism, Mormon, etc. would have as good a chance at being right, but I'm not lying so it doesn't look good for all the other denominations or religions, that don't go by what is in the King James Bible of 1611 verifying a physical salvation. The earth, planets, insects, dinosaurs, and the complexity of it all, needed a superior supreme being in charge of it all.

The World in the present form, the author of this nonfiction book can't see any hope, but as it reads in the last two verses in my K J Bible of 1611. "Behold, I will send you Elijah the prophet before the coming of the great and dreadful day of the Lord;" Malachi 4:5 "And he shall turn the heart of the fathers to the children, and the heart of the children to their Fathers, lest I come and smite the earth with a curse." 6 I believe I am Elijah.

Chapter 20

The Tower of Babel and Beyond

Is it possible that man in his advancement in history can bring down his own demise? That is what happened to Noah, and that generation in Genesis "And God saw that the wickedness of man was great in the earth, and every imagination of the thoughts of his heart was only evil continually." Genesis 6:5 "And it repented the Lord that he had made man on the earth, and it grieved him at his heart." 6 "But Noah found grace in the eyes of the Lord." 8 "And God said unto Noah, the end of all flesh is come before me; for the earth is filled with violence through them; and , behold I will destroy them with the earth." 13

At the Tower of Babel the word imagination comes up again. It is the for-runner of invention or change for mankind's existence. "And the Lord said, Behold the people is one, and they have all one language; and this they begin to do: and now nothing will be restrained from them, which they have imagined to do." Genesis 11:6

Where did the water come from that flooded the earth, when God said he would destroy both man, and beast, and the creeping thing, and the fowls of the air; with the earth, for it repented him that I have made them? Genesis 6:7 and 6:6 I thought God was love that you hear so much about.

It is a known fact that most of the dinosaurs were vegetation eaters what if there were above the earth as the Bible says a firmament or a layer of water circling the earth. That would be the catalyst for the growth of vegetation for the dinosaurs. I believe that would leave the entire earth at the same temperature. Etc. It reads that nothing is impossible with God, so why would this be beyond what he can do? "It is easier for a camel to go through the eye of a needle, than for a rich man to enter into the kingdom of God!." St Mark 10:25 "And they were astonished (out of measure,) saying among themselves, who then can be saved?" 26 "And Jesus looking upon them saith, with men it is impossible, but with God all things are possible." 27

The water that came down, as rain for forty days and nights, it could be from this firmament or layer of water that flooded the earth.

Second day Firmament

"And God said let there be a firmament in the midst of the waters, and let it divide the waters from the waters. Genesis 1:6 "And God made the firmament, and divided the waters which were under the firmament from the waters which were above the firmament: and it was so." 7 "And God called the firmament, "Heaven.---." 8 (Above the earth)

"And God said, let the waters bring forth abundantly the moving creature that hath life, and fowl that may fly above the earth in the (open firmament of heaven.)" Genesis 1:20

In the dictionary firmament = means to strengthen or a solid arch. Why couldn't a thickness of water lay on top of the solid arch that would circle the earth?

At the time of the Tower of Babel in Genesis "And the whole earth was of one language and of one speech." Genesis 11:1 (The peoples imagination started up) "And they said one to another, go to, let us make brick, and burn them thoroughly. (Dry them) And they had brick for stone, and slime had they for mortar." 3 "And they said, Go to, let us build us a city and a tower, whose top may reach unto heaven; and let us make us a name lest we be scattered abroad upon the face of the whole earth." 4 (They must have had a premonition of what was to come) "And the Lord came down, to see the city and the tower, which the children of men builded." 5

"And the Lord said, (Lord to me means the Spirit was with Him in Genesis 1:2 and 26) Behold, the people is one, and they have all one language; and this they begin to do: and now nothing will be restrained from them, which they have "imagined" to do" 6

Was the language all that was changed?

In 4 the word "face" is used, (by the Pilgrims) and 8 "face" of all the earth God used the word. Is it about or could it be at that time that mankind was scattered on the face of the earth or the earth was one land mass. "These are the three sons of Noah: and of them was the whole earth overspread." Genesis 9:19 Were the whole earth one large land mass that they could overspread it as it read's. Did they have a boat or ocean liner to go to Australia?

Confusion of languages

Was that all, just the languages were confounded, that they may not understand one another's speech. If you look at the earth it appears to me the land masses were separated and only now they are making a study scientifically of that fact.

In Genesis is mentioned the children of Noah. "And unto E-ber were born two sons: the name of one was Pe-leg; (for in his days was the earth divided;) and his brother's name was Jok'-tan." Genesis 10:25

Casper Star Tribune in April of 2016 "Age-old rocks may give clues to mining industry" by Heather Richards

The first scientist to suggest that the seven continents were once a single supercontinent was laughed out of the room.

In an article published April 1, 2016 in the online version of the geology journal Nature Geo-science, a team of scientist including Chamberlain argued that Siberia and North America were once connected, a discovery with important implications in the industry, which paid for the five-year study that culminated in the publication.

Rare earth metals like copper and nickel are crucial for modern technology, but finding those deposits used to be the work of prospectors. It was a tedious search. But mapping the history of the earth's surface will allow mining companies to pinpoint areas likely to have mineral deposits. Knowing where continents once connected means that if copper, for example, had been successfully mined in an area on the edge of Siberia, it is also likely in the part of North America that broke away from Siberia million of years ago.

With God, nothing is impossible it reads, why couldn't He have separated the supercontinent?

"Ah Lord God! behold, thou hast made the heaven and the earth by thy great power and stretched out arm, and there is nothing too hard for thee:" Jeremiah 32:17

Biblical movement of the Sun

It is my understanding that Russia believes the earth is stationary, and the sun travels around it. They are not the only one. Almost daily I hear the sun is either rising or sitting, and when I look at the moon and sun they seem to follow each other in the sky, the only difference is the brightness as it reads in Genesis.

The two books in one is "A Geocentricity Primer" by Gerardus D. Bouw, Ph.D. and "The Geocentric Bible 6" by Gordon Bane they try and prove the earth is stationary with the Sun moving around it. Both authors are no stranger to the scriptures in proving their point.

The most compelling verses that I have read is in Joshua as mentioned in their book called the long day, which is recorded by most all the major ancestors of the different nationalities, Africa, Central and South America, North America, and the Chinese, etc..

The defeat of the Amorites

"And the Lord said unto Joshua, fear them not: for I have delivered them into thine hand; there shall not a man of them stand before thee. Joshua 10:8 "And it came to pass, as they fled from before Israel, and were in the going down to Beth-hor-on, that the Lord cast down great stones from heaven upon them unto Azekah, and they died: they were more which died with hailstones than they whom the children of Israel slew with the sword." 11

The sun stands still

"Then spake Joshua to the Lord in the day when the Lord delivered up the Amorites before the children of Israel, and he said in the sight of Israel,

"Sun stand thou still upon Gib-eon;
And thou, Moon, in the valley of Aj-alon 12
And the sun stood still, and the moon stayed,
until the people had avenged themselves upon their enemies.
Is not this written in the book of Jash-er? So the sun stood still in the midst of heaven, and hasted not to go down (set) about a whole day." 13

"And there was no day like that before it or after it, that the Lord hearkened unto the voice of a man: for the Lord fought for Israel." 14

"The sun also ariseth, and the sun goeth down, and hasteth to his place where he arose." Ecclesiastes 1:5

"Fear before him, all the earth: the world also shall be stable, that it be not moved." 1 Chronicles 16:30 "Say among the heathen that the Lord reigneth: the world also will be established that it shall not be moved: he shall judge the people righteously." Psalm 96:10 "Who laid the foundations of the earth, that it should not be removed forever." 104:5

"Say among the heathen that the Lord reigneth: the world also shall be established that it shall not be moved:" Psalm 96:10

Noah

It is documented all over the earth of structures built, and a possible existence of space aliens of one kind or another. Structures that it appears, couldn't have been in existence with the material used or the vastness of the projects. What does this have to do with Noah?

How could we call a man human when he lived according to the Bible nine hundred and fifty years: "And all the days of Noah were nine hundred and fifty years: and he died." Genesis 9:29 I'm glad that it reads he died, or people would have another church with him in the attic as another patriarch.

Job acknowledges God's Justice

There are several verses that has to do with the end time, end of days, or the great and dreadful day of the Lord. "Behold I will send you Elijah the prophet before the coming of the great and dreadful day of the Lord:" Malachi 4:5

"He (God) is wise in heart, and mighty in strength: who hath hardened himself against him; (and have prospered?)' Job 9:4 "Which removed the mountains, and they know not; which overturned then (preachers of false doctrine) in his anger;" 5 "Which shaketh the earth out of her place, and the pillers tremble;" 6 "Which commandeth the sun, and it riseth not; and sealeth up the stars;" 7

"Therefore I will shake the heaven, and the earth shall remove out of her place, in the wrath of the Lord of hosts, and in the day of his fierce anger." Isaiah 13:13 "The earth is utterly broken down, the earth is clean (completely) dissolved, the earth is moved exceedingly." Isaiah 24:19 "The earth shall reel to and fro like a drunkard, and shall be removed like a cottage; and the transgression thereof shall be heavy upon it; and it shall fall, and not rise again." 20

In St Matthew is mentioned the tribulation that will come on the earth. "And Jesus answered and said unto them, Take heed that no man deceive you." St Matthew 24:4 "For then shall be great tribulation such as was not the beginning of the world to this time, no, nor ever shall be." 21 "And except those days should be shortened, there should no flesh be saved: but for the elect's sake those days shall be shortened." 22 "Immediately after the tribulation of those days shall the sun be darkened, and the moon shall not give her light, and the stars shall fall from heaven: and the powers of the heavens shall be shaken:" 29

"He that overcometh shall inherit all things; and I will be his God, and he shall be my son." Revelation 21:7 "But the fearful, (those that haven't seen any part of God St John 3:3) and unbelieving, and the abominable, and murderers, and whoremongers, and sorcerers, and idolaters, and all liars, shall have their part in the lake which burneth with fire and brimstone: which is the second death." 8 "Ye are of your father the devil, and the lusts of your father ye will do. He was a murderer from the beginning, and abode not in the truth, because there is no truth in him.

When he speaketh a lie, he speaketh of his own: for he is a liar, and the father of it." St John 8:44 "Hereafter I will not talk much with you: for the prince of this world cometh, and hath nothing in me." St John 14:30 That would be Satan and Paul. Isaiah 14:13-14

"And I saw a new heaven and a new earth: for the first heaven and the first earth were passed away; and there was no more sea." Revelation 21:1 "And I John saw the holy city, new Jerusalem, coming down from God out of heaven, prepared as a bride adorned for her husband." 2 "And God shall wipe away all tears from their eyes; and there shall be no more death, neither sorrow, nor crying, neither shall there be any more pain: for the former things are passed away." 4

"And he carried me away in the spirit to a great city, the holy Jerusalem, descending out of heaven from God," Revelation 21:10 "Having the glory of God:---" 11 "And I saw no temple therein: for the Lord God Almighty AND the Lamb are the temple of it." 22 "And there shall in no wise enter into it anything that defileth, neither whatsoever worketh abomination, or maketh a lie: but they which are written in the Lamb's book of life." 21:27 And there shall be no more curse: but the throne of God AND the Lamb shall be in it: and his servants shall serve him:" 22:3

"---God and of the Lamb." Revelation 22:1 "---God and of the Lamb---" 3 "He that is unjust, let him be unjust still: and he which is filthy, let him be filthy still: and he that is righteous, let him be righteous still: (God might mean those that believe they are righteous) and he that is holy, let him be holy still." 11

"Be ye therefore perfect, even as your Father which is in heaven is perfect." St Matthew 5:48

www.ingramcontent.com/pod-product-compliance
Lightning Source LLC
Chambersburg PA
CBHW071958070526
44583CB00015B/1239